# ABOVE
## THE GRASS

*Stories of My Life and My Roots*

**GARY P. PERKINS**

iUniverse®

**ABOVE THE GRASS**
**STORIES OF MY LIFE AND MY ROOTS**

iUniverse books may be ordered through booksellers or by contacting:

iUniverse
1663 Liberty Drive
Bloomington, IN 47403
www.iuniverse.com
1-800-Authors (1-800-288-4677)

ISBN: 978-1-4917-5099-5 (sc)
ISBN: 978-1-4917-5100-8 (e)

Library of Congress Control Number: 2014918739

Printed in the United States of America.

iUniverse rev. date: 11/22/2014

# AUTHOR'S NOTE

My life has been filled with much love, many happy times, and cherished memories, along with periods of strife, struggle, and recovery. *Above the Grass* is a narrative of my personal journey and my business accomplishments. It also provides information regarding my family history and my English/Cornish roots.

G. P. P.
October 8, 2014

To my daughter, Pamela Jane (Perkins) Padgett.
She inspired and encouraged me to record this history.

# CONTENTS

CHAPTER 1

# RED ALERT

"Now hear this. All hands go to red alert. I repeat: go to red alert. This is not a test!"

It was 1959, and I was in the peacetime United States Navy, aboard the USS *San Pablo*, AGS30, a geographic survey ship. This red alert caught the crew off guard. We had had drills before, and as a quartermaster "striker" (candidate for the rate of quartermaster), I knew my assignment, but could this alarm be for real?

As we scrambled to our duty stations, we were all wondering what was going on. Were we being attacked? Was there a Russian missile headed our way? Maybe it was simply a drill after all.

When I got to my duty station as portside lookout on the bridge, I picked up bits and pieces of scuttlebutt. The OOD, officer of the deck in temporary command of the ship, informed our navigation officer, Mr. Knight, that a Russian submarine had been spotted in Delaware Bay and we were to get our ship underway.

We were tied up at a pier in the Philadelphia Naval Shipyard, our home port on the Delaware River. One-third of the crew was on liberty, and the shore patrol had been ordered to round up as many of the liberty party as possible and get them back on board. We would be casting off shortly. The *San Pablo* was the only active navy ship in port. The other active-duty ship assigned to the Port of Philadelphia was the USS *Galveston*, which was out at sea on maneuvers at the time. The remaining naval vessels in the Philadelphia Naval Shipyard—and there were a lot of them—had been relegated to "mothball" status. These had been decommissioned, secured, and locked down. Some would later be sold as salvage and recycled into Gillette razor blades (as told to us by the "yardbirds," more formally known as shipyard workers).

While we were the only active ship within twenty miles or so of Delaware Bay, the *San Pablo* was not a combat vessel. There were antisubmarine (ASW) groups headed this way from Norfolk and other East Coast locations under this red alert alarm, but our ship was nearest to the target.

Our crew was scurrying now, going through check-down exercises in preparation for getting the ship underway and making the damage-control equipment checks in case we were to step up to general quarters status, or to man battle stations and be ready for direct conflict. At the same time, we couldn't believe that this was for real!

The other quartermasters were at their stations: Newman at the ship's log, Howard on the helm. QM3 Bowman was on liberty and one of the first to arrive back at the ship. He said to me, "I can't believe they sighted a Russian sub in the bay. How could they have gotten through our shoreline defense?" Bowman was on his second hitch with the navy, and I asked him if he had been on a red alert status before this. He said, "Not aboard this ship! All we have on board are small arms, so about all we can do is shoot survivors!"

I reminded him that our *San Pablo* could be the first vessel to challenge the Russian sub since it was fewer than thirty miles to the bay from where we were located on the Delaware River.

Bowman responded, "You may be right about that! This baby will do twenty-one knots with the four diesel engines driving twin screws. We could be down there in just over an hour. I hope to hell we have some help!"

The *San Pablo* had been a seaplane tender during WWII and had seen its share of combat. Rumor had it that the bridge had been destroyed by a Japanese kamikaze plane. This old, war-torn vessel displayed an array of campaign ribbons on the forward bridge bulkhead. In the mid-1950s, this ship, along with its sister ship USS *Maury*, had been converted to perform oceanography studies after the navy's seaplanes had been retired. The five-inch guns and antiaircraft weaponry had been stripped off, and the ship was refitted with precision depth-recording equipment and a science laboratory. We normally carried twelve or thirteen civilian scientists and technicians on board. The *San Pablo* and its twin, the *Maury*, were 310 feet long, about the size of a destroyer, but were built with a rounded icebreaker hull as opposed to the V-shaped hull of the destroyer.

Some of our liberty party had been located and returned to the ship by the time we got underway. We headed down the Delaware River, a familiar route for us, but this time there was a sense of excitement. We were going to see some action. There was a difference in the crew: bright-eyed and sharp in performance as we all went about our duties. The officers wore a sober expression and gave orders crisply, and the radio crackled constantly. Man, this was the real navy!

Now in 1959, we were steaming down the Delaware River to face our Cold War enemy in defense of our homeland. We had been underway for about half an hour. I was the starboard lookout on the flying bridge just outside the pilothouse, with binoculars in hand, scanning the distance ahead. There were two deck seamen standing their watch up forward on the forecastle, and in the pilothouse were the OOD, the chief boatswain, Navigation Officer Mr. Knight, fellow Quartermasters Howard and Newman, and our skipper, who was continuously engaged by radio with his superiors. We were flying our colors—the Union Jack fluttering on the bow, the Stars and Stripes at the stern, and our signal flags at the yardarm displayed our call sign of November, Bravo, Uniform, Kilo (N-B-U-K). We were cruising down the Delaware River, all four engines at "full speed ahead."

I was still thinking about Bowman's joke that our mission was to "shoot survivors" when activity suddenly picked up in the pilothouse. From my station just outside the starboard hatch, I couldn't hear clearly what was going on, but then the skipper went to the ship's microphone and gave the order to "Stand down from red alert!" With that order, our anticipated moment of fame was denied. We wouldn't be going to general quarters, and we wouldn't be facing down a Russian submarine. It was over.

When the opportunity came, I slipped inside the pilothouse and asked Newman for an explanation. He told me that air surveillance revealed that the submarine wasn't Russian. It was Greek. Apparently, when it surfaced and hoisted its colors, a local pleasure craft in the bay mistook the Greek flag as Russian. The star and crescent moon on a red background was mistakenly interpreted as a Russian hammer and sickle on a similar red background. Newman said the civilians must have notified authorities by ship-to-shore radio, and the alert was sounded shortly afterward.

This would be one of several interesting "adventures" during my two years aboard the *San Pablo*. I made the best of my tour of duty in the navy, and in one respect it was a welcome break from the pressure of working my way through college. I learned to tolerate the military discipline and to appreciate the moderate freedom from responsibility as an enlisted man: just follow orders and don't question the logic. "There's the right way, the wrong way, and then there's the navy way." As sailors, we learned to relax and enjoy the cruise. Sailors can have a pretty good time on just eighty dollars a month plus an extra five bucks for sea duty.

I experienced some mild disappointment in not getting into a skirmish with the Russians but at the same time felt relief in not having to enter a combat situation. I'm sure these mixed feelings are common among all military personnel who find themselves in harm's way. I heard a good deal of grousing among the crew about this lost opportunity to engage the Russians. I, too, felt a big letdown after the emotional buildup toward military action. Stationed up on the bridge, I would have been in the thick of the action. With a big shot of adrenalin, a military man doesn't dwell on the danger of the situation.

Now, after the nonaction was over, most of us felt some degree of depression. This brief adventure, however, convinced me that I was going to enjoy this tour with the US Navy. There was a certain romance about sailing the high seas and having an opportunity to see the world.

Instead of sitting in air-conditioned classrooms by day and trimming heads of lettuce and cabbage in the produce department of A&P at night, I had found myself marching around the "grinder" at the Great Lakes Naval Boot Camp with blistered feet in the hot July sun and carrying a fake rifle that we were forced to call our "piece." After nine weeks at boot camp, I had put in a request for sea duty and was assigned to the USS *San Pablo*. I then spent two weeks in the Brooklyn Navy Yard while the navy located the whereabouts of the ship … but that's another story.

CHAPTER 2

# DRAFTED BY THE NAVY

This was peacetime, the years after Korea and before Vietnam, but the Cold War between the superpowers brought a certain tension to American life. A few years ago, in elementary school, we had been taught how to "duck and roll" under our desks in the event of an enemy attack. We knew the Russians had missiles pointed at us and that those missiles had nuclear warheads. Our government had set up radioactive shelters in cities and towns coast to coast. Back in my hometown of Benton, Wisconsin, a small village of 850 people, the high-school gymnasium had served as the radioactive shelter, and that was typical in most small towns in the United States during the 1950s.

The military draft was in effect during the fifties and sixties, and I was fulfilling my military obligation. All young men, upon reaching sixteen years of age, were required to register with the local Selective Service Board. Most were then drafted into the US Army unless one chose to voluntarily enlist in one of the other branches.

I had graduated from high school at age seventeen and then registered with the board on my birthday three months later. I began classes at the business college in Rockford, Illinois, the following January. Shortly thereafter, I enlisted in the US Naval Reserve. The naval drill center was just a short distance away from the business college in Rockford. My purpose was to attend weekly drills with the Naval Reserve while attending college, thereby meeting my military obligation at the same time. This schedule proved to be a challenge because I was also working part-time at the A&P supermarket three nights a week and on Saturdays. As an accounting major, I had to spend a lot of extra time on study assignments, balancing debits and credits. The naval drills were held just one evening per week, but my part-time job and the heavy study requirements of the accounting classes left me little free time. After six months, I had settled into a tolerable work/study routine and was getting above-average grades in my business classes. In addition, our A&P supermarket had won the "Store of the Year" award for the Midwest Region. Each employee was awarded a prize; I chose an electric razor.

The business college at Rockford was small, confined to a single building downtown on Jefferson Street. I rented a sleeping room in an old, three-story rooming house on the north side, about twelve blocks from the school. My roommate, Jerry, was from a Chicago suburb, and we both lived on a pretty tight budget, eating a lot of McDonald's burgers, some cold cuts, bread, and peanut butter, which we smuggled into the house. Our room was on the third floor, so we had to quietly enter the back door, sneak through the kitchen, and get up the stairs with our booty. The front window opened over a porch roof, and we kept our milk and cold cuts out there on the gently sloping roof.

In a letter home in 1958, I told Mom and Dad that I had just $17.00 that would have to last until next week's payday at A&P. I also said, "Jerry and I got haircuts tonight. They charged us $1.75. Everything is higher down here!"

I had no car, so I walked the twelve blocks back and forth to school, then on work nights another nine blocks farther west to the A&P store. I went on a date with a girl from Scales Mound, Illinois, one night, and we walked about eight blocks from her rooming house to the movie theatre. After the movie, we walked back to her place in the pouring rain. She never went out with me again after that.

Then in June, with just six months of college behind me, everything abruptly changed. When I reported for reserve duty at a regular Tuesday night drill, I was told to report to the commanding officer. He informed me that the navy needed more people on active duty and that they were calling up naval reservists, primarily new recruits like me. I couldn't believe it! I saw all of my planning and hard work going down the drain. Then I thought of something: I reminded him that I was attending college. Couldn't my active duty service be deferred? He then agreed that, yes, it could probably be deferred. "What college are you attending?" When I told him it was the Rockford School of Business, he said, "Isn't that a private college? Only students at state colleges or universities are allowed a deferment."

So much for all of my planning! In July, I received orders to report to the US Naval Base at Great Lakes, Illinois, for nine weeks of boot camp as part of a two-year active tour of duty with the US Navy. Despite my disappointment of having to put my college education on hold, I found some humor in this minor crisis. I had joined the Naval Reserve to avoid being drafted by the army, only to have managed somehow to be drafted by the navy!

I was assigned to Camp Barry at the Great Lakes Training Center north of Waukegan, Illinois. I wrote home on July 11 and told my folks that my pay was $83.20 per month and that "my uniforms and clothing items cost $175.00, which I'm to pay for with payroll deductions."

Reveille was held every morning at four thirty, and lights-out was at nine thirty. This was the routine, seven days a week. The first couple of weeks weren't too bad at boot camp. We spent a good deal of our time on indoctrination and learning the routine. It seemed like we were constantly standing in line for one thing or another: for inoculations, uniforms and equipment issue, for meals to be eaten and for food trays to be stacked afterward. We lined up three times a day at the mess hall. By the third week, however, we stopped complaining about the lines, for life at Camp Berry became a great deal more challenging.

I was assigned to Company 306, one of eighty-eight men, and the commander in charge of our company was David L. Pitts, a name I will never forget. He was a boatswain's mate first class, a "lifer" with twelve years in the navy. We soon learned that he had a top reputation as a drill instructor and that he had commanded the "Honor Company" the last three times. The other commanders were always out to beat him by winning the top number of competitive flags during the eight-week basic training session.

He conducted inspections continually, some unannounced, so we were always washing our clothes and scrubbing our whites with powdered bleach, liquid Wisk, and a hand brush. I hated that chore and quickly learned that the tiniest speck on your white hat or blouse meant a failed inspection, and you were sent back to the laundry room while the rest of your company continued with their drills. We were in danger of falling behind the others, so we soon learned how to scrub the sweat stains out of our white hatbands.

Our company went on to win seventeen more competition flags to total twenty-three at graduation, and we were named Color Company, making it four in a row for Commander Pitts. It was a close finish because we had difficulty winning that third drill flag. There were a couple of guys who couldn't march to save their butts. They just weren't coordinated enough to keep one foot ahead of the other. I don't know how many times Pitts would call us all out on the "grinder" (tarmac) to line up and march at three in the morning. "You're going to keep at it until you get it right." He had us line up and march to the mess hall a couple of times. No other company was made to do this. Pitts was obsessed. We lost eighteen members of our company during basic training. Two were discharged for mental issues; the others were "set back" by Pitts for "further training." He was determined to win the Color Company award.

When graduation day came, our Company 306 lined up at the head of the parade with those twenty-three flags. As Color Company, we were allowed to wear white leggings and guard belts, similar to those sailors on Honor Guard. We were marching briskly now in perfect cadence, with flags flying and the band playing "Anchors Aweigh"! It made the hair on my neck stand up! We were all proud as peacocks and, to a man, felt that Commander David L. Pitts was our hero, perhaps second only to John Wayne.

# CHAPTER 3

# CHILDHOOD IN THE 1940S

As a youngster, I had always thought that I would be an infantry soldier. Four of my dad's brothers joined the army during WWII, and I was old enough to remember them coming home after the war. As kids growing up in Benton, we often played "Army," using snowballs and dirt clods for artillery. We built and commanded "forts" in the neighborhood and held ranks like captain, lieutenant, or platoon sergeant. We had a vivid imagination, growing up in this small town during the 1940s.

The mines around Benton were all going strong when we lived in this home between 1939 and 1945 during WWII. The mine owners sent their drill bits to Probst's blacksmith shop to be reground and sharpened. I watched with fascination as Ambrose "Ambie" Probst fired up his open furnace and heated the ends of those long iron bars of various lengths. He would heat the end with star-shaped "teeth" to a red, then orange, then white color. He would then take it to the huge anvil where he pounded it and shaped it with special tools, sparks flying. When he finally dunked it into a shallow barrel of cold water, it would hiss loudly, and steam would billow up in a big cloud. He repeated the process several times until the piece was finished to his satisfaction. It was much the same process with the horseshoes and other iron pieces that needed to be cut or shaped. He had a hand bellows to fire the open-pit furnace. It was operated by a rope that he pulled around an overhead pulley. I would spend hours watching him at work, and he would talk to me throughout the time, occasionally taking the time to explain a process.

My dad worked in the mines at that time, and he would arrive home in late afternoon. In the summer, he would spend the early evening hours working in our vegetable garden. We always had a big garden. The two-story house had been converted to a duplex dwelling. We rented the downstairs, and the Delbert Symons family rented the upper level. Barbara ("Babs") Symons was my age, and Joyce was the same age as my sister Ruth. I believe Babs was my earliest playmate.

I had a dog when we lived on Depot Street. He was a mixed-breed terrier named Spot. He was white with brown and black spots and had a black face with white around one eye. I can still remember vividly the sight of the poor dog after he was run over by a car. It happened on the side street next to our house, the street that ran west toward Grandma and Grandpa Perkins's house. I ran over to Spot right after it happened. He was screeching and yelping, in obvious pain. The car had run over his head, and his eyeball was sticking out! It was a shocking sight. My mother came running out of the house, picked Spot up in her arms, then ran to one of our neighbors' houses and asked them to drive her and Spot to the veterinarian's office in Cuba City. Spot recovered okay, but he never went near the street again.

Our Grandpa Cook lived with us in Benton. After losing his farm, he decided to "break up housekeeping," as they called it in those days. He was a widower who had lost his wife, my mother's mother, back in 1927 when she died from high blood pressure that caused her lungs to rupture. She was only forty-nine years of age when she died. My mother was only nineteen years old at the time of her mother's death.

Grandpa Cook had always found time for prospecting throughout his life and continued that habit until he reached his midseventies. When he lived with us at the house across from the blacksmith shop, he would often go prospecting in the farmers' fields and pastures around Benton. He had worked hard all his life, and prospecting had provided him with an outlet—made him feel productive, I suppose, and kept him physically fit. Mom would pack sandwiches for him in his "dinner bucket," together with a thermos of hot coffee, cream and sugar added, and he would leave the house on foot. When I asked, "Where are you going, Grandpa?" his response was always, "For a walk in the country."

Later on, at the age of four, I asked my mother to make me a lunch because I wanted to take a "walk in the country." She laughed and said, "Okay," and packed me a lunch, thinking I would be taking my imaginary walk in our big backyard where I spent most of my time outdoors. She said later that I had always been good about staying in our yard and away from the street traffic, so she didn't expect that I would wander off. But this day was different. When she looked out the kitchen window later that morning, I was nowhere to be seen. She went outside, called my name, walked all around the house, looked up and down both intersecting streets, then asked the neighbor ladies if anyone had seen me. One said yes, she had seen me walking down the sidewalk past her house with my straw hat on (like the hat that Grandpa wore when he took his walk in the country), and she also mentioned that I had been carrying a dinner pail.

I can imagine my mother scurrying around and getting more and more stressed by the minute. She was always a nervous person, a bit high-strung, and I know she must have felt terrible about telling me it was okay to "take a walk in the country." Until now, she had no reason to think that I would actually walk out of our neighborhood.

Our family didn't own a car at that time, and my parents, in their entire lifetime, never had a telephone, so my mother left Ruth with our neighbor, Grace Symons, and hiked all around the neighborhood looking every which way to see if she could spot me trudging along. When she reached Main Street, she turned east toward the downtown area. She had only gone two or three blocks on Main when Charlotte Murray drove up alongside her, with me in the car. "Are you missing someone?" she asked. The Murrays lived about a half mile southeast of town on the New Diggings road, and Charlotte had looked out her kitchen window and saw me trudging along the road, all alone, with my straw hat and dinner pail. *Why, that looks like Jeanette and Percy's boy*, she thought to herself. She went out on her front porch and asked, "Where are you going, Gary?"

"For a walk in the country," I responded.

She persuaded me to get into her car, and she then drove me into town where she met Mom hiking down Main Street with a worried look on her face. Obviously, my mother was greatly relieved and happy to see me. She told that story many times over the years.

I didn't have many playmates in the immediate neighborhood, and my sister Ruth was just a toddler at that time. Babs Symons lived in the upstairs apartment, and Carol Peacock lived across the street from us. Carol was two years older than Babs and me. They always wanted to play house and other girl-type stuff, so I usually went off on my own. I had a two-wheel scooter, a tricycle, and a lot of toy cars and trucks to play with. The toys at that time were often made of wood with wooden wheels because most of the steel and rubber was needed for the war effort in the early 1940s. On rainy days, I would stay inside and play, sometimes with my set of Tinkertoys or Lincoln Logs.

Richard Troy was two years older than me and lived a block and a half away with his grandmother. When I was about five years old, I was allowed to walk down to his house and play, and, in turn, he would come up to our house quite often. I appreciated having a boy as a childhood playmate and would leave Babs and Carol to play on their own. My mom took a picture of Richard and me one afternoon when we were "fishing" out of a big washtub on our front porch. I had my straw hat on, and I guess I looked a bit like Tom Sawyer. Richard's grandma would treat us to roasted peanuts in the shell, and it was Richard who showed me the proper technique for cracking a peanut shell cleanly. It's surprising to me how many people have never learned the proper method of cracking a peanut shell.

Dad still worked at the Old Mulcahy Mine located between Benton and Shullsburg. Mom was pregnant with my sister Judy, and I guess we could now afford to rent the larger, single-family house up on Main Street, so we moved up there next to the "white church," which was the locals' name for the Methodist Church. This was a two-story house with three bedrooms and an indoor bathroom, and it had a big porch that wrapped around the front and along the side where there was a second entry into the dining room. The garden in back was the size of a city lot and had both raspberry and blackberry bushes along the front and one side of the garden, next to the Methodist Church cemetery. Mom put up berry preserves and jelly every fall, along with canned vegetables and pickles from the garden. She squeezed juice from the berries by dumping them into a cloth bag that was tied to the center of a broomstick. This contraption was suspended over the backs of two kitchen chairs. My job was to twist the bag every few minutes to compress the berries, causing the juice to drip into a pan beneath the bag. I guess this would be considered to be a "forerunner" to the modern electric juicer.

Judy was born shortly after we moved to the house on Main, and I began my first year of school the next month when I was enrolled in the first grade. We didn't have kindergarten in Benton then. My mother had to practically drag me to school. I hated it. Most of my friends were younger, and they didn't have to go.

We had a neighborhood "gang" consisting of four of my cousins, Gordon and Carl Farrey and Delos and Jack Mullikin, and neighborhood friends Ben Temple, Pete White, "Leaky" Fawcett, "Pots" Robbins, and a few others. We roamed the west-end neighborhoods and playgrounds, Depot Hill and the creek bottom, all in the west end of Benton. The creek was popular because boys are often attracted to water and related mud. One of our favorite pastimes was to build go-karts out of coaster wagon parts and any other salvage we could scrounge up from our dads' garages. (More on this later.) We constructed "forts" down by the creek and up on top of the big rock pile left after the closure of the Frontier Mine on Wes Robson's farm at the west edge of town. The rock pile was probably fifty feet high, ideal for an imaginary mountain. It was a great setting for playing "Cavalry and Indians" and for building forts, but we had to be on alert for an occasional rattlesnake.

The Second World War was on at this time, and most of our fathers worked in the lead and zinc mines around Benton. The big dump trucks passed by our house on a regular basis, loaded with ore from the area mines. Once in a while, our gang would do some "mining" in my dad's big garden in the fall while it lay dormant. We would dig a shaft with shovels and haul the dirt away in coaster wagons, our "dump trucks." We got a bit too ambitious one time, though, and sunk a shaft about eight feet deep. At age six or seven, it seemed to be that deep. At any rate, it was way over our heads as we dug through the rich black loam, the red clay, then gray-colored clay, sandstone shale, and more red, gray, and black clay. It was really hard work, and we had to hoist the dirt and heavy clay from the shaft with a rope and bucket because, at that young age, we didn't know how to engineer a winch and failed to scrounge up a large pulley that would have aided in the hoisting process.

By midafternoon, the "mining crew" had grown to eight or ten members plus a couple of girl spectators cautiously standing clear of the muddy worksite. This crowd caught the attention of my mother at the kitchen window, and she came out of the house to check on us. When she discovered how deep we had dug the hole, she got real excited and told us, "Fill in that right now before it caves in on you!" Water had begun to seep into the bottom of the shaft by now. It was real mucky to work down there when your shoes collected an inch or two of heavy clay, so suspending the mining operation and filling up the shaft wasn't such a bad idea. We had had enough of mining, and of course Mom was right: it was a bit hazardous.

In the winter months, we used to sleigh ride down Depot Hill. The paved street was long, fairly steep, ran about three or four city blocks, and at the bottom we would fly over the railroad track crossing at the lumber yard and then have to make an immediate ninety-degree right turn before the big oil storage tanks. The Village crew would spread sand on the street surface, so we would guide our sled next to the curb where there was no sand and then skid around the end of a dangerous culvert pipe before bounding over the tracks just before the sharp turn. If anyone dragged their feet to slow their rate of speed, they were labeled "sissies," and none of us wanted that! When the hill was icy and super fast, we would sometimes miss the turn past the tracks, drop down a steep bank, through a barbed-wire fence, and then drop into the creek (or go skidding across if it was frozen). I was usually one of the first to try anything daring. I was never reckless but felt compelled to overcome any fear by calculating the risk, determining the best route, then going for it! I inspected the barbed-wire fence, for example, to locate the best place to pass under it if I had to (Plan B if I missed the turn). I got skinned up more than a few times, tore my jacket on the barbed wire, and landed in the creek more than once. That required a trip home to change clothes. The water was ice cold. In summer, we ran this same course with the go-karts and often with the same results if we missed the turn at the bottom.

My dad's brother, Uncle "Rip" Perkins, had been the lead janitor at the Benton schools for many years, and he unlocked the gymnasium for "open gym" on Saturday mornings in the winter months. It was great for pickup games for all ages and a great escape from the harsh winter weather.

There was neither television nor video games in those days, so we amused ourselves with engineering and building projects as well as the daring feats of skill. I don't remember ever being bored at that age. Our gang could always gather and collectively think of something to do: catch pigeons under the viaduct (sometimes wing them with BB guns to make for an easier capture), "hunt" bumblebees with our BB guns, or shoot rats at the village dump with a .22-caliber rifle.

For the captured pigeons, we built chicken-wire cages or coops and kept them well fed with field corn stolen from a nearby field and cracked on a sidewalk with a hammer. We each had a variety of pigeons, all different colors. The mostly white ones were preferred. There was a lot of pigeon trading, two gray pigeons for one white/brown bird, as an example. I don't believe any cash changed hands. There was sport in hunting bumblebees because if you missed with the BB gun, you were apt to get stung.

We often skied in the wintertime at Wes Robson's pasture with the really steep hill and sometimes at Fowlers' farm across the highway. Our skis were wooden with a leather strap that buckled over the toes of our rubber boots. Hardly any of us owned ski poles. We also built a long, heavy bobsled with a two-by-ten plank bolted to two sets of two-by-six runners that could be towed behind a car or farm tractor to the top of a big hill on one of the country roads packed with snow. We built snow houses and forts by freezing blocks of snow into ice, then stacking them like bricks as high as we could reach. Sometimes we would lay some old scrap boards across the top to support a snow roof, but we seldom took the time to do that.

Snowball fights were common, and the ice-block forts were the scenes of many battles. There would usually be a couple of forts in the west-end neighborhood, and we would station two volunteers to guard our forts while we formed a raiding party to invade the enemy fort. It wasn't always the guys, either. Sometimes the girls would join in the raid or stay behind on guard detail. When our fort became overrun and knocked down, we would rebuild it. Sometimes our fort would get smashed by the enemy late at night while no one was there to guard it. We would have to rebuild it quickly, before the snow melted, and get back into the skirmish. If a new fort was constructed, we would hear about it pretty fast. A scouting party was sent out to spy on the new fort and bring back an intelligence report. Then we would gather round and plan a strategy, whether it would be a straight-on attack or some type of flanking maneuver. The key was to pick a time for the raid that would give us an advantage, and then assign responsibilities. If we were shorthanded, we would sometimes attack at dusk when some of the enemy had gone home for supper.

It seemed like we had a lot more winter snows in those days, and these activities were popular throughout the winter months. It was always a disappointment when the snow melted in the spring, because there would be no more snow-fort building. One year, we were able to extend our battle season when the Bowman family built a new house in our neighborhood. They brought equipment in and dug the basement, eight feet deep, leaving big piles of clay around the site. We had a couple of weeks to play "War" at the building site before the crew came to lay block. We employed trench warfare and the big, heavy artillery (large clods of red clay). They really hurt when you got hit! In our view, the pain made it a more realistic experience. At night we would use flashlights as decoys. We would set the lighted flashlights on top of a pile of dirt and, while the enemy was throwing the missiles at lights, we would crawl around and attack them on their flank. Our neighborhood had a great infantry. Forward scout was my favorite assignment, smearing my face with mud and crawling around in the dirt amid flying clods of rock-hard clay. What a rush that was!

We would often climb mulberry or plum trees and eat fruit and berries. Green apples with salt always tasted best when they were stolen. The bruise on a green apple tasted sweeter, so at times we would tap it on a fire hydrant or pipe frame of some playground equipment to create a bruise. We found it advisable to post a guard to give us advanced warning. Watermelon was fun to steal, but most gardens were close by a house, so it was difficult to get away with a successful raid in town. We found Mr. Fowler's farm at the edge of town to be ideal. His garden was a distance away from the farmhouse and separated by a grove of trees. We would steal a nice big melon and scamper up the hill to our secret hiding place in the old rock pile, a leftover from the Fowler mine.

We played baseball down at the ballpark near the lumberyard or, back in the day, when we were younger, we would play ball in someone's yard. Gordy, Carl, and I used to play in their driveway when there was just the three of us. We would pitch rubber or tennis balls with the garage doors as a backstop, the three of us—pitcher, catcher, and batter—taking turns. We were Cubs fans, so I was Dee Fondy, Gordy was Roy Smalley, and Carl was Andy Pafko. After the "game," we were instructed by Aunt Blanche (Gordy and Carl's mother) to clean all of the ball marks off the white garage door with a scrub brush, soap, and water.

One spring afternoon, I jauntily walked the four blocks down to Gordy and Carl's house with my glove slipped over the bat handle and the bat over my shoulder, expecting to play ball in their driveway. But just as we got lined up, Aunt Blanche came to the kitchen window and said, "Now don't forget to weed the strawberry patch, boys. Like I told you last night, I want that done before you play ball!" So we spent most of the morning on our hands and knees, pulling weeds one by one, carefully working around the young strawberry plants. It was a complete waste of a good morning, and I couldn't have had worse timing!

My dad cut my hair when I was very young. He had a pair of hand clippers that tended to pull, rather than cut, at times. After he wrapped a towel around my shoulders and pinned it at the back of my neck, I would make a face in preparation for the hair-pulling ordeal. The clippers didn't pull my hair that often, but I never knew when it would happen, so I maintained a grimace at all times.

Dad didn't chop my hair up too much, but when I reached the age of eight or nine years, I insisted on going to the barbershop in Benton to get a professional cut like the rest of my buddies. The Vaughn barbershop was owned by two brothers, "Bubbins" and "Dutch." Bubbins gave the better haircut, whereas Dutch cut faster but rather "choppy." My mother would say, "Now when you get your haircut today, wait for Bubbins. Don't let Dutch cut your hair!"

When it came four o'clock at the Vaughn barbershop, the brothers would take a couple of dollars out of the till and ask one of the patrons to go next door to Rollie's Tavern and bring back a couple of beers. I was in the chair at four o'clock a couple of times when Bubbins would interrupt the snip-snip of the scissors to take a swig of beer from the bottle that sat on the back bar next to the clippers and the rose-scented hair tonic. I could hear the "glug-glug" sound as he took a couple of swallows and then resumed the snip-snip of the scissors. After a couple of minutes, Bubbins would give out a healthy burp in midsnip. They enjoyed that bottle of cold beer every afternoon before closing shop and going home for supper. I guess it must have sharpened their appetite.

Shortly after the end of World War II, my dad was laid off at the mine when the price level dropped for lead ore. It was in the spring, and I remember he had been spading the garden when Frank Calvert drove into our driveway. He told Dad that he was in need of some help at his farm operation. He owned two dairy farms north of Benton where he milked Holsteins, raised pigs and Hereford beef cattle. He had most of his acreage in corn, hay, and soybeans. He knew Dad had the necessary experience after being raised on a farm and, later on, working for Wes Robson as a hired hand on his dairy farm before he went to work in the mines. I stood nearby as Frank laid out the terms of employment, including weekly wage. He also owned a rental house in Benton and told Dad that he could move his family into the house on a rent-free basis as part of the deal.

The whole time that Frank was talking, my dad was down on one knee next to the garden, quietly cleaning the round-mouth spade. He scarcely looked up as Frank went on and on in a soft voice. Finally, when Calvert had completed his verbal offer, he asked, "Can you start working for me on Monday morning, Haggens?" ("Haggens" was my dad's nickname.)

My dad answered, "I suppose I can."

That was undoubtedly the most unusual job interview, offer, and acceptance I have ever witnessed in my lifetime. That's the way I remember my dad, though, very laid back, and he never seemed to worry about things. If he did, he kept it to himself. Of course, I was only nine years old when this event took place and was not aware of some private discussions Mom and Dad may have had after he had been laid off at the mine. I'm sure they were concerned about their future and the need for family income. Dad may have had some other employment possibilities, but if he did, I wasn't aware of them.

Shortly after Dad began working for Calvert, we moved into the old, two-story house just two blocks away from the house on Main Street and just one a block from the school. The house was drafty, had no inside plumbing, and no central heat. We burned wood and coal in the stoves. There was a flattop cooking stove in the kitchen and a large heating stove in the living room at the front of the house. One of my chores after school during winter months was splitting wood and keeping the wood boxes filled.

Uncle Harry Cook, my mother's brother, had a large, thirty-inch portable saw that he would take into the woods, and he and my dad, Grandpa Cook, and Duffy Mullikin would cut firewood in late summer for all three families. I often went along to help, and sometimes the Mullikin boys were there too. The tree limbs had been cleaned of small branches prior to the sawing operation where three men would hold the long limbs or logs as Uncle Harry guided them into the stationary saw blade. With all of this manpower, we would soon have a huge pile of firewood that we would then load by hand into a truck. My dad would usually bring the two-ton flatbed truck from the farm. It had sideboards and a dump bed, so we didn't have to unload it by hand. We were often out in the woods during the early fall season when it was crisp and cold, and I really liked the smell of freshly cut hardwoods in the cold autumn air.

We moved into the hundred-year-old house in Benton as per the terms of employment of Dad's new job. The house required a lot of fuel in the winter months because it was not insulated and had windows seven feet in height. When winter winds blew, the curtains would sway to and fro as air infiltrated around the gaps in those big, old, single-pane windows. In the bitter cold of a Wisconsin winter, the only warm place was next to the stove. Since there was no indoor plumbing, we also had to acclimate to the use of an outdoor privy. It had two holes separated by a full-height partition and two separate entry doors to the structure. I often told people that we had the only "duplex outhouse" in town. It was an oversized structure and was anchored with steel fence posts set into concrete. There was no way it could be tipped over as a Halloween prank.

I took my routine Saturday bath in a washtub next to the kitchen stove. We all took turns at the tub, so the kitchen was "off limits" during those Saturday baths.

Grandpa Cook had the warmest upstairs bedroom, above the living room stove. My sisters had the other front bedroom where the stovepipe came through the floor, and this kept their room somewhat warm in the winter. I had the rear bedroom upstairs where there was a small register cut into the floor, which brought a bit of heat up from the kitchen, but my windows would ice up in the wintertime. I had to jump into bed and curl up in one place until the bed warmed up. My mother would put flannel sheets on the beds in winter, and that was a big improvement over the icy cotton sheets.

One of my classmates, Bill Cherry, lived next door. Harold and Allen Farrey lived just up the street, and the Bainbridge brothers were across the street. Another classmate, Ben Temple, lived on a nearby farm that was inside the village limits. They drove their milk cows across Main Street twice each day. This required the traffic to stop in both directions on State Highway 11. The farm was there long before the village of Benton had been established. Temple's cows sometimes cut through the corner of the schoolyard and left unwanted deposits that we tried to avoid during play at recess time.

The Village of Benton was formerly known as Cottonwood Hill, and the Dennis Murphy home of 1838, including the adjoining Cottonwood

Farm, became the Temple home. My friend and classmate Ben and his family were descendants of the Murphys.

This little mining hamlet in the Wisconsin Territory was founded by Andrew Murphy in 1827. The Murphys built the water-powered feed mill east of the village in 1828–29. Dennis and James Murphy, two of Andrew's five sons, platted the village and donated land for all three churches and cemeteries in town. Dennis's son Matt Murphy, an attorney who grew wealthy through mining and real estate, gave money to build the county courthouse in Darlington. A statue of Matt Murphy stands in front of the courthouse with an added Irish green bowtie.

One of the three churches was Roman Catholic, established by Father Samuel Mazzuchelli. (To the Irish miners, he was known as "Matthew Kelly.") He had been sent to this lead region to minister to the whites and Indians. He started some twenty-five churches in these mining towns. He also possessed an impressive architectural skill and designed the church in Cottonwood Hill (later known as Benton), Shullsburg, Sinsinawa, and New Diggings. He also founded a nunnery for the Sinsinawa Dominican Sisters near the Sinsinawa Mound to the west of Benton.

Cottonwood Hill gained a nickname by local miners of "Swindlers' Ridge" due to numerous shady deals over mining rights and landowners being cheated out of the bountiful lead ore revenue by slick lawyers from outside the area. But then in 1845, the village was renamed Benton in honor of respected Senator Thomas Hart Benton from

Missouri who had actively promoted the interests of this lead and zinc mining region in southwestern Wisconsin.

\* \* \* \* \* \*

Our neighborhood gang became the engineering team that turned out several go-karts. The first two models would roll over on the tight turns, so I came up with the concept of using forty-inch-wide axles and a lower chassis. We cut the axles from steel pipe with my dad's hacksaw, and Grandpa Cook helped us find some rusty bolts and fittings from the many coffee cans used for storage in our garage. The race cart was really fast and would slide sideways on the gravel surface at the bottom of Depot Hill, but it never tipped over after we widened the wheelbase. (Years later, General Motors introduced the "wide-track" Pontiac. It was quite apparent that we were way ahead of our time in this Benton neighborhood.) With the wider tracking, our car slid through the turn and splashed into the creek a few times. We cut ourselves on the barbed-wire fence, but it was the fastest racer in Benton. Roger and Ray Farrey used to have the fastest cart until we put this baby on the track!

Then, later on, Bill got the idea that we ought to have a cab with a top on the go-kart. There was some argument about that proposal, but he won out, so we nailed some upright framing and used a scrap of plywood for a roof over the seat. It never performed the same after that modification. It was top-heavy, sluggish, and just plain ugly. Years later we could have called it the "Edsel," but at that time, in 1950, we christened it the "Bum Buggy" after we had put that clunky cab over the seat. By this time, we had painted and repainted it several times. We could buy a half pint of enamel at reasonable cost at the Gambles store in Cuba City or at the Benton Lumber Yard, so we enjoyed painting our bikes and coaster wagons once or twice each summer, choosing a different color each time and adding some "creative trim" for contrast. We weren't artistic enough to paint freehand, so we used a lot of masking tape.

We played tackle football in Bill's yard because they had a double corner lot. When some of the bigger boys joined the game, we would play "two-hand touch" to maintain a fair level of competition. The game would get pretty rough at times, so I would wear two pairs of denim jeans to protect my knees and hips from the hard winter ground and occasional rocks in the yard. I remember running a pass pattern one day, and the ball was thrown off target. I veered right, looking back over my shoulder, and got literally "clotheslined." After that I was not only aware of where the defensive player was but also watched for Mrs. Cherry's clothesline.

* * * * * *

After that difficult first year of school, I did much better and began receiving some good grades. That first-grade year was a bad experience for me, though, and I was almost held back. My teacher was Charlene Gray, and she was a strict disciplinarian. I didn't want to be in school that first year, and she had no patience for my lackadaisical approach to study. She began to call me "Pokey Perkins," and some of the other kids from the other end of town picked on me and pushed me around at recess time. I had never been involved in fistfights at this point of my life, and this was a new experience. My feelings would get hurt more than anything else because I couldn't understand the reason for the hostility. I tried not to react to taunts and avoided confrontations whenever possible.

Once I realized that I would have to stay in school, I managed to adjust, became a good student, and gained the respect of the rest of my new classmates. Second grade went a lot better for me. By fifth grade, I had grown considerably and was one of the tallest in my class of twenty-four students. Elaine Welsh was also tall and gangly at that age, and they called us "Daddy Longlegs" and "Momma Longlegs." I had a crush on her in the fifth grade, but she never knew about that.

On Saturdays and also during summer school vacation, at about the age of twelve, I would spend hours at the Calvert farm where my dad worked. It was about a half mile northwest of Benton, and it was an easy ride up there on my bike. George Calvert was in my class at school, and we became close friends. Howard Schloeman was also in my class, and his family rented the house next to the Calvert farm, so the three of us spent a lot of time at the farm. We learned to drive tractor, cultivate corn, and haul hay bales on a wagon behind the tractor. We experimented with chewing tobacco and corn-silk cigarettes. Howard and I could handle the chewing tobacco pretty well, but it often made George sick to his stomach. We chewed Red Man, the same brand that my dad chewed. He told us that the tobacco kept the dust out of his throat when working around the dry, dusty hay or oat chaff. He had that Cornish dry sense of humor, so we couldn't always tell whether he was serious.

My dad had some unique sayings, and a couple of them come to mind here. For example, when he discovered a flat tire on the car, "Well now, that's a helluva note!" Or when there was more of the story to be told: "That wasn't the half of it."

We also learned a lot about life on the farm. In those days, parents didn't often explain the facts of life. Dad would let us watch the cows being bred by the big Holstein bull, and sometimes we would catch the hogs in action. The three of us would discuss these observations and make note of the animals' physical differences and techniques. We would talk things over, George, Howard, and I, and on at least one occasion, we smuggled some "dirty" magazines up into the haymow.

At the age of sixteen, my first paying job at the Calvert farm was hoeing corn. My job was to walk between the rows of hybrid corn and hoe out the "volunteers," the nonhybrid sprouts that came up between the rows. I was paid fifty cents an hour by Frank Calvert and had to go down to the post office in Benton to get my Social Security card. I spent some pretty long days in that thirty-acre cornfield and earned some serious blisters along with the twenty dollars a week.

# CHAPTER 4

# THE PERKINS FAMILY IN BENTON

Life aboard the USS *San Pablo* had fallen into a more normal routine following the red alert scare in Delaware Bay. We had sailed out of our home port of Philadelphia and were now cruising in the deep water of the Atlantic.

This was my first time on the ocean, and once the eastern shoreline was out of sight, it seemed to me that the ship was sailing in a "basin," an illusion that the water surface was higher at the horizon in all directions and that the ship was at a lower level. I don't know if other sailors felt the same sensation, but that's the way it seemed to me.

My initial duties aboard ship were dull and boring after a short time: chipping paint (an endless task), maintaining the lines (or ropes), stowing deck gear, and standing daily watches. As a deckhand, I was required to stand four-hour watches and was assigned to the upper deck lookout position on either the port or starboard side. My duties were to scan the horizon with binoculars, and if I sighted a vessel, I was to inform the bridge officer of its bearing by reading the compass at my lookout duty station. We often traveled for days without sighting another vessel. Of course, the radar man on watch would spot the blip of a vessel long before it came into sight on the horizon, so he would normally give me a heads-up so I could more easily spot it when it came into view.

I was beginning to enjoy life in the navy in spite of the grunt work and occasional boredom. Life at sea certainly beat boot camp by a long shot.

I must say, however, that boot camp, while painful and harsh during those nine weeks, is an experience that benefits any young man, and some more than others. It prepares one psychologically for life beyond the military in addition to providing the recruit with superb physical conditioning. The training in my group at Great Lakes was taken to an extreme, however. We had close to ninety recruits in Company 306, but only seventy of us made the grade and graduated nine weeks later. Our company had more "washouts" than the others because of our demanding company commander, David L. Pitts, a fiery, redheaded first-class boatswain's mate from Alabama. He was a tough disciplinarian, sharp in tongue and dress with his starched whites and spit-shined boots. He let us know on the first day of camp, "We have only one objective, and that is to be Color Company. We're going to win every competitive award, and we will march at the head of the parade on graduation day with all flags flying. I'll tell you right now, a lot of you aren't going to be able to cut it!"

He was much more demanding than the other company leaders. While we performed well in the athletic competitions, he repeatedly called us out onto the "grinder" at three in the morning for extra marching drills because we had so many guys who failed to catch on to the cadence and didn't seem to know left from right. My boots were too large, and in spite of wearing three pairs of socks, blisters developed on both of my heels. I stuffed pieces of white handkerchief inside my socks, but the blisters became infected, and my ankles swelled so much that I had to tug hard to get my boots on each morning. The pain would shoot up my legs when I first got them on, but after a slow, gingerly walk around the barracks, the pain would diminish. If I kept moving throughout the day, the pain was tolerable, but I could feel the fluid draining from the blisters on both heels, and my socks would be wet when I removed them at lights-out. I toughed it out for about a week, because if any of us lost as much as three days in sick bay, we would be set back a week and reassigned to another company. I was determined to stay with 306 and didn't want to be one of those guys who couldn't cut it. We had already lost several guys by now. Pitts had managed to get rid of the guys with "two left feet" and one bed-wetter from Kentucky.

The swelling worsened. It was pure torture to pull those damn boots on every morning, and I finally reported to sickbay when it got so bad that I could hardly walk. They gave me shots for the infection, put me in bed with my feet elevated, and I soaked my ankles in Epsom salts four times a day. I managed to rejoin my company on the third day.

Just as Pitts promised, we won all of the competitive flags at least once, and we led the parade at graduation as Color Company 306. Pitts was a tough nut. He had challenged us and pissed us off more than a few times, but he succeeded in firing us up. It was a proud moment for the remaining seventy recruits who hung in there and made it through the nine-week program with that salty, old boatswain's mate.

Gary USN, 1958

My aunt Arlene and uncle Tom Ewing drove up to Great Lakes for my graduation, a three-hour trip from their home in Beloit, Wisconsin. They had made this trip before. Their son Ben had served in the navy and had graduated from Great Lakes a few years earlier. Seeing cousin Ben in uniform and listening to some of his "sea stories" had influenced my decision to join the navy. Two other cousins on the Cook side of the family, Donald and Dale Farrey, were sailors during WWII, but the Perkinses were army vets. Four of my dad's brothers were soldiers during that war, and three of them saw action in Europe.

\* \* \* \* \* \*

My father, William Percy, was born on November 27, 1902. He was the second oldest of ten children born to Thomas and Lilla Jane (Robbins) Perkins. Their firstborn son, Thomas Emery, died in infancy, an event that was all too common in those days.

My dad grew up on a farm about a mile south of Benton, Wisconsin, near the Old Ollie Belle mine. His father, Tom, was a miner and a tenant farmer who raised crops and livestock on his small dairy farm. He shared the proceeds with the landowner. This arrangement was commonly known as "farming on shares." Tom and Lilla Jane were of Cornish/Irish descent, and their children were born two to three years apart. They were always a close-knit family and blessed with a lively sense of humor, both common traits of the Cornish heritage.

My father, known primarily by his middle name of Percy, didn't go to school until his sister Bertha, two years younger, reached school age. They walked about two miles into Benton and had to cross a swinging bridge over the Fever River. Dad told me that when he and Bertha started out for that very first day of school, they discovered a big, old rattlesnake sunning itself in the center of the bridge. At that point, Dad said, "Come on, Bertha, let's go back home." They started their schooling a day later.

Dad and one of his brothers, Charles James Foster Perkins ("Foss"), were close in age and played together whenever they had finished their daily chores on the farm. In the wintertime when the river was frozen, they broke holes in the ice and caught mud turtles that they had spotted beneath the ice, loaded them onto a sled, and took them home. Dad said that their mother, my grandma Perkins, made them take the turtles back where they found them. Another time, he and Foss spotted a redheaded woodpecker up in a tree near the farm, so they decided to try to catch it. They climbed up the tree to a hollowed area where the woodpecker was nested. Dad said he was a bit tentative about reaching in there bare-handed, so he said to Foss, "Give me your shirt." He then wrapped the shirt around his hand and reached into the hole. Immediately there was a loud squawk and a flutter of wings as the woodpecker flew out of the tree … with Foss's red plaid shirt snagged onto the bird's claw! They scrambled back down from the tree and chased across the field to where the shirt had fallen when the woodpecker finally shed it. Dad said, "Foss sure didn't want to go home to Mother without his shirt."

Percy Perkins, ca. 1917

My father picked up the nickname of "Haggens" when he was in school. He said he didn't know where that name came from or how he was tagged with it, but it stayed with him throughout his life. His friends and some of his brothers called him "Haggens" at various times, but his parents always called him Percy. I never heard him called by his first name of William. Ironically, one of his younger brothers was called "Bill," yet his given name was Glenn. Nicknames were common in Benton.

Dad was a good student, and when he was in the fifth grade at Benton, his teacher asked him to take Herby Hardman out in the hallway and help him with his reader. A generation later, I was asked to take Herby's son Gene out in that same hallway, at the same window seat, in the same school building, to help him with his phonics.

Grandpa Tom Perkins was a teamster for the mining companies during the boom of World War I. He hauled lead and zinc ore from the mines to the National Roaster near Cuba City by team and wagon. He shoveled the ore onto the wagon at the mine and then shoveled it off at the roaster, all by hand in those days. He also had morning and evening chores at the farm, and there were crops to plant in the spring and to harvest in the fall each year. Sometime after the war, my grandparents, Tom and Lilla Jane, moved their family into the village of Benton, where they rented a home on the west end of town. It was next door to Grandpa's sister who had married Bernie Treganza, another Cornish American. My dad's youngest siblings, Carl ("Pat"), Glenn ("Bill"), and Wilbur ("Willie"), were born in the village of Benton.

The Perkinses were all of moderate height, about five feet seven inches at most, and of average build. They enjoyed a happy family life. Their Cornish heritage gave them a strong sense of pride and strong moral values. They were independent people, good with their hands, and enjoyed the outdoor life. Most had vegetable gardens. The mothers and daughters loved to cook, bake, and "put up" fruits and vegetables from their gardens. They made several varieties of pickles from cucumbers, beets, and crabapples, as well as candies and peanut brittle at Christmastime. Much of the food in those days was produced on the farm or in the vegetable gardens in town.

While the Perkins boys all went to school at Benton, they were mostly self-taught when it came to the many skills they mastered. Foss and Clarence ("Clary") were finish carpenters and cabinetmakers, while Pat was a framer in rough carpentry. Robert Irvin ("Rip") and Bill were bricklayers, and many of the chimneys and fireplaces around Benton were built by one of the Perkins brothers. When the Benton Public School was built during the Great Depression of the 1930s, Rip made seventy-five cents an hour as a mason while most of the workers on this national WPA project, including my grandfather Cook, made the normal rate of sixty cents an hour for unskilled labor.

Foss, Bill, and Willie served in the army during World War II. Pat also enlisted but was given an early discharge at Camp Grant in Rockford, Illinois, due to medical reasons. He was very disappointed about not being able to join the service with his brothers. Both Foss and Bill enlisted at the early stage of the war, prior to the attack on Pearl Harbor. Foss was the first to sign up in March 1941 at age thirty-five. Uncle Bill was twenty-two when he enlisted on the Fourth of July of the same year. They both signed up for a three-year obligation. Uncle Willie also enlisted in the army in September of 1942. He had just turned twenty-one when he volunteered "for the duration of the war plus six months." All of them were single without dependents and entered the US Army at a grade of private.

Uncle Foss strung telephone and telegraph lines for the army in Europe as the front line of battle moved forward. He was in field artillery and used the phone lines to direct gunnery fire from base camp to forward targets on the front line.

Uncle Bill served in the Second Cavalry, Fourth Army, which was commanded by General George Patton. He attained the grade of sergeant in charge of maintenance and parts in the Fourth Army Support Group. He had eight soldiers reporting to him. He said they were often short of repair parts near the front lines and had to be innovative to keep all the tanks, trucks, and other vehicles running.

His unit saw duty in France, Belgium, and Germany. In December 1944, the Germans mounted a huge offensive from Germany, across the border into Belgium. It was known as the Battle of the Bulge. After some early success, the Germans' forward offensive was halted by the 101st Airborne Division at the small town of Bastogne. The paratroopers, heavily outnumbered, found themselves completely surrounded by German troops. Bastogne sat on an important crossroads, and the 101st was ordered to hold the town at all costs. If the Germans were to take Bastogne, they would have a clear path to Antwerp, and the Allied Forces couldn't afford to let this happen. The "Screaming Eagles" of the 101st took heavy casualties in the bitter cold of December but managed to hold off the Germans until two American armored divisions could be brought into the battle. One of those was Patton's Fourth Army, whose tank corps, in ten days of snow and freezing temperatures, sped over two hundred miles from the south and, with no time to rest, broke through the German Panzer unit the day after Christmas and saved the 101st from being totally wiped out. It took several more days of tough fighting to drive the German tanks and troops back into Germany. The battle at Bastogne became a major turning point of the war and was to become the final major offensive of the German army. Their failure at the Battle of the Bulge broke the Germans' fighting spirit and was the beginning of the end for the Nazis.

Uncle Willie also served in an armored division in Europe. He was a member of a six-man crew in a tank destroyer, a half-track vehicle that traveled faster than a tank but, due to its light armor, was vulnerable to a direct hit by enemy fire. On the battlefields of France, an artillery shell hit their vehicle, and it caught fire. The three crewmen in the lower stations were burned to death, but Willie and two other crewmen in the upper chamber managed to get out. Willie's clothes were on fire, and by rolling around on the ground, he managed to put out the flames. He was severely burned and spent about six months in an army hospital. Willie had to have skin grafted to portions of his face and hands. His facial skin remained rather pink in color and pockmarked, and he suffered the permanent loss of his earlobes.

Prior to his injury, Willie was awarded the Bronze Star for achievement against the enemy. He also was awarded the good conduct ribbon plus the E.T.O. ribbon with several battle stars. None of the Perkins brothers spoke much about their wartime experiences, but in a report that was published in the *Benton Advocate*, Willie's platoon described how he won the Bronze Star:

> During a recent battle, Cpl Willie ventured into enemy territory, not realizing at the time where he was. Walking along enemy trenches looking for souvenirs, he stumbled upon two Germans whom he thought were dead.
>
> Stepping over the first one, stooping to pick up a German Luger, he noticed the second one blinking an eye. Stepping back, Cpl Willie shouted, "Achtung" (Attention!), at the same time covering them both with his sub-machine gun.
>
> He marched them back to where they were questioned by the Interrogating Officer, who learned that they were a dangerous Bazooka team. They also disclosed the positions of two other Bazooka teams and they were quickly eliminated.

The three brothers were separated during the war except for one occasion. Bill said he had an opportunity to visit Foss, and they met at the town of Rosenheim in Bavaria. As a youngster, I remember when they came home from the war and brought war souvenirs with them: flags, German bayonets, insignias, and other paraphernalia. I also remember a German dinner fork that was impressive to me because it was so much larger than our American dinnerware. I was about seven years of age at the time.

\* \* \* \* \* \*

Thomas Perkins Family, 1951

Grandma and Grandpa Perkins celebrated their fiftieth wedding anniversary at their home in Benton in 1951. At that time, they lived in a big ranch-style home with a daylight basement, which was located one block south of Main Street, near the school. I believe Uncle Willie put up most of the money for the house, and his brothers built it for their parents. At the time of their fiftieth anniversary, a photograph was taken of them and their nine adult children.

We often had large family gatherings at their house, especially at Thanksgiving and Christmas, and occasionally on Easter Sunday. The Tom and Lilla Perkins family had grown considerably by the early 1950s: Percy, Jeanette, and their children, Gary, Ruth, and Judy; Bertha and Foss, both single and living at home; Rip, Margaret, and their children, Donna and Bonnie; Grace and Wilbur Peebles with their children, Carol and Wayne; Clary, Elva Jane, and their children, Kay, Tom, Sharon and Fred; Carl (Pat), Esther, and children, Susan and John; Bill, Jean, and their boys, Jimmy and Joe; and Willie, also single and living at home. All of the families lived in Benton except for Uncle Bill and his family in Blue River, an hour and a half north of Benton, and Grace and her family in Galena, Illinois, a half hour south of Benton.

I remember that we always had two Christmases when I was young. We would open gifts at our house on Christmas morning, then go down to Grandma and Grandpa's house in the afternoon. There would be more gifts under their tree for us. The Perkins family became so large that we began to draw names for gifts, so you never knew in advance whom your gift would be from. Grandma always bought a small gift for each of her grandchildren and, later, for the great-grandchildren as the family grew in size. I'm sure Uncle Willie helped her finance this tradition when the family grew so large.

Grandpa Tom Perkins was an avid gardener, as were most of his sons. He would work the garden with a hand cultivator that, unlike a garden hoe, had long, curved claws. He wore twill pants with suspenders and a light blue chambray shirt. He always wore a felt hat that had sweat stains spreading above the band. When cultivating his garden, he would spit Red Man tobacco juice when he reached the end of the row. He maintained a large garden during his time as a tenant farmer just east of Benton, and again later when they lived in three different houses in the village of Benton at various times. He would typically select a large house with an empty lot next door that he could cultivate for his vegetable garden. When his sons built him a new home, the house was situated on one lot and the garden on the one adjacent. I remember he had two or three crabapple trees so Grandma and Aunt Bertha could make pickled crabapples for the Christmas season.

Grandpa Perkins also had beautiful flower gardens, with plants in bloom from spring to fall: tulips (Grandma's favorite), lilies, irises, gladiola, and many others. My mother said that when I was born, Dad went to Grandpa's house and picked a fresh bouquet of flowers for her every evening. Dad didn't have a car at the time, and my uncle Rip drove him to Hazel Green to visit me and Mom in the hospital. New mothers and their babies stayed in the hospital for a week or longer at that time; Mom must have had a beautiful collection of flowers when we were ready to go home!

When we gathered for a holiday, Grandma and Aunt Bertha would prepare most of the food: baked beans, home-baked buns, potatoes, squash, and vegetables. They always had sweet chunk pickles, apple butter, pickled crabapples and beets that were put up in the fall and stored in the basement along with the canned fruit and Uncle Foss's homemade sauerkraut and horseradish. They would roast a big turkey or two, and Uncle Pat would bake a ham and bring it over to his folks' house, along with a pie or two that he had baked. Some of the others would bring desserts and salads. We always had plenty to eat, and during those holiday gatherings, we often ate in three shifts, the children first, then a couple more groups, whoever was ready to sit down at the long table. Grandma and Aunt Bertha always waited and sat down with the last group. It was always an informal, happy time at

Grandma and Grandpa's house. The table was large when all the leaves were inserted, and there was never a shortage of food.

I remember there was always a lot of lively conversation, and Uncles Rip and Clary grew hard of hearing over the years, so you had to talk pretty loud to make yourself heard. Rip was a great storyteller and hunched his shoulders when he laughed. He became the unofficial counselor at the high school after being janitor there for all those years. It was the teachers, not the students, who came to him for advice, asking, "What would you do, Rip?"

Uncle Foss never did marry and lived with his folks. He enjoyed having all of us kids around during the holidays. He would get down on the floor with his nephews to help them put Erector sets or Tinkertoy models together. He was a carpenter, and because he never married, he was pretty independent. On the other hand, maybe he was too independent to get married. When he accepted a carpentry job, remodeling or additions or whatever, he would never commit to a date for when the job would start or when it would be finished. The customer would have to bide his time until Foss showed up to do the job. He was always busy, with jobs on a waiting list. Sometimes his brothers would help him on the weekends or in the evenings when they got home from work at their regular jobs. Foss was observed shingling a steep roof on a two-story house in Benton when he was seventy-three years old. When someone in town informed his sister, Bertha, that he had seen Foss up on the roof, Bertha said, "Oh, it couldn't have been Foss. He hasn't done any shingling in ten years." The neighbor responded that he could have sworn it was Foss that he had seen up on Watsons' roof, but wisely thought it best to not pursue the subject any further.

Foss, like his father, was a great gardener and took over the family garden plot after Grandpa died. He raised peanuts one year and roasted them in the oven. When Bob O'Flahrity and I stopped by one day to admire his garden, Foss told Bob that the secret to his healthy potatoes was that he planted an onion in every hill. When Bob questioned the reasoning for an onion being planted, Foss told him that the onion made the potato's eyes water, and the extra moisture kept the potato healthy.

Uncle Clary worked at the mines for most of his adult life. He was an avid fisherman and sometimes would go fishing at sunrise before he went to work at the mine. He, too, was a carpenter, and sometimes he and Foss would work on a job together. Both of them were proud and independent, so once in a while there would be a disagreement on how to proceed on a project. As I recall, there was never any spirited argument or harsh words spoken. If they couldn't reach an agreement, Foss would calmly pick up his tools and go home. Maybe he'd be back the next day or the day after, but it was as though nothing had happened. He was a man truly at peace with the world, and he avoided any direct conflict. Perhaps this was due to some harrowing experiences at the front lines in Europe during the war, but more likely it was just his nature. I think he simply felt that it didn't pay to get excited over the small things in life, and his brothers seemed to have this same calm disposition.

Both Foss and Clary liked to tinker with things. Clary made a miniature wood-turning lathe out of an old sewing machine, and Uncle Foss also made one. They each claimed responsibility, so I don't know which uncle had the original version. Clary was still using his contraption when he was eighty years of age, making finials for the tops of hall trees and quilt racks that he had constructed for his family. He made a lot of furniture over the years and enjoyed cabinetmaking as a lifetime hobby. As a miner, he was used to hard labor. He bought the old house in Benton when he was first married, and he later dug out the basement using a pick and shovel. He hauled the dirt out by wheelbarrow and dumped it into his garden behind the house. It took him a long time to finish this project, working at night after his shift at the mine.

Clary's first wife died shortly after Kay was born, so Grandma and Aunt Bertha took care of her most of the time while Clary was at work. Years later, Clary married Elva Jane Palfrey, and they had three more children, Tom, Sharon, and Fred. Clary liked the outdoors, and he took his family camping and fishing in the summer months. Uncle Willie took a job at the Benton post office after he came home from the war, and years later became the postmaster. Everyone picked up his or her mail at the post office in those early years, because there was no home delivery of mail. The post office was a community focal point in Benton, where everyone kept abreast of news and gossip around town. Willie was always a jolly person with a ready smile, and everyone in town liked him. He was the youngest of the family, and he, like Foss and Bertha, never married.

Robert Irvin Perkins, forever known as "Rip," was the first of the family to finish school. He graduated from Benton High School in 1926. My father, Percy, Foss, and Bertha were the three eldest of the family, and they had quit school after sixth grade to help at home on the farm. Jobs were hard to find when Rip graduated from high school, so he worked at laying brick with a carpenter in town and picked up on the craft rather quickly. He later took a job as a mason on a WPA project in Benton, building the new school. He married Margaret Driscoll from Benton, and they went to Beloit where Rip began training as a machinist. He liked that trade and was doing very well, but Margaret didn't like living away from Benton, so they moved back home. The only job opening he could find at that time in Benton was at the school. He became one of the janitors. Rip was good with his hands and could do almost anything, from maintenance on the boiler system to refinishing the gymnasium floor to building cabinets and shelves. He was called upon constantly by Benton residents to perform house repairs or to build fireplaces and chimneys for them. Small towns have a high percentage of elderly citizens, and many of them are widows who need help with house repairs. If they needed something done, they would be told, "Call Rip." When he finally retired from the school, he had served there for some forty-two years. The school administration and faculty hosted a retirement party for him and then presented him with a "cushy" recliner and an inscribed bronze dustpan.

# MY FATHER, "HAGGENS"

In 1958, just prior to my graduation from Naval Boot Camp at the Great Lakes Naval Training Center, I made a formal request for sea duty and was later assigned to the USS *San Pablo*, an old seaplane tender from the WWII period. The navy orders instructed me to travel to the Brooklyn Navy Yard in New York City, where I was to board the ship. Upon my arrival at the base, they had no record of the *San Pablo* being there, so I was assigned a bunk in the barracks and given daily work detail in the mess hall. After two weeks, the navy finally informed me that the *San Pablo* was in Philadelphia, where it had been for the past six months, and I also learned that Philadelphia was its home port! The navy had screwed up my orders and had sent me to Brooklyn by mistake. It was okay by me, though; I had liberty every night while I was there and managed to see some of the sights in New York City. Eighteen was the legal drinking age in "The Big Apple" at that time, so that was an added bonus, because most of the sights I saw were in the bars of Brooklyn.

When I finally boarded the *San Pablo* in the Philadelphia Naval Shipyard, it was in dry dock, undergoing routine repairs. A few years earlier, when seaplanes had become obsolete, the ship's guns were removed, and it was converted for oceanographic exploration duty, one of only two navy ships that performed that type of work. In later years, the oceanographic studies would be performed by a new governmental agency called NOAA. In 1958, however, the *San Pablo's* primary role in oceanography was to map the ocean bottom in selected regions of the Atlantic and, at the same time, track the ocean currents, variations in water temperatures, and winch up sample material from the ocean floor. We had about a dozen civilian scientists and technicians on board the *San Pablo* charged with performing the analytical tasks, along with our crew of about 150 sailors.

We knew that the precision topographical maps we made of the ocean floor were to be used by cable-laying ships to string communication cable across the Atlantic. What we didn't know at the time was that the cables would become the means for transmitting radio communication to and from the European and African continents when tracking our astronauts during the early days of NASA. There were no space satellites in those days. All communication was performed by radio on trans-oceanic cable.

The *San Pablo* was typically on station, at assigned locations in the Atlantic, for up to three months at a time with no escort vessels, so we felt like we were aboard the only ship in the ocean. At times we were deep-sea anchored to the ocean bottom, with gear strung out all round the ship, just "lying to" and rocking with the waves and swells. When we finally got some shore liberty in places like Halifax or St. Johns in Nova Scotia during summer months, or in the South Atlantic at Caribbean ports of Bermuda, Puerto Rico, Santo Domingo, or Andros Island, we were really ready to party. Unfortunately, it doesn't take long for a sailor to go through his cash, and that was especially true in the 1950s when military pay was quite low. As a seaman apprentice, I was paid eighty-seven dollars in cash every two weeks.

When I first went aboard ship as a newly assigned seaman apprentice, my duties consisted primarily of chipping paint. I was assigned to the deck crew, and we painted anything that didn't move.

I rather enjoyed the painting, but it was the surface preparation that was most demanding. It's well known that ships made of steel will rust, and the rust had to be removed before painting. We sometimes used air-powered, cup-style wire brushes, but most of the time we were required to use the "hand-powered" brush or steel scraper.

When the rust had been removed and the shiny metal revealed, we would apply a coat of yellow zinc chromate by brush, then a red primer. From that point, one of only three colors was to be applied, as per navy regulation. Deck surfaces were painted a specific dark gray; the bulkheads (walls) were painted a haze gray; and the overhead (ceiling) surfaces were white. In my day, all paint was applied on board ship with a brush.

Like most sailors, I didn't write home as often as I should have. Mom was writing to me on a regular basis with news from home, and I was pleasantly surprised when I would get an occasional letter from Dad. I'm sure he had written only after repeated urging by my mother because I had never known him to write a letter before this time. Mom said they both looked forward to my letters, and when Dad would come home from work of an evening, he would say, "We haven't heard from Gary for a while."

In a letter home on October 24, 1958, I wrote:

> *Dear Mom and Dad,*
>
> *I've been working pretty hard since I came aboard. I got put in the Deck Division. As you probably know, I work mostly on topside ... scraping, chipping, and sanding old paint off and putting new on. Most of the time we use*

*air-powered tools. They are a lot like small jackhammers, and they make a racket too.*

*Last week we chipped paint off the sides and bottom of the chain locker. It is a compartment that the anchor chain drops into when the anchor is hoisted. This chamber is about six feet in diameter and thirty feet deep. When we came out of there, we were really dirty. Our faces were as black as night. We had to wear respirators, but even then we got dirt in our mouth and lungs. It takes about three days to get it all out of your skin.*

*I recently got "promoted" though. Now I am in charge of the Petty Officers' head. In civilian language, that means I clean the bathroom. It's a real racket. I can just take my time.*

*We go into dry dock next month. We will then start painting the sides and larger parts of the ship. The civilian yard workers (sailors call them "yard birds") work on the ship too.*

*We are in the Philadelphia Naval Base, which is on the Delaware River between Philadelphia and Jersey City. I came over here by bus on the Jersey Turnpike. It took about two hours.*

*We have different divisions on the ship: Deck, Operations, (radio and radar), Supply, Engineering, Navigation, etc. The crew is divided into three sections. One section is on duty at a time, and they stand the watches. Our normal workday is 8:00 a.m. to 3:40 p.m., and then the section on duty stands watches. When we are in port, one section stands the watches, and the other two are given liberty on a rotation basis. Consequently, the first weekend you have duty, the next weekend you have forty-eight-hour liberty, then the third weekend you have seventy-two-hour liberty.*

*I'm trying for a chance to get out of Deck Division whenever there is an opening. I may put in for Electronics Technician school. It's very hard to get a school while on this ship because they don't like to let you go. But if I can strike for E.T., it's a wide-open rate, and I could advance to a lot better rating. It would be good training for the outside too, when I'm discharged.*

*By the way, I got a letter from Grandma Perkins today, and she had a lot of news and also sent me the* Benton Advocate. *Grandma sent me the dollar I gave her for that phone call. I wanted her to keep that.*

*Love, Gary*

* * * * * *

By my teenage years, my parents had placed an inordinate amount of trust in me. They set some basic rules, but I had a tremendous amount of freedom, and they basically left the decisions for my future to my own judgment.

I think there were a couple of reasons for this. They were raised at a time when the man of the house was the sole breadwinner, and he made all of the major decisions for the family. I was the eldest, the son who was approaching manhood. They felt that they had taught me well, that I had learned sound values from their example. While they must have had some apprehension about my actions as a teenager, they apparently believed that I was a morally sound young man. This was during the early 1950s when families were fairly stable and the world as a whole was relatively peaceful, so they were confident that I would be ready to take on the responsibilities of manhood and select my own course in life.

The second reason for granting me all of this freedom of choice was that they perhaps felt that I was better educated than they had been at my age. I would be venturing out into the world on a much higher plane than from where they had started. My father, "Haggens," didn't vocalize his thoughts or feelings, and he relied on my mother to speak for both of them when she often told of how proud they were, and I knew that their admiration for me was sincere. Ironically, while they had me on a lofty perch, I didn't feel that I deserved their high level of confidence, for I had low self-esteem as a teenager, and, to a degree, that characteristic remained with me throughout my adult life.

Both my parents were good students when they were in school and were intelligent people, but neither had attended school beyond the age of twelve or thirteen. In those days, the eldest were allowed or, in some cases, required by the parents to quit school after sixth grade to work at home.

My mother completed eighth grade, graduating from classes in a one-room schoolhouse in Leadmine, Wisconsin. She said she started high-school classes in Benton, but the girls there were a bit "snooty." She was not comfortable in that environment, so she stopped going. I believe she started working at the age of fifteen as a "hired girl" for Mrs. Ella Fowler in Benton, at an hourly wage of fifty cents.

Dad stayed home after sixth grade to help out on the farm. His father, Tom Perkins, was a teamster who hauled ore from the mine to the smelter by horse and wagon. He was also a tenant farmer, and there were always a good number of chores to perform. Grandpa Tom Perkins kept his job as a teamster and later worked at the roaster/smelter all through the Great Depression. He earned good wages while many others either had no work at that time or were consigned to government construction projects at fifty to seventy-five cents an hour. I believe my dad worked at home on the farm for quite a few years and also for other farmers in the Benton vicinity to earn some extra wages. Bertha and Foss had also quit school after the sixth grade, and Robert (Rip) was the first member of the Tom Perkins family to finish high school, graduating in 1926. His four younger brothers and his sister Grace all finished school and also graduated from Benton High School.

It was fairly common in those days for a farmer to hire outside help. Farm operations were very much labor-intensive. The farm implements were horse-drawn in most cases, and any mechanization was pretty simple and basic. In his thirties, Dad was the hired hand on Wes Robson's farm where he met my mother who also worked for the Robsons, performing domestic chores. She had ended a brief marriage to a Darlington man who was a hard worker but was not much of a family man. Fortunately, there were no children born to that marriage.

Percy, Jeanette, 1939

My parents were married in 1939 and rented a home in the west end of Benton, one block south of Main Street. It was a lower apartment in a two-story home that had been converted to serve two families. As was common in the late 1930s, there was no indoor plumbing and no central heat in the home. The place was heated by a stove in the living room and a wood-burning cook stove in the kitchen. They burned both lump coal and wood.

Percy and Gary, 1939

My father was thirty-seven, and my mother was thirty-one when I was born. I'm sure that I was unduly pampered as a young child, because I had arrived later in life for them. In all of those early pictures, my clothes were crisp and clean, and my hair was neatly combed. I was the picture of a perfect little gentleman like the young models in those Sears Roebuck & Company catalogs. When I was young, Dad would take me uptown for groceries on Saturday night. He would cash his paycheck at the store when he picked up the groceries from the list that Mom had prepared for him. We would bring the groceries home, and then Dad would go back downtown to have a few beers with his friends at Williams' Bar. This was his regular routine on a Saturday night.

On Sunday mornings, he and I would go downtown to Peacock's Drug Store to get the Sunday issue of the *Milwaukee Journal*. Next door was Tut Horsley's variety store, and he had the best ice cream in town. So after Dad got the paper, we would go next door for ice cream. My favorite was raspberry ripple. Tut often worked on Sundays, so I always got an extra big scoop. I didn't fare as well when Sophie Kitto was working at the store. She was pretty tight with her boss's resources, and a scoop of ice cream was much smaller when Sophie served it. (I also remember my mother telling us that during WWII, when Grandma Perkins or Bertha had packages to ship overseas to my uncles who were serving in the war, after wrapping the packages in brown paper, they would take them to Tut's store to have them tied with cotton cord, which Tut had on a large spool in his store. Tut never charged for the string needed for the packages, but if Sophie was working, she would measure and charge for it so as not to cheat her boss out of money.)

Our family seldom attended church on Sundays. Sometimes my mother would take my sisters and me to the Primitive Methodist Church on the west end of town, which was known locally as the "Brick Church." Some of the other Perkins families were members of that church, and there are, at present, six generations of Perkinses buried in the church cemetery, including my great-grandfather, James Perkins, the first of the family to come to America in 1863. My sisters and I often went to Sunday school at the urging of our mother, until we reached the upper grades in school. Dad only went to church a few times at Easter or Christmas.

One of my favorite memories about Sundays at our house was the roast beef dinner. In the Midwest, dinner is served at midday, and on Sundays, roast beef was a family favorite. Mom always made perfect beef gravy, and my sister Ruth came to call it "Sunday gravy" when she was little. She would exclaim, "Oh boy! We're having Sunday gravy!" My dad learned to make very good beef gravy too, when my mother was recovering from rheumatic fever and he took over some of the cooking chores. Sometimes he would stir the gravy on the stove with one hand while holding a cold bottle of Schlitz beer in his other hand—a little aperitif before Sunday dinner. On rare occasions, we would enjoy Sunday gravy on a Wednesday or Thursday!

I believe Dad was hired at the Old Mulcahy mine west of Shullsburg in 1941, a couple of years after I was born. He worked there until the end of World War II, when the price of lead and zinc fell off and most of the smaller mines closed. I don't think Dad much enjoyed working at the mine, because he was an outdoor type. I know he liked farming much better. He enjoyed working the soil, tending livestock, and being outdoors in the elements. During those years at the mine, he worked high up in the derrick on the "grizzly," which allowed him to be outdoors for part of the time. I don't know if he requested the position or if he was simply fortunate in his job assignment, but I'm sure that he preferred this to working underground, or "below the grass," the term used by the old-time Cornish miners. As the grizzly man, he was stationed at the uppermost level of the derrick, and when the winch man hoisted the fully loaded "can" up from the mineshaft, it would rise to the top of the derrick where it would be hooked by the workman called "the hooker" and dumped onto the grizzly platform: a set of heavy iron bars positioned horizontally over a chute. The parallel bars caught the big boulders and let the smaller rock and ore pass through and down the chute for further processing. He would then roll the big boulders off into a steel four-wheeled cart that ran on iron tracks along the top of the huge rock pile. By hand, he pushed the cart out to the end of the track and dumped it by releasing a trip lever.

He took me to work with him when I was about four or five years old, and I got my first look at the lead and zinc mining process. I only have a few recollections from that age, but I still remember the strong smell of acid and carbide in the changing room. The miners rode up from below ground in the can. They wore rubber suits and hard hats with mounted carbide lamps. They removed the wet rubber suits in the changing room that had a ceiling height of at least twenty feet. There was a huge stove in the center to provide heat, and the men would hang their rubber suits on hooks that were mounted on a long wooden plank, then hoist them up toward the ceiling, where they would drip dry for the next workday. The highlight of my visit to the mine that day was the ride on the grizzly cart. Dad helped me up onto the cartload of boulders and then pushed it down the track with me on board. From atop the rock pile, I could see for miles in all directions. After I climbed off at the end of the track, he dumped the cart and then gave me a ride back again. But he cautioned me, "Don't tell your mother about this!"

Percy and Gary, ca. 1943

I spent some quality time with my dad in those early years. He was a good gardener and raised a variety of vegetables. He taught me how to prepare the soil, how to cut seed potatoes, how to set out tomato plants, and of course, how to properly weed a garden! He would build cabinets, whatnot shelf units, and other wooden items with hand tools. Later on, he purchased an electric drill, which I believe was the only power tool that he ever owned. I would stick with him like glue, always eager to learn. We would sand the finished product by hand and then apply a coat or two of paint or varnish. I helped him build a miniature desk with pigeonholes for my sister Ruth. Dad was a very quiet and patient man who never said much unless you asked a question. But whenever he did speak, it was usually important. He was not a man for idle chatter.

We would hear an occasional story from him, and, like all of the Perkins brothers, he could tell them pretty well. Many times he couldn't get through the story without laughing because they were generally humorous stories or anecdotes about some of the local characters in Benton or about something that occurred at work. I remember one story he told about the Cassidys, father and son. Jimmy Cassidy, in his forties, still lived at home with his father. His mother, I think, ran off because she could no longer live with the two of them. Jimmy and his father, Ochre, were both pretty eccentric, or as people around Benton would say, "They were odd." Anyway, my dad told of seeing the two of them driving their Model A Ford past the Calvert farm one cold winter day. The road was a glare of ice, and the turn in front of the farm was sharp and steeply banked. Ochre was driving about as slowly as he could go without killing the motor, and when they got to the turn in the road, he stopped and made Jimmy get out and push against the side of the Model A from the lower side of the road as they slowly crept around the banked curve. They obviously believed this procedure would prevent the old Ford from sliding into the ditch. When Dad would tell stories like this, he would punctuate them with his own laughter, briefly interrupting the narrative. "Oh," he'd say, "I can't tell it for laughing!"

When I was very young, he would recite this poem to me and my sisters. I believe it had three verses, but I can only remember a part of it:

> My name is Jimmy Brown, and I came from Buffalo town.
> I've traveled the wide world over, and I've traveled the wide world round.
> I've had my ups and downs in life, and better days I'd seen
> When I met that dirty scoundrel: his name was Jimmy Green.

I don't know how my father came to memorize that verse. It may have been a study assignment in school, or perhaps someone in the family had passed it on to him. I never knew him to sit down and read a book. He devoted his time to his job and providing for his family. He was good to us. We always had presents for our birthdays and for Christmas. There were some lean times after the mine closed, but his children were his first priority. Our parents made extreme sacrifices to get us through school, but we always had wholesome food and good, warm clothing in the winter months. Dad was a proud man who was determined to provide for his family, but at the same time, he was strong in principle. He refused to take factory work, as had many of the men in Benton after the mines closed, and chose not to work below ground during those years of employment at the mine. I think his lifelong dream was to be a farmer, raising crops and livestock. As he grew older, I think he may have become regretful of not pursuing that dream. We never had talks about what he was feeling, and he always kept his thoughts to himself, so I am speculating here to some extent. He had a lot of time for introspection during those long hours of boredom when tilling the land for Calvert.

He would not take on the personal debt required to invest in a farm operation. After WWII, the government offered low-interest loans to potential farmers, but when we talked about it, he said, "I would never borrow that much money, Gary." When I reminded him that some of my friends' fathers had taken jobs at the factories in nearby Dubuque, Iowa, after the mines closed, he told me that he could never work in a factory. He needed to be in open space. There had to have been some Cornish genes in play there: his pride and independence became more evident to me in later years after I had learned more about my Cornish heritage. My father was all about family. We were close as a family unit and close to our extended Perkins family—cousins, aunts and uncles, grandparents. The belief in strong family ties is another characteristic of the Cornish people.

Percy (or "Haggens" to some) was only five seven and slight of build, but he was a big man in my eyes and in the respect shown to him by others who knew him. He was a hardworking, dependable man in a very literal sense. His hands were big and rough; two of his fingers had been chewed up by a corn chopper. I went with him to the doctor's office the day of the accident and watched intently while Dr. Bent cut away the loose flesh, then stitched up the two fingers. It was done without anesthetic.

He felt satisfied after a good day's work. He was a man who felt the need to produce tangible results with his strong hands and back. He would come home from work of an evening and say, "Well, we got ten loads of corn in the crib today," or, "We baled forty acres of hay and got it in the barn before the rain came." In the spring and summer, after a typical ten-hour workday, he would come home and work in his vegetable garden with hand tools like his father had done before him: spade, hoe, or the claw-tooth cultivator. That was his therapy, his way of relaxing, with his silent thoughts and the smell of the soil.

Dad was a throwback, I think, to his Cornish and Irish ancestry. His grandfather began working in the mines of Cornwall with pick and shovel at the age of eleven. He was one of the "tinners," the hard-rock miners who punched through solid granite with hand tools powered by nothing more than their muscles and their steadfast determination. These men had a need to be physically productive, to see the tangible results of their labor. For many men, hand work and the visible fruits of their labor fill a therapeutic need. I've known doctors, lawyers, and other professionals who took up a woodworking hobby to satisfy their need to work with their hands after a long day of mental stress. This need for physical work in my dad's case was satisfied by farm work at the Calvert's after the mine closed. He loved farming, and based upon comments I overheard from some of his peers, Dad had a real talent for that line of work.

Percy Perkins, 1955

He worked at the Calvert farms for twenty years before his health failed him and he died in January 1965. There were two farms owned by Frank Calvert, who performed no physical labor himself. He was known to have what they called the "Gray Sickness," though my mother said she thought he was simply "allergic to work." Frank was the youngest of his family, perhaps the favorite son, and inherited the Calvert family farm from his father, Tom. Frank hired extra help at harvest time for the two farms, and my dad oversaw operations at both locations. Unlike some hired men, he was both competent and dependable, and that left Frank with plenty of spare time to spend in town after taking care of his administrative duties at the farm. You could often find him in town drinking coffee with friends at the café.

Frank's son George and I were good friends, and I spent most of the summer, Saturdays, and occasionally weekdays after school at the farm. It was a half mile north of Benton, an easy ride on my bike. Dad taught George and me how to drive a tractor when we were maybe twelve years old. Then as we got bigger and stronger, we would help with the haying, a labor-intensive process that lasted two to three weeks. Often the men would put up three crops of hay if they had good summer weather. George and I stuck with Dad most of the time around the farm, and he taught us a lot about caring for the livestock. They raised Hereford beef cattle, Holstein dairy cattle, hogs, and—for a few years—Frank bought a couple thousand young turkeys in the spring, fed them all summer, and marketed them in the fall. There were always lots of chores on the farm, and we learned a lot as we volunteered our help. To be honest, I was the only volunteer because George had his required duties. I volunteered to help him and my dad because I enjoyed my part-time experience on the farm. There was a lot more to be done besides simply feeding the livestock twice a day. We assisted in herding young cattle into a pen, where they would be dehorned. We would latch their heads in a stanchion, the horns would be sawed off, and the bleeder veins pinched off and cauterized. Catching young pigs and lifting them up by their hind legs so they could be neutered was really hard work for youngsters. The pig was heavy, kicked like crazy, and when we finally got it raised up by the hind legs, Dad would castrate it with a sharp pocketknife and douse it with a disinfectant. We would then release that hog and chase down another one.

The dirtiest job I remember was when we helped the men cut the beaks off the turkeys. Turkeys are really stupid. We had to help erect separation pens to prevent the young turkeys from piling up and suffocating each other. In a heavy rain, they would raise their heads with mouths open and drown! To prevent this, they had to be herded inside one of the barns. Turkeys can't be driven like other livestock. We had to use a fence gate, one man on each end, and gradually push the turkeys into the barn. The "debeaking" process almost did me in that summer. It was a hot July day in Wisconsin, and we had herded about a thousand turkeys into the barn and closed the doors. George and I were charged with catching those turkeys, one by one, and lugging them over to the electric knife station. The top beak had to be cut off to prevent the turkeys from picking each other's eyes out. The knife was similar to a small guillotine and heated by electric current until it was white hot. The heat would cauterize the wound as the beak was cut. We would grab a turkey by the legs, sometimes grasping only one leg and struggling to get hold of the other, while the turkey was beating us up with its flapping wings. When we finally got it to the knife, we would poke a finger in its mouth and position its upper beak on the metal plate beneath the knife blade. One of the men operated the guillotine knife. There was a loud hiss as it cut off the top beak, and the odor from the cutting was something awful. With no air circulation in the closed barn, the inside temperature of about a hundred degrees, and the terrible smell, it was all I could do to keep my breakfast down. There were three hired hands helping George and me catch the turkeys, but it was late afternoon by the time we debeaked a thousand of those damn turkeys.

Driving the tractors was a lot more fun, and we liked the field work. There is nothing like the smell of freshly turned soil in the early spring of the year. Plowing had to be done in a straight line, so Dad would usually "open up" the field by plowing the initial round or two, and then we would follow his furrow to continue the plowing. There were a lot of fields to plow, so two or three tractors were fitted up with two- to four-bottom plows, depending upon the size of the tractor.

The neighboring farmers usually got together for haying or combining of oats. The three Calvert brothers and sometimes Bill Harper, who lived nearby, would pool their equipment and manpower to get the crops harvested while weather permitted. The women would cook the midday dinner for the crew, and we would all eat hearty. George's mom made the best pork chop gravy I ever tasted.

Having the opportunity to spend time where my dad worked, I admired him for his knowledge of farming. I noticed early on that he had natural leadership qualities and that he had the respect of the other farmers and hired hands. After a break for lunch, he would be the first one to climb up on his tractor to continue his task, and the others would follow. He pulled the hay baler with the big Farmall Model M, and the rest of us would load the wagons, haul the hay, and stack it in the barn loft. When the oats were ripe, he would operate the combine, and the crews would haul the grain back to the granary and unload the trucks. Haggens would always set the pace. He led by example in his own quiet way. Naturally, George and his younger brother, John, spent a lot more time than I did on the farm with Dad, and they learned a lot from him. He would joke around with us sometimes but always made sure we had work to perform and enjoyed teaching us new tasks and techniques on farming.

I observed on numerous occasions where Frank would come to Haggens in the barn and say, "When do you think we ought to cut hay up at the Story Farm?" or, "I'm thinking of putting the lower forty in soybeans this year. What do you think?"

My mother was deeply depressed for years after Dad died in 1965, and it was not her nature to be depressed. Percy, as she always called him, was her rock and her life's love. They had a very happy marriage. I can remember them carrying on at night in the downstairs bedroom, "Hee-hee, Percy! Stop that!" This would be followed by the sound of giggles coming from my sisters' bedroom.

Dad was really sick before he died, and no one knows how long he suffered because he was never one to complain about anything like that, so one never knew. Until then, he had only gone to a doctor one time that I remember. It wasn't until after his death that we learned he probably had primary biliary cirrhosis. We found it to be a genetic trait in our family. My sister Ruth would die of it some twenty-eight years later. She was in her early fifties. My youngest sister, Judy, is required to take medication for the rest of her life to keep this same ailment under control. Dad, in the last stages of the disease, turned yellow with jaundice, was exhausted every night after work, was unusually quiet, and kept to himself. He finally heeded my mother's pleading and went to the doctor. They opened up his liver at the University of Wisconsin Hospital in Madison, but it was too late to do much for him. The cirrhosis was severely advanced. He sat at home in a rocking chair with a catheter that had been inserted to drain fluid from his body into a jug that sat on the floor by his chair.

Throughout my life, I've tried to live up to him—not to heed his words, because there weren't many of those, but to copy his deeds and follow his example. He was a great man to have as a father.

I shaved him for the last time at the hospital, and he knew his time was up. The sparkle in his eyes was gone and had been replaced by a sad, resigned look. He died on January 25, 1965.

So many things that I should have said but didn't.

# CHAPTER 6

# THE ROBBINS FAMILY: EARLY MINING IN WISCONSIN

*December 3, 1958*

*Dear Mom,*

    *Well, I won't be home for Christmas, but I will be home for New Years! From December 27 to January 4. I may catch a ride to Toledo with one of my buddies, then hitchhike from there. If that doesn't work out, I'll fly into Madison. The train takes fifteen hours just to get to Chicago, and it would be faster to hitchhike.*

    *Today was my lucky day! At about 0900, the boatswain's mate came up to me and said, "Perkins, effective right now, you are in Operations Division. Pack your gear and move out!" So I am now in a new compartment. It really surprised me, as I didn't even put in for the transfer, even though I did want one. My first choice would have been for electronics technician, but now they are going to make me a quartermaster? I told the chief that I didn't want to be a quartermaster striker and wasn't interested in it. When the navigation officer, Mr. Knight, heard that I wasn't going to take QM and wanted to go back into the Deck Division, he called me up to the Ward Room and we had a little talk. He did most of the talking. I told him I didn't want to spend my time in the navy as a quartermaster, as it was of no use on the outside. He agreed on that point but said I should be a QM striker and then when something opens up for ET, I could switch. Anyway, all the "deck apes" are congratulating me on my transfer, and I guess things will work out. At least I'm up on the bridge of the ship where all the action is.*

*Hope this finds everyone "ship-shape"!*

*Merry Christmas,*

*Gary*

This would be my first Christmas away from home. We were a close family, and the holidays of Thanksgiving, Christmas, and Easter were always a happy time for all of us. Both my mom's and dad's families were large, and my two sisters and I had many cousins.

Grandma Perkins also came from a large family. Lilla Jane Robbins was the eldest of twelve, but her parents, Charles and Hanna Maria (Redfern) Robbins, lost four of the twelve in infancy. Her mother, Hannah, was the daughter of Robert and Jane Redfern. Lilla was born in New Diggings, another small town in the southwestern Wisconsin lead and zinc mining region, in June 1882. Her father, Charles, was born in New Diggings as well and had worked in the mines as a young man. Then, as with many Cornish miners, he turned to farming when the ore prices fell off. He began farming around Benton a few years after Lilla Jane was born.

Grandma's paternal grandparents, John and Grace (Vail) Robbins, were among the early settlers of New Diggings. They were both born in Cornwall and married in Ireland, where their first child, Harriett, was born in 1840. Within the next two years, they had returned to Cornwall, where three more children were born. John and Grace came to America in the early 1850s with four young children and first settled in Hardscrabble (present-day Hazel Green), another small mining town in southwestern Wisconsin, then moved five miles east to New Diggings. Grandma's father, Charles, was their fifth child, born in New Diggings on St. Patrick's Day 1855. John and Grace had four more children, but of those, Sam died at age two, and Henry drowned as a young man.

There were five mining towns in southwestern Wisconsin near the Fever River lead region: Hazel Green (Hardscrabble), Benton (Swindlers' Ridge), Shullsburg, Leadmine, and New Diggings. All were located within a ten-mile radius and had sprung to life from the mining camps that had been established in 1826 to 1827. The Robbins family came to the region during this time of turmoil following the Black Hawk War when the Huron and Winnebago Indian tribes were attempting to recapture their former homeland from the miners.

When Wisconsin was granted statehood in 1848, they chose to name it the "Badger State," a tribute to the digging and burrowing of the early miners who were fondly called "badgers." In fact, when the rush was on for "gray gold" and the ore (lead sulfide known as "galena") was near the surface, many young miners didn't take the time to build permanent dwelling, instead choosing temporary shelter in a dug-out cave. Many of these badgers carved into the face of limestone bluffs along the Fever River for their shelter.

The first Cornishman to arrive in this area was Francis Clyma, born in Perranzabuloe in 1792. In the year of 1827, he reached the diggings in Galena, Illinois, where the Fever River from the Wisconsin Territory emptied into the Mississippi River. His wife, the former Frances Maynard of St. Ives, Cornwall, joined him after he had gotten settled in the New Diggings area that lay north, up the Fever River valley. Hundreds of Cornishmen from the Camborne mining region in West Cornwall came to America in the 1830s, and by 1850 they were estimated to be about five thousand. The Indians had used crude methods in mining the surface lead often found in caves and hillsides. They smelted the ore over an open fire pit. When the early American miners migrated to this Wisconsin lead region from Kentucky, Illinois, Missouri, and central Tennessee, the Indians were driven west across the Mississippi. This prompted the hostilities that led to the Black Hawk War of 1832. Colonel Henry Dodge, the former marshal of Missouri Territory and a miner himself, organized and led the badgers against the Indians at the famous Battle of Bad Axe in what is now southwestern Wisconsin. Reportedly, the miners were a fairly rough, ragtag outfit and not well disciplined, so there was a lot of confusion during the battle. It was apparently a series of scattered skirmishes rather than a pitched battle, and when the dust finally settled, the miners went back to their diggings.

The US government took control of the mining and issued leases to both the Indians and the Americans. There was no upfront cost for a lease; the government took a percentage of the ore. These early miners burrowed drifts into the side of a hill or dug shallow pits on the surface as they followed the vein of lead. When they struck solid rock or water, both the Indian and American miners would abandon the lease and seek another location for their diggings. By the 1830s, the Cornishmen began arriving on the scene, and they were delighted to take over these abandoned diggings. They were delighted because they needed no capital. The Cornishman was an early entrepreneur who craved independence. Furthermore, he had been a tinner or copper-seeker in Cornwall, where miners worked on "tribute" rather than wages. Tribute was a term used for working on a percentage basis. If they produced ore in these Wisconsin diggings, they were simply required to pay the government a percentage of their take. They were experienced miners who knew how to work successfully "below the grass"—underground—in a skillful and efficient manner. They had that uncanny ability to anticipate the direction of the vein of ore, knew how to break through the rock, and could fashion a hand pump to remove the water from the shaft. They would follow the ore deep underground and run horizontal drifts, shored up with timbers for safety. The limestone they found in Wisconsin was much easier to work than the extremely hard granite of Cornwall.

The early miners' income would fluctuate, and there would be some hard times, so they depended on the womenfolk to carefully manage the household. The Cornishmen, with their expertise in mining, were accomplished masons. They built solid houses cut from the local limestone, and they were efficient in size. The doorways and ceiling beams were often less than six feet high. They wasted no material on excess, and smaller rooms were easier to heat during those cold Wisconsin winters. Furniture was crafted for more than one use: a table could be hinged over to become a bunk bed, for example.

By the mid-1840s, the surface diggings for lead had been replaced by mines with shafts ever deeper, long horizontal drifts, and a new technology brought to Wisconsin by the Cornish and some Irish miners. This technology was developed through the process of tin mining in their homeland. The earlier method of tin streaming led to digging into the bluffs and hillsides as they followed the lodes and veins of mineral. These early miners could not dig very deep before striking water, but the eighteenth-century invention of a pumping engine would clear the works of water. Early makers of the walking beam pump were the Harveys of Hayle, Cornwall. This machine was first powered by a horse and later by a steam engine.

Mining was an extremely dangerous occupation prior to the twentieth century. In addition to accidents, many miners fell victim to and died early of phthisis and silicosis from bad ventilation.

Life itself was hard in those days, and many early American settlers died at a young age. When my great-grandfather Charles Robbins was a child of five years, his mother, Grace, was killed by lightning while hanging clothes on the line behind the house. Then, two years later, his father John Robbins was killed by wild Indians near Marengo, Iowa. John and a group of fellow miners had formed a wagon train and were headed from Wisconsin to the Colorado mines when he met his fate.

A call had been made for experienced Cornish miners to work the gold ore and placer diggings in Colorado near Pike's Peak in Gilpin County. These shallow diggings had begun to play out, and the financial backers wanted to bring in the more experienced Cornish and Irish miners. The earliest miners seeking gold in Colorado came there from California, and, when the mining grew more difficult, many of the workings were abandoned. So when the call went out for more expertise, the "hard-rock" miners who had been working the mines of southwestern Wisconsin, the Upper Peninsula of Michigan, and others directly from Cornwall made the difficult trek to Pike's Peak to replace the American miners. These Cornish miners, who came to be called the "Cousin Jacks," had lengthy experience in underground work, "below the grass," and they contributed much to improving mining technique in America.

John Robbins had left his family in New Diggings, Wisconsin, and was answering that call when he joined the wagon train to Pike's Peak and lost his life in Iowa.

In later years, his son Charles married Hannah Redfern, and they raised their family in the Fever River mining region near the frontier mining towns of Benton and New Diggings in southwestern Wisconsin. The informative booklet *A Tour Guide to the Mines,* by Loren Farrey, also describes the three major mines in Benton. The Frontier mine was the premier mine with a zinc ore body some fifty feet in thickness. It had a mill, a rail siding, and boarding houses for its several hundred employees. Two other large mining operations were the Treganza and Calvert mines.

Benton and New Diggings, a few miles to the south, were both at the center of operations throughout much of the mining era in this region. There were a large number of highly productive mines, ore-processing mills, and a railroad facility for transport. By the early part of the twentieth century, zinc in this region had replaced lead as the primary metal. This was due to a growing demand for zinc coupled with the fact that the local lead production had been eclipsed by the enormous growth of the Missouri, Colorado, Utah, and Idaho lead-mining regions.

From Loren Farrey's *A Tour Guide to the Mines*:

> At the turn of the twentieth century, the little village of Benton was perhaps the most prominently identified mining camp in the great zinc and lead region of the upper Mississippi Valley. A remarkable number of strikes of zinc ore had been made in and within a five-mile radius of the community which truly made Benton the hub of the growing zinc mining activity.
>
> A mining report from 1907 lists the mines in or near the village of Benton as the Looney, Dawson, Frontier, Century, Whaley, and Peacock mines. In a straight line to the north were the Beacon Hill, Wiseman, Lucky Three, Quinlan, Forcite, Wilkinson, Pine Tree, Eagle,

Rico, Roosevelt, Baxter, Gritty Six, Trego, Meekers Grove, Dall, Cook, and Cuba City Lead and Zinc mines.

To the northeast were found the Crawhall, Pratt, Shaffer, Corr, Pittsburgh-Benton, Etna, Fairy-Queen, and Iowa mines. To the East were the Dunn, Helena, Grant, Weiskircher, Swift-Rooney, Coltman, Leadmine, Jug Handle, Etna Open Cut, Amalgamated, Empress, Monarch, Stubbs, Ivo, Booty, Lafayette, Murphy, Chicago-Benton, Ollie Belle, Penna-Benton, Jack of Diamonds, Eureka, and Aragon Mines.

And to the south of Benton were the Fox, Little Bennie, Good Hope, Rowley, Tunnel Hill, Northwestern, Big Dad, Little Dad, Big Tom Syndicate, Illinois Lead and Zinc, Mills, Square Deal, Winnebago, Kennedy, King Bee, Hazel Green, Murphy, Jefferson, Scrabble Creek, and the General Custer mines.

All of the mines were in operation and fully equipped with buildings, machinery, and steam or electrical power for operation. A number had boarding houses or other accommodations for the many miners they employed, many of whom were recruited from around the country and the world.

By 1917, the greatest year of zinc production in the region, many of these mines were still operating and scores of new ones had opened. Benton, Leadmine, New Diggings, Buncombe, Shullsburg, and Hazel Green became true boom towns.

A number of the Cornish miners came to the Benton area in the early 1840s, and also a large number of lead miners from the North

Yorkshire and County Durham regions of England. There were also a great many Irish immigrants, some with experience in working with stone, who ably entered into mine work.

Many families from the Germanic states also emigrated here, but most of them took up farming. Many farmers grew wealthy from the mining speculation. Farmers' royalties from mining rights amounted to 7 to 10 percent of the value of ore produced. During the period of 1892 to 1905, one mine near Benton paid the landowner nearly $3 million in royalties. In most cases, stock in most of the mines was not held by local citizens, but rather by investors, particularly from Chicago, Pittsburgh, and New York. Therefore, most of the money made by the local mines left the area.

During the mining boom of 1906 to 1918, more labor was in demand. News had spread throughout Europe and elsewhere that brought an influx of "Italians, Serbs, Hungarians, Finns, Austrians, Czechs, Poles, Danes, Norwegians, Swedes, Negroes, Bulgarians, Mexicans, one Chinaman, and two Yazoo Indians," by one local man's account.

A brief history of mining in this region was published in the *Benton Advocate* on September 17, 1954:

> The Wisconsin zinc district is located in southwestern Wisconsin, with slight extensions into the adjacent states of Illinois and Iowa. It is an irregular-shaped quadrilateral that has a maximum length, north and south, of 60 miles, by a width, east and west, of 60 miles.
>
> It lies 150 miles northwest of Chicago and 300 miles north of St. Louis, which later was the principal lead and zinc market of this country.
>
> Mining by whites began in this district in 1788, when Julian Dubuque, a French settler, obtained a lease

from the Indians to dig lead where the city of Dubuque now stands. The occurrence of lead was known to the Indians prior to this, but they made little, if any, use of it.

By 1820, lead was being mined around Galena, Illinois and by 1830 the mining had extended throughout the southwestern portion of Wisconsin.

From 1830 to 1861, mining for lead was actively prosecuted throughout the entire district, which became the principal source of lead in this country. The total output was estimated at approximately 500,000 tons or about $40,000,000.00 in value in 1861. Up to this time, the work was largely in the surface clays and open crevices, and when the water level was reached (at depths ranging from 30 to 80 feet) work was abandoned for a new lease because of the inability to pump water with their crude outfits. The mining was very primitive, and it was carried on by innumerable small groups of miners who leased lots of 100 feet or more on a vein or crevice on a basis of 25% royalty to the land owners.

Since 1845, lead production has decreased from 1000 to 5000 tons a year, and this district has been surpassed in production due to enormous growth in other areas of the country. At present (1954), Benton has more mining companies in operation than any other camp in the Wisconsin lead and zinc region. This fact surely makes Benton the 'Banner Mining Town' of this district.

After the untimely deaths of his mother and father, Charles Robbins and his younger siblings were probably cared for by the four older brothers and sisters. According to family records, he spent his early years in the mines around New Diggings and Benton, and then later turned to farming. His marriage to Hannah Redfern bore twelve children, my grandmother Lilla Jane being the oldest surviving child.

Tom and Lilla Jane Perkins, 1901

It would be fitting, then, that she would also marry miner Thomas Perkins, a second-generation American of common Cornish ancestry. Thomas, one of the sons of James Perkins, was also born and raised in the Benton-New Diggings mining region.

# CHAPTER 7

# JAMES PERKINS: MINING IN AMERICA

After a series of brief shakedown runs in Delaware Bay following the dry-dock refitting, the USS *San Pablo* embarked on its first real cruise. Our mission was to venture south to the US Naval Base in Guantanamo Bay, Cuba, and be tested for combat readiness.

The young seamen like me had been forewarned by the experienced members of the crew that the waters around Cape Hatteras on the Virginia coast would be a challenge. They said the cape waters were always rough, and that certainly turned out to be an understatement. As we approached the cape, the ship began rolling and pitching as huge swells rolled in from our port side. Then it got much worse. I couldn't remember ever being so sick. A full day of vomiting left me with the dry heaves, and the ache in my gut caused me to stumble around, bent over, as the ship's deck heaved up and down beneath my feet. With the severe pitching of the deck, and in my weakened condition, my knees would buckle at times. I wasn't the only young sailor who carried a bucket around in one hand while clutching the rail with the other. We had to tough it out and man our assigned stations and stand watch on schedule. The old ship would rear up, shudder, and slam back into the oncoming waves and ocean swell. Munching soda crackers gave me some relief by soaking up some of the bitter stomach acid as I bounced around the ship, grabbing the nearest fixed object to keep my footing. It didn't help much to lie in my bunk when I came off duty. The below-deck quarters were stuffy, and you had to wrap an arm around one of the bunk chains to remain in the bunk, so I didn't get a whole lot of sleep on this voyage. I was now beginning to understand why my dad's brothers joined the army.

I also thought about my great-grandfather James Perkins, who had crossed the Atlantic in a small wooden ship back in 1863. He would have been about the same age as I was at this time. His trip was undoubtedly more miserable than mine, and that thought bucked me up a bit: "I can get through this. There are better days ahead."

I finally recovered after a couple of days in Guantanamo, or GITMO in navy talk. From the base, our ship and crew ventured out into the Caribbean several times, where the US Navy inspection squad put us under simulated battle conditions. They tested our response time to repair damage from "torpedo hits" and "artillery fire." At the end of the three-day exercise, we were pronounced fit and combat-ready. However, we did suffer some real damage. When one of the inspection officers tossed a live hand grenade over the side to simulate a torpedo hit, the explosion blew one of our hull plates loose, and we began to take on water. One of our damage-control crews managed to patch up the seam in the hull while we hightailed it back to GITMO for repairs.

This old seaplane tender had taken some hits during WWII, and a Japanese kamikaze attack had destroyed the port side of the bridge, so we knew the old girl wasn't 100 percent fit. Despite all the necessary repairs, there had to be a whole bunch of loose rivets. When the navy later converted the *San Pablo* for oceanography, they removed all of the five-inch cannons and forty-millimeter gun turrets, so that left us with no firepower. When they pronounced us "fit and combat-ready" for battle, we had to wonder what our role would be on this old boat with no guns.

Once I got my sea legs, I was enjoying the tour in the Caribbean as we cruised to the first of our oceanography assignments. The weather was warm and clear, and the sun setting on the ocean was a beautiful sight. The view was unobstructed as the sun, like a big, orange globe, slowly sank into the ocean.

I now spent my days, as a quartermaster striker, in the pilothouse on the bridge deck. I was learning to read and update navigational charts, logging weather observations every four hours, and making entries in the ship's log. At night, I stood my four-hour watch on the bridge, rotating each week from the four-to-eight watch to the eight-to-twelve watch, and then came the dreaded twelve-to-four midwatch. As we cruised the South Atlantic week after week with no land in sight, the watches were boring for the most part, and I had a lot of time on my hands ... time to think about my life and my family members back home. Again I thought about James Perkins, my ancestor who ventured so far from his home in England to a new life in America. As I gazed out upon the empty ocean, I had my hopes and dreams for the future. I wondered what hopes and dreams James had as he gazed out over the water on his trip to America.

\* \* \* \* \* \*

According to family history, James Perkins sailed out of England at the age of twenty-one in the year of 1863 and was accompanied by an

aunt and uncle, whom I believe were John and Mary Ann Bennett.
They settled in Dog Hollow, a very small mining community near the
Wisconsin/Illinois state line. As a young miner, James spent time in
Colorado, the Upper Peninsula of Michigan, and in the Johnstown area
of Pennsylvania before returning to Wisconsin and settling down near
Benton to raise his family.

The Cornishmen were attracted to Colorado because of the gold that
had been discovered in the Pike's Peak area around 1859. As the surface
gold and placer diggings played out, the Cornish miners replaced the
American miners during the mid-1860s. With their extensive experience
in underground work, they contributed much to improving the mining
techniques in their new homeland. They were skillful in sinking shafts
and seemed to have an uncanny sense for following the vein of ore. They
had developed mechanical aids, such as the Cornish walking beam
pump for removing water from the underground recesses.

They often took up work at a digging that was previously abandoned
by less skillful miners. They introduced their contract system of working
on tribute, meaning a 10 percent to 15 percent share of the proceeds
from the sale of minerals extracted. At other times they were hired at
a daily wage of $2.50. In this time period, the Cornish miners were in
demand, and they could live well at this wage level.

The initial excitement over the gold discovered in Gilpin County and
Pike's Peak had begun to wane by the time James Perkins arrived there
around 1865. This mining area was high up in the Rocky Mountains,
at about eight thousand feet elevation, and it was a dangerous trek to
get there. The rough mountain roads from Denver were steep and
narrow. Clear Creek lay to the south of this mining area and Boulder
to the north. No railroads served the area until 1878, so travel was by
horseback or wagon teams.

Perhaps James Perkins's destination was Central City, described at the time as "the richest square mile on earth." The road from Idaho Springs to Central City was a perilous shelf-road of dust (or mud) that twisted and turned for nine miles up Virginia Canyon. Idaho Springs served as a base camp where the miners rested before making the grand assault. James probably stayed in one of the boarding houses in Idaho Springs, many of which were maintained by "Cousin Jennies." One such dwelling was owned by Selina Bickford and Edith Brent who hailed from Calstock, Cornwall. James Perkins's family had lived in Calstock for a time. His younger brother, George, was born there, so he may have found some warm hospitality and enjoyed lively conversation at this particular boarding house: a "Cousin Jack" sparking with a couple of "Cousin Jennies" from Calstock? It could have happened.

The Cornish arriving in Colorado were described in Arthur Cecil Todd's book, *The Cornish Miner in America*, as "robust, stout chested, pink-cheeked lads from the tin mines of Cornwall. There is very little brawling ... an occasional mix-up with the Irish. People were struck by their lingo: the dropped 'h' and haphazard insertion: ''ow art 'e getting hon, you?' A miner thrown off a horse: 'Dam she; I could ride she if it wudn' for the dam dinner pail.'"

Stories in Todd's book reflect the lives of these simple people. At Nevadaville, Colorado, a Cornishman by the name of Nankervis ran a butcher's shop that sported a large stuffed owl for decoration on a shelf above the counter.

"'Ow much for the broad-faced chicken?" asked a Cousin Jenny.

"That edn' no chicken. Tes an owl."

"I dun't care 'ow owl 'ee be; 'ee'll do for my boarders."

Most were illiterate and could neither read nor write, but their pride and independence prevented them from confessing their illiteracy.

By the later 1860s, the Pike's Peak excitement proved to be a deception, and Colorado mining experienced a depression. James apparently left that region along with many other miners.

In northern Wisconsin and the adjacent Upper Peninsula of Michigan, copper and iron mining drew the Cousin Jacks. Two-thirds of the miners in this region were Cornish and Irish. In James's case, he was a mix of both nationalities and undoubtedly felt at home in the UP. Because of the harsh weather, many of the miners were migrants who went south with the onset of the bitter winter winds off Lake Superior and returned to the diggings after the spring thaw. It's likely that James was one of those who migrated between the Benton area in southwestern Wisconsin and the northern region. He may have worked in the copper mines of the UP. Negaunee, Michigan, was known as "Cornish Town," and James perhaps worked in that area, at Ishpeming or around the Port of Marquette where the miners earned a substantial wage of two dollars per day at that time.

He wasn't up north but for one or two summers because on June 7, 1866, he married Eliza Jane Hocking at Galena, Illinois, ten miles south of Benton. The next year, they left for Pennsylvania after their first child, Martha Jane, was born.

It must have been the iron mining that drew him to Johnstown in Pennsylvania. Could he have had some distant relatives there? (The twenty-first ward in the city of Johnstown was formerly known as Perkinsville until 1869.)

Johnstown was the acknowledged birthplace of the American steel industry. As described in records of the Cambria County, Pennsylvania Historical Society:

The ore bed was in the center of the Johnstown basin. Its eastern outcrop was a short distance west of Conemaugh, well up the hillside above the railroad. From there it ran under Prospect appearing at water level at Hinkston Run. The bed was quite extensive and was sufficient limestone to make it self-fluxing in the furnaces. It probably benched at all of the Cambria furnaces. The ore was of a carbonate of iron that contained an average of 30% of iron and was mined as late as 1875 when it was wholly replaced by the cheaper and far richer lake ores.

It should be noted that the iron ores from the Upper Great Lakes region were extracted by the open-pit method, and Cornishmen weren't fond of the open-pit style of mining.

Johnstown lay on the western slope of the Allegheny Mountains, situated on a broad flat, completely encircled by mountains, at the confluence of the Stony Creek with the little Conemaugh. In the center of the town, a large basin was formed by the damming of the Conemaugh to accommodate the great fleet of canal boats plying between Johnstown and Pittsburgh. The basin was surrounded by warehouses, boat yards, and other conveniences for receiving and delivering goods. Some eight or ten lines for transportation had forwarding houses there, and during the summer it was a stirring, busy place. The dwellings were generally very well built—many of them brick. The water was pure, and the mountain air was clear. There were four churches at the time: Catholic, Presbyterian, Methodist, and Lutheran.

There was a large demand for steel rails for the railroad industry during the boom period of 1869 through 1871. In Johnstown, the Cambria Mining Company employed about four thousand men in its works and mine. There were some railroad shops, planing mills, flour mills, and several newspapers. Only the men employed by the Cambria Company and their families lived on the flats and made ground. The

Cambria Company owned all of this and made it a rule not to sell it, but to lease it. The company put rows of two-story frame tenements close together on their land close to the works. The land they chose was not far above the water at normal times. During the ordinary spring floods, the water rose so high that it flowed into the cellars of the tenements. James and Eliza perhaps lived in one of the tenement houses when their second child, Elizabeth, was born in 1868.

We're not sure how long James and his family remained in Johnstown—perhaps just a couple of years—before returning to southwestern Wisconsin. It's a possibility that iron mining didn't appeal to James, or maybe Eliza Jane grew tired of a wet basement every spring or maybe she missed her Hocking family and was homesick. In any case, they packed up and went back home to the Fever River mining area and remained there to raise their family, which later grew to nine children.

What made these young miners pull up stakes and go from place to place? Were they hoping to strike it rich or was it simply an attempt to make the most of an American dream ... find that one place that would provide a rewarding future for them and their families? The Cousin Jacks were in demand, there was good money to be made, and after years of hardship in the "old country," they were attempting to make the most of their newfound opportunity.

In *A Century of Iron and Men*, Harlan Hatcher wrote:

> The Cornishmen were among the greatest of the mining captains, those immensely able underground technicians who were always observing and studying the progress of the workings and seemed, almost by intuition, to follow the crazy convolutions of the rock formations. It was a matter of high personal ambition with them to get out at least expense the maximum of

clean ore, to avoid digging through waste rock and to guard the safety of the miners. Experienced geologists also learned to listen carefully to the words of these experienced captains on the nature and position of the ore deposits. Several of the Cornishmen became famous, even legendary, on the range, for their physical strength, their ability to wrestle, handle a drill and were known to load more ore than the next man.

# CHAPTER 8

# THE COOK FAMILY

In February 1960, I was aboard the USS *San Pablo* in the Caribbean when my maternal grandfather, Bert Cook, died at age eighty-four. He had made his home with us in Benton since the late 1930s.

Because he was a member of our household as I was growing up in Benton, we were very close. We spent time together fishing and playing cards. He was fond of the "seven-up" card game where you played for points: high, low, jack, and the game. I would ride my bike downtown, running errands for him. Grandpa would give me money to buy his Horseshoe brand of plug tobacco or a couple of Red Dot cigars and tell me to buy myself an ice-cream cone from any remaining change.

In the winter, he and I would shovel snow from the sidewalks. He had a particular technique and taught it to me as a youngster: make one long scoop straight ahead on the right side of the walk, then three or four horizontal swipes to the left. We used common scoop shovels in those days. I often used one from the coal bin. Grandpa was fussy about gardening too. In the summer, we spent time together hoeing and cultivating my dad's garden to keep it free of weeds. As he worked, he took care not to spit any tobacco juice on the vegetable plants.

We kept an empty tin can handy so we could collect worms as we worked up the garden. Then we would hike out of town and cross a couple of cornfields to the gravel road leading to Bryant's Bridge, where we would fish the Fever River. As an energetic young kid, I liked to work up and down the river, casting for black bass while Grandpa would locate his favorite spot on the river bank, shaded by a nearby tree, and there he stayed, fish or no fish. He stowed a short piece of pine board under a tree on the riverbank. He would retrieve it when we arrived at the river and use it as a seat when the ground was soggy.

I have a vivid memory of the two of us sitting next to the river under the shade tree, eating a lunch that Mom had packed for us. Grandpa preferred a thick slab of cheddar cheese sandwiched between slices of homemade bread. He drank his coffee with milk and sugar while I washed my sandwich down with lemon soda pop.

My grandpa Cook's grandfather hailed from Pennsylvania. There is a saying, "Too many cooks in the kitchen!" Well, John P. Cook had five wives at different times, so he definitely had a lot of different cooks in his kitchen!

He was born on March 19, 1798, in Washington County, Pennsylvania. As of this writing, we have no confirmed records indicating his exact place of birth or his parents' names. One of our relatives claims that his first marriage to Armanella Leverine bore one child, but that fact has never been verified.

He married a second time, to Sophronia R. Smith in 1832 in Marion County, Indiana, where she was born. It was there in Indiana that John P. received a grant of eighty acres of land. This land grant was dated October 23, 1834, and signed by US President Andrew Jackson.

John and Sophronia had four children, with the two eldest, Phebe [sic] and my great-grandfather Timothy, being born on the farm in

Marion County. It is said that John later traveled from Indiana to Jenkynsville, Wisconsin Territory, with his wife and the two children by cart hitched to a yoke of oxen. He would have been one of the earliest settlers in this region just a mile or two south of "Buzzards Roost," a town that later became known as Jenkynsville. Two more children, Lydia and John, were born in Jenkynsville in 1840 and 1843.

HeritageQuest.com provides this information:

> When the Northwestern Territory was ceded to the United States by Virginia in 1784, it embraced only the territory lying between the Ohio and the Mississippi Rivers, and north to the northern limits of the United States. It coincided with the area now embraced in the States of Ohio, Indiana, Michigan, Illinois, Wisconsin, and that portion of Minnesota lying on the east side of the Mississippi River. The United States itself at that period extended no further west than the Mississippi River; but by the purchase of Louisiana in 1803, the western boundary of the United States was extended to the Rocky Mountains and the Northern Pacific Ocean. The new territory thus added to the National domain, and subsequently opened to settlement, has been called the "New Northwest," in contradistinction from the old "Northwestern Territory."

Wisconsin was granted statehood in 1848, and the John P. Cook family was listed in the 1850 census of Lafayette County. By this time, he had married a third wife, Mealisa Mallory, and had become stepfather to her two children, Napoleon and Elizabeth. There were now six children in his household. This census report indicates that he owned a farm of 160 acres valued at $2,000. John homesteaded this property through a land grant signed by President James Polk.

We have no record of what caused the death of my great-great-grandmother Sophronia (Smith) Cook in 1848, but John married Mealisa in 1849, followed by two other marriages, Mary Rouse and Julia Oldham, over the next ten-year period. There is no evidence that these latter marriages bore any children.

John's eldest son, my great-grandfather Timothy Smith Cook, who was born on the Indiana farm in 1838, had come with the family to Wisconsin when he was one or two years of age. He was raised on the farm south of Jenkynsville, and it was toward the end of the US Civil War, in February 1865, that he and his brother, John Garland Cook, decided to enlist in the Union Army. It was close to the time that their father, John P., had passed on, and this leads us to believe that John P. may have kept his sons out of the war, and they then wasted no time in enlisting following his death. Another theory is that John P. left a young widow in her forties, Julia (Oldham) Cook, and the boys may not have gotten along well with the young stepmother. They may have chosen to leave the farm for that reason, or she may have kicked them out.

Timothy was a volunteer with Company E, 154th Regiment of the Illinois Infantry. He and his brother had enlisted across the state line at Dixon, Illinois. He served at the rank of private, and military records indicate that he was one of the soldiers assigned to guard a train near Chattanooga, Tennessee. Those records also indicate that he was a musician.

He was honorably discharged at Memphis at the end of the war on September 21, 1865, and was granted a pension of six dollars a month due to having a hernia on his right side. As a civilian, this pension was renewed year after year because of the persistence of the hernia. "He couldn't do full day's work," according to the signed affidavits sworn by neighbors and acquaintances.

He was physically handicapped for most of his life following the war. First of all, there was the matter of the hernia. In those days, a surgical procedure to repair a hernia was unknown, and it must have been difficult for him to endure the nagging pain of it. The pension from the army of six dollars a month hardly seems adequate, even in those days.

Then there was the matter of a broken ankle. From records obtained in the US Archives, he had applied for disability compensation due to a broken ankle suffered after an accident with a team and wagon. At the time of the accident, Timothy was farming near Seymour, Wisconsin, in the township of Jenkynsville. He was fifty-two years of age and had been married to his second wife, Sarah Ann Kendall, for about seven years. The two of them were taking the team and wagon down the road when the horses apparently spooked and ran off, tipping the wagon over into a ditch. Melinda Downs, a neighbor, saw the horses running toward her down the highway, and she managed to run out and catch them by the harness. After settling the horses, she saw Timothy's wife, Sarah, out on the road, and she led the horses back to the scene of the accident. It was then that she discovered that Timothy's ankle was severely broken and he was lying on the ground.

All of this was written up by Melinda Downs in an affidavit where she went on to say, "And I know it wasn't caused by any vicious habits, as he always was and is now a man of strict morals." The affidavit was sworn August 2, 1891.

Timothy was first married to Janet Riddle shortly after the Civil War. She was born in Scotland (or England), and they had seven children, but three of them died in infancy. My grandfather Adelbert "Bert" Cook was the sixth. He was born on July 16, 1875.

Timothy's second marriage, to Sarah Kendall, who was seventeen years younger than him, bore four more children. Of the eight surviving children, seven remained in the Wisconsin and Minnesota region, while my great-aunt Lylia was employed as an executive secretary by the federal government in Washington, DC. She never married and later retired to Florida, where she lived until her death.

My great-grandfather Timothy must have made many friends in the army. When he died in 1911, his obituary read that there were "a number of troops" in attendance at his funeral at Cuba City, Wisconsin. He had become senile shortly before his death at age seventy-four. He spent his retirement years in Cuba City, and most residents knew him quite well. They told of him walking downtown at midday carrying a lantern. When asked about it, he said to them, "I have the lantern just in case I don't get home before dark." He was only a few blocks from the house. I don't know if that story is true or not, but my grandfather Bert (his son), also experienced those periods of senility when he reached his eighties. Family members said he had "hardening of the arteries," which caused confusion and mental lapses, but in both of those cases it was probably Alzheimer's disease, which went undiagnosed in those days.

Bert and Cora Cook, 1902

Grandpa Bert Cook farmed north of Benton near the unincorporated town of Jenkynsville. He had a small dairy farm. He married Cora Ellen Raisbeck. Their firstborn, Delbert, died at age seventeen of influenza, and the youngest child, Harvey, died in infancy. When Harvey died, that left Harry, the oldest surviving child, with four sisters.

The girls all helped out with chores at the farm. Blanche was the oldest of the four sisters. My mother, Mary Jeanette, was next, then Phoebe Arlene. Melva Florence was the youngest. There were cows to be milked, chickens and pigs to be fed, and eggs to be gathered. Blanche and Jeanette helped out with the baking and the canning of fruit and vegetables from the garden.

My grandpa Cook was one of the first in the farming community to purchase an automobile. It was a Ford Model T. Jeanette and her sisters took pride in this modern conveyance and kept it washed and cleaned. They obviously inherited some of Grandpa's traits. He always fussed over his tools and equipment, keeping his knives sharp and his tools and farm implements scraped clean and well lubricated between seasonal chores.

His son Harry, however, was less disciplined in that regard. As a teenager, Harry enjoyed going into Benton to party on Saturday nights with brother Delbert and some of his friends, and perhaps to drive to one of the local dance halls. My mother recalled that on one particular Saturday night when their parents had gone away for the weekend, he and Delbert sneaked the Model T out of the shed and took it to town. When the girls went out to the barnyard on Sunday morning to do their chores, there sat the precious car completely splattered with mud! She said that she and Blanche were "just sick about it," so they and younger sister Arlene quickly got some rags and buckets of water. They hurried to clean up the Ford so that "Pop" wouldn't notice it when he returned home. They wanted to protect their two brothers so they wouldn't get into trouble. Of course, Harry was the instigator, as usual, and Pop wouldn't have been happy if he had found that Harry had taken the car without permission.

Jeanette would drive the Model T on occasion and take her younger sisters into town and back and, in the summer, to the county fair in Darlington, Wisconsin. The Cook sisters were good friends with the Schwartz girls of Darlington, so they often went there to visit on Sundays. Sometimes they would all ride in the Model T with Jeanette driving, touring the county roads around Darlington. The young girls knew all of the popular songs of the day and would sing as they rode.

Mom told of another time when she drove sisters Blanche and Arlene out in the country to pick berries. Families in those days often saved the empty Karo brand corn-syrup pails and scrubbed them out for general household use. The girls took a few of them with them because, with their wire bails, they found them handy for picking berries. On this particular day, having filled the pails with berries, Jeanette cranked up the Ford and they were clambering into the car for the return trip when they noticed gasoline leaking from beneath the engine compartment. The gas tank was leaking. At Jeanette's direction, the girls emptied their pails of berries, and then Arlene, being the youngest, was told to crawl under the car and catch the stream of gasoline in each pail. They then drove the few miles home, knowing that they had reserve fuel in case the tank went dry. They arrived home without any berries but had an interesting story to tell!

Bert used a team of horses for most of the farm work. Once in a while, the two oldest girls, Jeanette and Blanche, would ride the old horses bareback. Jeanette would always talk Blanche into riding Nellie, who Jeanette thought was "mean and spunky." My mother was always a nervous and cautious person, an unusual trait for a farm girl, but Blanche was much more adventuresome and a better match for Nellie.

Milk from their farm was hauled to the creamery near Jenkynsville that produced butter and cheese. Jeanette usually drove the cart and single horse, hauling the milk to the creamery. The cart at that time had a couple of loose spokes in one wheel, and it would "clickety-clack" as it rolled along. Neighbor Annie Oliver said she could hear the cart go by on the gravel road in front of their place, and she would say to her family, "There goes Jeanette to the creamery."

Their mother, Cora, was always well-organized around the house, just as husband, Bert (known as "Pop" by his children), was always fussy with his tools and equipment. She had a fixed schedule for household chores that the girls were to follow, and it only varied when absolutely necessary. My mother said her mother, Cora, wasn't severe about it, just well-disciplined, perhaps a trait of the Raisbeck family. Monday was always wash day, Tuesday was for ironing, mending was done on Wednesday, upstairs cleaning Thursday, and the downstairs was cleaned on Friday. Saturday was baking day.

As was typical with most farm families, they went to church on Sunday after putting a roast in the oven. A big Sunday dinner was served at midday following church. Sometimes they would be joined at the table by guests, relatives, or close family friends. At other times on Sunday afternoons, they would have visitors or would go to visit. There were scarcely any telephones in the early twentieth century, so it was common for families to make personal visits. It was their way of keeping in touch with family and close friends.

On a larger scale, a family reunion would be organized during the summer months. There would be a Cherry/Raisbeck reunion, a Cook reunion, or (on my dad's side of the family) a Perkins family gathering, often with thirty to forty people attending. These were sometimes held at a family farm, where picnic tables were set up under shade trees in the yard, or the dinner would be served in the large farmhouse kitchen. It was more common, however, to reserve a shelter house at a community park in Shullsburg or Benton for this large group of adults and children. The families were quite large for the most part, and there were lots of cousins of all ages.

There was no television during the early half of the twentieth century, and because many of the families had no telephone, these gatherings were important in maintaining social contact. The women brought precooked dishes "to pass," such as baked beans, vegetable casseroles, desserts, and salads. One family would volunteer to bring a baked ham, another some fried chicken, a baked turkey, or roast beef. Deviled eggs and home-canned pickles often provided a special treat. There was always more than enough food to go around.

There would be jugs of homemade lemonade, with slices of fresh lemon floating amid the ice chips. Coffee would be brought in thermoses or boiled in a large porcelain coffee pot over a pit fire. The shelter houses at the village park had fire pits, and, in later years, the parks had iron barbeque grills located throughout the park where the kids could cook their hot dogs and burgers. There would also be soda pop available, and each family brought their own glasses, plates, and flatware.

The men would gather in groups to discuss the mining or crop farming, the impact of the previous winter's weather, and how it affected the spring field work. Some would pitch horseshoes if there was a court available. The women would catch up on family news and health issues, and the children would amuse themselves at the park. Baseball or softball was the favorite pastime, and some of the adults would join in. The park in Shullsburg had a municipal swimming pool. That was a great diversion on a hot summer day in the Midwest. I never knew my dad to wear a short-sleeve shirt despite the warm summer weather. He always rolled up the sleeves of his long-sleeve shirts. After the swimming and baseball, it was back to the picnic area for supper and more cake or pie for dessert. A family reunion normally lasted all afternoon. Some families left earlier because there was milking and other chores to be done at the farm.

There were also social gatherings at harvest time on the farms. The men would combine labor and equipment for threshing the oats and sometimes when putting up a large crop of hay. These would be held at one family farm then another until all of the crops had been harvested. The women would bring food, lemonade, and coffee; the kids would come along just for the fun of it. The older ones would help with the food preparation, and the younger ones would play ball on the expansive lawn or spend time exploring the barns and livestock pens.

In 1923, my grandpa Bert Cook lost his farm north of Leadmine, and there are conflicting stories about how this happened. According to my aunt Melva, Grandpa was making payments to the bank through a third party for some reason, and some payments never got to the bank. This resulted in a foreclosure. Another version concerned the local creamery. As a normal practice, farmers in the area consigned their milk to the creamery and were then paid when the products, primarily butter and cheese, were processed or sold. Some said that the creamery got behind in their payments to the farmers, and then, suddenly, the creamery building burned down. It was reported that a truck was seen at the creamery after dark on the night before it burned, and many suspected that it was being loaded with butter and cheese that night before the fire.

Whatever happened, Melva suspected that our Grandpa Bert may have placed too much trust in other people. I knew him as a kind, tenderhearted person who could have been susceptible to a scheming individual.

In 1924, Bert, his wife, Cora, and their youngest child, three-year-old Melva, moved into Benton. Jeanette was married and living in

Darlington, Blanche was married to LaVerne Farrey, Harry had married Zetta Ewing, and Phoebe Arlene had married Tom Ewing, Zetta's brother. Three years after Bert and Cora had moved to Benton, Cora died suddenly of heart failure. She had always experienced "fainting spells," according to my mother. She apparently suffered from high blood pressure, which led to lung hemorrhage. People seldom visited a doctor in those days.

Melva, now six years old when her mother died, went to live with my mother, Jeanette, and her first husband, Delbert Reichling, in Darlington. This first marriage failed, however, and the divorce papers were recorded in Marshfield, Wisconsin, on August 17, 1935. She married my dad, William Percy Perkins, in 1939, and they made their home in Benton where my father was raised.

\* \* \* \* \* \*

My parents met while both were working for Wes and Jen Robson, farmers at the west edge of Benton. Dad ("Haggens") had been working for Wes as the hired hand for some time when Wes and Jen hired my mother at the dairy farm as the "hired girl" who helped with the cooking and housework. Farm work starts early in the day, and Jeanette, having been away from the farm life for ten years, developed a habit of oversleeping on occasion. Wes cured her of that habit by secretly tying a cowbell under her bed. The string from the cowbell stretched down through the floor register to the kitchen below. When the bell started clanging in the morning, she got out of bed in a hurry!

Wes Robson was a heavy drinker, an apparent alcoholic, and his health "turned poorly" when he reach his sixties. He was bedridden toward the end and died of a bad liver. Wes was over six feet tall and in his heyday was known to get on top of the bar at one of the taverns in

Benton and lead the singing. My dad more or less took responsibility for the day-to-day running of the farm as Wes's health deteriorated.

* * * * * *

After Mom and Dad were married, Grandpa Cook and Melva moved into their home in Benton. Melva had just one year of high school remaining. She graduated in May 1939, and I was born in August of the same year. Grandpa paid my mother for his and Melva's room and board. He also worked at the vegetable canning plant in nearby Cuba City during the harvest months and spent his free time prospecting around Benton for lead and zinc, his lifetime hobby.

Some of Grandpa's family had moved away from the small village of Benton to Beloit, Milwaukee, and the Twin Cities (Minneapolis-St. Paul), so when they were able to come home for a visit, it was a special time for him. My mother would cook a big Sunday dinner for the visitors, and "Pop" would enjoy having more of his family around. He was all smiles and justifiably proud of them. The Cooks and Raisbecks, as well as the Perkins family, had all been blessed with a keen sense of humor, so these gatherings were a primary source of entertainment in those days, and a host of family memories were recounted during these family visits.

# CHAPTER 9

# CELTIC CORNWALL AND IRELAND

The ancestry of the Robbins and Perkins families made their homes in Ireland as well as in Cornwall, England. It's known that Cornwall, on the southwestern tip of the British Isles, traded with Ireland and maintained a favorable relationship with the Irish, primarily because they were both of Celtic origin. The people in County Cornwall, for the most part, were somewhat disloyal to the king of England and rose up against the king's Royal Army on more than one occasion. Frequent periods of famine and a difficult life in both societies, combined with religious persecution, was cause for many families to relocate from Cornwall to Ireland and vice versa.

These Celts migrated by sea between southern Ireland and Hayle estuary of Western Cornwall in St. Ives Bay. The estuary is an encircling arm protecting the shallow and yellow sands at the mouth of the Hayle River on the northwest coast.

Our Perkins family has a double tie between Cornwall and Ireland. While Thomas Perkins was born in England (most likely in Cornwall), he married Catherine Creed in County Waterford, Ireland. From that union, James and his two older sisters, Mary Ann and Martha, were born in Waterford, as was their mother, Catherine, according to the British census. When James was quite young, the Thomas Perkins family relocated to Calstock, Cornwall, where George, the youngest sibling, was born in 1846. Thomas was a miner and spent his lifetime at that vocation as the means of providing for his family. By the time of the 1851 British census, his family had again relocated across the River Tamar to the Bere Peninsula in the town of Bere Alston.

Son James left England for America in the year of 1863 at the age of twenty-one. He reportedly came over with an aunt and uncle, possibly the Bennetts, but it is unknown whether any of his siblings made the journey at the same time. On June 7, 1866, he married Eliza Jane Hocking in Galena, Illinois, just a few miles south of the New Diggings, Wisconsin, mining area. Eliza Jane, born in the mining village of Illogan, Cornwall, in the Camborne District, had come to America years earlier with her parents, William and Eleanor Hocking. William was also a miner and had settled his family in the Wisconsin mining region as well.

James and Eliza Jane Perkins raised a large family in the Benton/ New Diggings area, and one of their sons, my grandfather Thomas, married Lilla Jane Robbins, the eldest child of Charles and Hannah (Redfern) Robbins. Charles's parents were both born in Cornwall, but they also had married in Ireland, this being the second Cornwall/ Ireland family connection.

Few Americans know much about Cornwall, the southernmost county located in the "tail" of the British Isles. Its two peninsulas, dissimilar in size, resemble a pincer informally known as the "Claw of Cornwall." The River Tamar, fifty-seven miles in length, almost separates this county from Devon and the main body of England.

Almost a country within a country, Cornwall remained somewhat isolated from the rest of England throughout history. In many ways, it had closer ties to Ireland than to London. In addition to their common Celtic ancestry, the Cornish practiced the same religion for a time and shared common hardships of famine and hostile environment. Life in Cornwall was especially difficult at times due to the harsh environment of the rugged, windswept coasts. The county was isolated from the rest of England because, with few bridges, the Tamar served as a form of barrier. When England was under Roman rule, Cornwall was further isolated. The Romans seldom crossed the Tamar, and none of the international trade flowed into or out of the Cornish ports during their period of rule. The Celtic background of the Cornish people, in common with the Irish and Scots, and their isolation from the rest of England, strengthened their fierce independence. The Cornish citizenry resented English rule and rose up against the Saxons and other authorities who imposed upon the Cornish their religious beliefs or their way of life. There was a quiet yet sturdy reserve in the Cornish character. The peasants spoke very little, and they grew to become quite tolerant of poverty and hardship.

They were also tempered by the environment. Gales and storms frequent both the north and south coasts of Cornwall. There is a long history of shipwrecks, primarily on the northern coast where the "land pirates" were afforded the opportunity to loot the wrecks. Coastal winds are severe, and hurricanes of sand were known to bury a hamlet or, on other occasions, would uncover a village that had been buried years earlier in a previous storm. The scenic northern coast is known for its lashing rain and roar of the sea. "A man wants two other men to hold the hair on his head," said an ancient Cornishman. The weather is changeable in Cornwall: "a shower every day of the week and two on Sundays." Inland there is some farming, but fruit doesn't ripen until November. There is little snow or frost in winter. Flowers bloom in February.

While Britons in the north, beyond the River Tamar, tilled the soil and grazed cattle, the first settlers near Lands End in Cornwall streamed tin and traded their mineral wealth with Iberian and Mediterranean people. These early Celtic adventurers were from Mediterranean lands, near the Aegean and Mirtoon Seas. Many had wrecked on the rugged coasts of Cornwall. They are believed to have found a haven in Cornwall and to have influenced the Cornish bloodlines. Short and dark, they are said to have been Celts who had migrated from the present-day French coastal area to Brittany, Ireland, Wales, and Scotland as well as to this Cornish region.

Daphne du Maurier wrote in *Vanishing Cornwall*:

> There is in the Cornish character, smoldering beneath the surface, a fiery independence, or stubborn pride. Some of this could be due to centuries of isolation after the Roman conquest of Britain when trade with the Mediterranean countries was cut off from Cornwall, but it is believed that most of their legacy was to the dark-haired invaders from an earlier time, 1400 BC, who were described as "dark-eyed seamen with narrow waists and braided hair from Knossos." It is further believed that the Cornish people share a common ancestry with the Irish further west.

A. L. Rowse writes: "Cornishmen, from the beginning, have always dug for wealth. They remain tinners, copper-seekers, quarries, slate-breakers, farmers." When he describes them as "an earthy people with an earthy knowledge," he means that as a salutatory description. In America, they provided expertise in mining gold and silver as well as the lead and zinc in southwestern Wisconsin and other regions of the country. They were known as "hard-rock" miners, as opposed to the Welsh, for example, who were known to mine primarily coal. These stubborn and independent Cornish were an earthy people known to pound through solid granite with pick, gad, and shovel; hence, they were "hard-rock" miners.

During the Bronze Age, these tinners were at work in Cornwall. Those first early explorers from the Mediterranean lands who settled around the River Hayle in the western part of Cornwall found the tin ore amid the mixture of sand and stone that had washed down in the streams from the granite hills. The tin, blended with copper ore discovered earlier in Ireland, could be made into bronze that was formed into weapons. Domestic uses for the bronze came later: cups, plates, linings of pots and pans, bells, and many other uses. Later it was found that Cornwall held the greatest deposits of tin in all of Europe.

The earliest method of ore extraction was by "streaming" the gravel from the rock face where the veins of ore were exposed. The lighter waste washed away, leaving the heavier ore-laden stones, which were pounded into grain and then smelted in a furnace. This mining technology did not advance for centuries. These early tinners were self-enterprising. They could set up on any stream in the wastelands, work in the open, and keep their profits. The ore was hauled by horse and wagon to the furnace for smelting after being pounded into grain.

It was during the reign of Richard I in the twelfth century that the tinners of Cornwall were burdened with the first code of laws. It was called the Charter for the Stanneries (as the industry came to be called). A tinner could dig where and how he liked, and he was still his own master, but the lord of manor who owned the land would receive his toll. The tinner, after paying a tax on the tin after it was smelted, was a free artisan who could keep his profits, but if there were no profits, he was the loser.

The tinner worked in the open, up on the moors or along the riverbanks, with a pick and shovel. He would take a lease, or "set," from the landowner, usually for a one-year period, then pay him either a fixed amount or a percentage of the tin found. The miner's family—men, women, and children—all worked in the mine, and if the miner prospered, he would employ other men as well. If the "set" was a distance from his hamlet, he would construct a moor house close by the diggings. The structure would offer bare and sparse quarters for the miner.

Later, when the surface ore became exhausted, the tinner had to dig for the ore. This extra expense had to be financed by people with wealth: the more successful tinners or landowners willing to gamble for huge profits. The tinner remained independent by working for himself and paying his financial partner an agreed-upon sum or a percentage of the profits, called "tribute."

By the fifteenth century, the surface ore had been mined, and tinners were required to dig tunnels and burrows underground. Copper was also discovered in Cornwall, and it turned out to be abundant. The mines grew deeper, however, and horizontal drifts were run. Shafts were sunk deeper, and tunnels were longer. The work became harder, and accidents were frequent. The air below ground became hot and stagnant, and the toil became more dangerous with cave-ins and drownings. Mining became a big-money investment.

As mining in Cornwall became a major industry, more and more middlemen provided the required capital. Merchants and affluent tinners loaned money to the independent miners, and some of the landowners formed their own mining companies. These companies would then employ the miners to work for flat wages, but many Cornishmen stubbornly and courageously maintained their independence by toiling on "tribute," a percentage of the profits. This was a difficult choice for the miners, as profits could swing wildly at times, and many miners found themselves in desperate straits. To avoid starvation, many would raid the nearest market town for food to feed their families. At these times, they often lived on potatoes and barley gruel and lived in a small, overcrowded cottage. During the boom times, there was much celebrating by those miners who had a share in the profits. The partying was rough and rowdy, accompanied by heavy drinking, cockfights, and fistfights. The tinners were feared and considered to be savages by many of the common citizenry, who couldn't understand and were suspicious of those miners who chose not to work for a regular wage and the security that went with steady pay. For this courageous group of tinners, mining was in their blood, and they desired no other occupation.

In the early nineteenth century, the price of tin and now copper mined near the River Tamar reached an all-time high. It was boom time again in the mining business, and that lasted throughout the industrial revolution. "Foreigners from Up-Country" began to get controlling interests in the mines, and capitalism took control from the former venturers. The miners now worked long hours for low wages. The average lifespan of a miner was forty-seven years.

It was at this time in history that my great-grandfather, James Perkins, born in Waterford of an Irish mother, began working near the River Tamar. The family had been located in Calstock, Cornwall, around 1846, and then moved across the river to the village of Bere Alston in Devon by 1850. Three years later, James went to work at a mine at the young age of eleven. He undoubtedly worked at the same mine where his oldest sister, Mary Ann, was working. Child labor was common at this time, but as a rule, children were not permitted to work underground, "below the grass."

Cornwall, by this time, had become the largest producer of copper in the world, providing two-thirds of the world's supply. That wouldn't last much longer, however. By the early 1860s, the bottom began to fall out of the market when copper was discovered near Lake Victoria, and tin deposits were discovered in Malaysia. Labor and production costs were lower in those areas of Africa and Malaysia, so mines in Cornwall were forced to close, putting thousands of miners out of work by the end of the nineteenth century. A third of the mining population left Cornwall and southern England prior to 1900. Among those was a young but experienced miner, James Perkins, who at age twenty-one migrated to America. This was 1863, in the midst of the American Civil War. Many miners at this time arrived at the Port of New Orleans and traveled up the Mississippi River to reach the lead district of southwestern Wisconsin.

In 1866, James married Eliza Jane Hocking, whose family had come to America in 1848, the same year that Wisconsin gained statehood. Her parents were William and Eleanor Hocking from Illogan, Cornwall. Eleanor was a Jenkyn, born in Cornwall on Christmas Day 1821. The Hocking family had settled at Coon Branch in the southwestern Wisconsin mining region.

# CHAPTER 10

# RELIGION IN CORNWALL

"Religion to the Cornish is bred to the bone, taking varying forms through successive generations," Daphne du Maurier wrote in *Vanishing Cornwall*.

The Cornish people accepted religion, yet they had a deep sense of superstition. Half wondering, half afraid, a reliance on the old magic never died away during their successive conversions to the Roman Catholic, Anglican, and then Methodist religions. Some were converted forcefully, others voluntarily, but there was always an unconscious longing to turn back to older cults and superstitions.

Spells, charms, curses, and wishes sometimes had more power over the witches and fairies that came and went at will. There were the "knackers" who hammered and howled from deep within the mines, and the "piskies" who haunted the Cornish household.

From earliest times, the Mediterranean settlers worshipped the Earth Mother, goddess of fertility who brought life to the world. Granite stones and rocks were her work. She had power over all things, inanimate and living. To these early Celtic settlers, standing and leaning stones held magic. Today, near Lanyon, there remains Men-an-tol, a large stone with a hole in the center. It was believed that if one crawled through this divine stone nine times against the sun, a serious affliction or disease would be "backened."

Madron Well, near Penzance in West Cornwall, had healing powers that could cure the tetters or cramp. Water from the well was known to have healed a cripple.

The Celtic races brought a different cult of sky gods, sun gods, spirits of trees and woodlands. The Earth Goddess notwithstanding, the gods were predominately male.

The Cornish were extremely superstitious. They would not eat hare. The best apple tree in the orchard, sprinkled with cider at Christmas, would bring good fortune. The voice of a drowned person was heard shortly after the drowning near the shore or river where he or she was lost. As a cure for smallpox and measles, live fowl would be plucked and hung upside down in the patient's bedroom. The Cornish miners believed that a woman in a mine would bring bad luck to the miners or disaster to the mine, and if a miner's candle went out three times or fell off a ledge or wall, somebody was at home playing with his wife.

The British church came into existence in the third century, when Britain was a province of the Roman Empire. It was a missionary church with figures such as St. Illtud, St. Ninian, and St. Patrick evangelizing in the Celtic regions of Scotland, Ireland, Wales, and Cornwall. The later invasions by the pagan Angles, Saxons, and Jutes in the fifth century destroyed the organization of the church in England.

In the year 597, a mission sent by Pope Gregory the Great and led by St. Augustine of Canterbury landed in Kent and began converting these pagans of England. This eventually became known as the Church of England, which initially acknowledged the authority of the pope.

Cornwall retained the Romano-British church, as did the other Celtic regions of Ireland, Scotland, and Wales. This religion in Cornwall was reinforced by monks from Ireland and Wales sailing up the Hayle estuary, teaching and baptizing the Cornish in their Catholic faith. Churches were built throughout the county, and ecclesiastical order was established to a great degree.

However, the old sense of superstition and magic in Cornwall never fully died. When the Church of England broke with Rome and ordered the destruction of the Roman Catholic Mass and prayer books, some of the Cornish people sought a deeper consolation in the magic of before. Others held Mass secretly in private homes.

Resentment grew as the Church of England grew more authoritative, and the Cornish rebelled. A contingent of the Saxon army entered Cornwall, under the direction of the Church of England, to confiscate and burn the Catholic prayer books.

In AD 825, a vicious battle was fought between the Cornish and the West Saxons at Slaughter Bridge above Camelford. There was a great Celtic leader called Arthur, who united the various tribes as they fought the invading Saxons. The Cornish, lacking in weapons, were severely defeated in hand-to-hand combat, and Arthur was mortally wounded.

Most historians claim that this battle at Slaughter Bridge became the basis of the legend of King Arthur. John Leland wrote years later of King Arthur's final battle with Mordred at a river in Cornwall. Slaughter Bridge over the River Camel is the exact location, according to local tradition. Truth and legend became intermingled, and some say Camelot took its name from the River Camel.

The present-day legend of King Arthur comes from the writings of Geoffrey of Monmouth, who had heard about Arthur, the Celtic leader of the Cornish tribes, and subsequently invented the stories of King

Arthur and the Round Table. Nevertheless, Arthur represents the spirit of Cornwall and reminds people of their Celtic past.

The battle at Slaughter Bridge was one of several instances of rebellion by the isolated and independent Cornish people. In one of the later rebellions, in AD 1497, the issue wasn't religion. They fought the army of King Henry VII over the taxes he imposed to finance his Scottish war. There was great poverty among the Cornish tin workers at this time, and they resented having to pay toward a war that had little to do with them.

Michael Joseph and Thomas Flamark roused the populace into open rebellion. They led an ill-clad, ill-armed force to march to London. Supporters were collected along the way, and in Somerset, Lord Audley took command of the army. By the time it reached Blackheath near London, there were several thousand men armed with staves, pitchforks, and homemade weapons. On June 17, 1497, they were surrounded by the king's army of ten thousand men. The battle was brief, and two hundred Cornishmen died. Lord Audley and Flamark were captured on the battlefield and Joseph as he fled toward Greenwich. They were taken to the Tower of London, Flamark and Joseph being executed ten days later, with Lord Audley being beheaded at Tower Hill one day later.

The Cornish were a spiritual people. Their Celtic superstitions and a Christian religion played a central role in their survival. Life was hard. The land yielded minerals, but the mining was cyclical. There were boom times where a man could well provide for his family, and then there would be the times of desperation when the demand for minerals weakened. The land yielded crops reluctantly, and the windswept coastline was a harsh environment, so mining remained the primary industry in Cornwall. A stubborn, independent character sustained these miners in their physically challenging and dangerous toil "below the grass." Religion offered them brief glimpses of brightness during the darker times of their lives. These darker times were punctuated with public drunkenness, fighting, and other sinful behavior at the public houses when the tinners sought to relieve their frustration and sense of failure. These hard-rock miners bore up mineral riches from the bowels of the earth and thus fulfilled their inborn need for productivity. Their attendance at church on Sundays provided these families with a bigger picture of life. They could momentarily rise up from their day-to-day focus on mere survival to a vision of hopefulness and reward at the end of their toil. They prayed for better days ahead and a better future for their children. For many tinners, a Sunday church service also offered them an opportunity to serve penance for their sinful behavior at the public house on the previous Saturday evening.

There was no freedom of choice in England, however. The form of religion was dictated at the whim of the monarchy, and the theology changed several times throughout history. At the Reformation, the church became divided between those who continued to accept papal authority and the various Protestant churches that repudiated it. The Church of England was among the churches that broke with Rome. In the reign of Mary Tudor, the Church of England once again submitted to papal authority, and then this policy was reversed when Elizabeth I came to the throne in 1558.

At the end of the sixteenth century and into the next, tensions arose within the Church of England as Puritan critics argued for further changes to make it more like the churches of Geneva or Scotland. These tensions over theological and liturgical issues were among the factors that led to the English Civil War.

Finally, in 1689, a settlement was reached whereby the Church of England remained the established church but with ever-increasing religious and civil rights being granted to other Christians, those of other faiths, and to those professing no faith at all. Hence, an important freedom of religious choice was envisioned for the people of the British Commonwealth. It may have been envisioned, but it wasn't commonly practiced.

In 1743, John Wesley crossed the River Tamar and traveled west into Cornwall to introduce the Methodist religion to the populace. Despite recent compromise in restrictions, his activities were performed unlawfully within the jurisdiction of the Church of England, so he often traveled by night and was transported by local citizenry to secret hiding places.

He had to be hidden from some of the locals as well. John Wesley wasn't accepted at first by the wary and stubborn Cornishmen. His services were held primarily outdoors, where he preached Hellfire revival as those willing to listen transported themselves from tears and lamentations to confession, falling on their knees, to eventually experience the joy of salvation. At this point, the entire gathering would burst into song.

He gradually won the tinners over as wave after wave of converts sang praises to God. The former drinking, hurling, fighting, and all manner of wicked behavior were replaced by a more peaceful assemblage. The lions became lambs, praising God.

Throughout the next forty years, John Wesley won over the hearts of the people, and Wesley's Methodism conquered the former apathy, despair, and general lawlessness of the Cornish tin miners. Their drunkenness declined, and they obeyed the Word of God. Their behavior changed for the better as time passed. Their spiritual renewal helped to sustain the miners and their families when mining went completely bust years later.

The open-air preaching gave way to Methodist chapels appearing in almost every town as this turned into a more "respectable" religion.

The more prosperous members of the community joined the church as it became less Hellfire and less dynamic.

With a cooling of the former religious fervor under Wesley, two local preachers in the Wesleyan Church had become zealous, consecrated men of God. They wanted to restore the original passion of the church, convert more of the populace, and bring them to Christ. Hugh Bourne and William Clowes organized a full-day meeting spent entirely in prayer and preaching in May 1807, and this was followed by others, held in the open air, where many souls were converted to Christ. Yet, even though Methodism had been founded by that great open-air preacher, John Wesley, the two local preachers, Bourne and Clowes, together with their large number of converts, were refused admittance into the Wesleyan Church.

This "camp meeting community" then was finally driven by necessity to the founding of a place for themselves and their new converts in the year of 1810. Hugh Bourne declared, "It now appeared to be the will of God that we, as a Camp Meeting Community, should form classes and take upon us the care of churches in the fear of God." In February 1812, the people took on the name of the Society of the Primitive Methodists.

Many of the members of this new church society were miners and their families, some of whom were already migrating to America. It was felt that the work should be strengthened there. In Pennsylvania, the societies attained considerable strength from 1829 to 1840, and in 1842, nine miners, most likely from Cornwall, settled in the lead-mining region of southwestern Wisconsin and northwestern Illinois and formed themselves into a Primitive Methodist Society. Their work was greatly blessed by God and spread to other parts. As these societies multiplied, they came to be known as the Western Conference while the churches of Pennsylvania and New York made up the Eastern Conference of the Primitive Methodist Society.

The Primitive Methodist Church in Benton, Wisconsin, has five generations of our Perkins family interred in its cemetery, as well as many other relatives of the Perkins, Robbins, and Hocking families, most of whom were miners. This little, red-brick church on the west end of town was where my sisters and I, along with many cousins, attended Sunday school and a week or two of vacation Bible school each summer. Ruth, Judy, and I attended at the urging of our mother. She herself did not attend church service very often but felt that my sisters and I should be there. I remember us going with her to a tent meeting once or twice too. A traveling evangelist would come to Benton and hold a "revival" meeting in an open-air tent. I remember my mother dragging my sisters and me to such meetings at the Village Park in Benton a couple of times. There would be a lot of hymns sung and a lot of passionate, Hellfire preaching. As the two-hour affair wound down, many would walk up to the makeshift altar, kneel down before the traveling evangelist, and as the congregation softly sang the hymn, "Just as I Am," the candidates for salvation would make a silent confession. The evangelist would then kneel down next to each of them, place a hand on their shoulder, and offer a prayer of redemption. When this ritual was completed, the entire congregation would stand and sing a rousing hymn in celebration of these souls having been brought to salvation. I was among those souls a couple of times. Jesus saves!

CHAPTER 11

# MY EARLY YEARS IN BENTON

My mother, Jeanette, as most mothers of her generation, was the central focus of our family. When my father worked at the mine during my early years, he brought home a good paycheck, and my grandpa Bert Cook, who lived with us, also contributed a portion of his Social Security pension check to pay for his room and board. I believe I was in third grade when the old Mulcahy mine closed and my dad took the job at Calvert's farm. We moved over to the big, two-story house on Galena Street with neither indoor plumbing nor central heat. My mother was a very frugal person, having recently experienced the hardships of the Great Depression of the 1930s. She baked quite often, and she canned vegetables from our large garden. In the fall, she would buy a three-gallon tin of cherries and flats of peaches or pears, which would be canned or processed into preserves and pie filling. Our cellar shelves were always full of canned fruits, pickles, and vegetables. She put up "chili sauce," which was similar to a mild salsa, in pint jars. I can remember going down to the cellar to bring up canned goods for supper. The house on Galena Street had a damp and dark cellar. It had a dirt floor, and there was a large coal bin in one corner. Occasionally I would forget to wipe my shoes before reentering the kitchen and would be told to mop up the dirt and coal dust from the linoleum floor.

We didn't have central heat in the rented house on Galena Street, and one of my designated chores was to go down to the cellar, fill the coal bucket, and carry it back upstairs to the kitchen. We had outside stairs to the cellar, and my dad had placed a series of wooden planks end to end to serve as a sidewalk between the back door to the kitchen and the outside cellar door. He taught me how to break the larger clumps of coal by tapping them "cross-grain" so they wouldn't shatter into thin, shale-like pieces.

On bitterly cold winter days, Mom hung the clothes inside the house on wash day, and the damp clothes always made the house seem warmer because of the increased humidity. Dad drove nails into the woodwork near the top of the windows from which Mom could string the clothesline back and forth across the kitchen. We would all have to duck under the clothes on the line as we passed through the kitchen on wash day. The old flattop, coal-fired cook stove would provide plenty of heat to dry the laundry.

We always had clean clothes to wear and were fed a well-rounded diet, with vegetables at every meal. We normally ate together as a family. When Dad took the farm job at Calvert's, and we lived in this house on Galena Street, he would get home later in the day, and we would wait for him until six o'clock or later so we could all sit down together for the evening supper meal. In the Midwest, we normally had a big meal at midday with meat, potatoes, and gravy. Dad's farm job was only a half mile from town, so he would come home and join us for the midday dinner. Mom always boiled extra potatoes at noon and would fry up the leftover "spuds" for our evening supper. We always had a plate of bread on the table, either homemade or store-bought, and a small, flat dish with a chunk of creamery butter. The dish of butter was placed in a cupboard after the meal was over. It wasn't stored in the refrigerator, because it would get too hard. We often had homemade dessert (pie or cake) or canned fruit or gelatin salad, but if there was none, my dad and Grandpa Cook would choose saltine crackers or bread with dark Karo syrup as a dessert substitute. Sometimes Dad would buy sorghum when it was in season.

Some of our meat came from the Calvert farm where Dad worked. He often would be given a side of pork in the fall when they butchered. If his boss had a good year, we would get a quarter of beef. We had no freezer, so Dad would rent a locker at the processing plant in Cuba City to store the meat. Grocery shopping was done at the Rock Store in Benton on Saturday night after Dad got home from work with his paycheck. Two or three times a month, he would make the five-mile drive to Cuba City to get frozen meat from our rented locker. Our locker consisted of a large, deep metal drawer, and sometimes it took a while to sort through all of the frozen packages to select the half dozen we wanted. It was bitterly cold in there, and my teeth would be chattering by the time we got done.

My parents were both raised on a self-sufficient farm where most of the food was grown or butchered. Of course my dad, too, had experienced the Great Depression, so they were both frugal, very conservative. All purchases were made on a cash basis, and that was not unusual in the 1940s and fifties. Much of our shopping was done by catalog mail order to Sears, Spiegel, or Montgomery Ward. Mom would fill out the order form, and I was often sent on my bike with the cash to buy a money order at the post office, stuff it with the order form into the envelope, and mail it off. When I was young, I thought that was a pretty important job. Sometimes she would let me keep a dime for an ice-cream cone from Tut's store.

It would take two or three weeks for the mail-order package to arrive, and if she had ordered something for us kids, we would get pretty anxious. The mail came to the post office because we didn't have home delivery of mail in Benton. When the package arrived, there would be a notice in our postal box, which we would give to the postmaster, my uncle Willie Perkins, and he would hand the package through the window. If the package was large, he would bring it out the side door, and I would have to haul it home in my coaster wagon.

I never saw my mother drive a car. She had driven a Model T Ford when she was young and lived at the Cook farm, but once she left the farm and got married, she never drove again. Dad would drive her to Cuba City or Platteville to shop once or twice a month, usually on a Saturday night, because Dad worked six days a week and the stores were never open on Sundays in those days. Once in a great while, she would take us kids to Dubuque to do some serious shopping. We would go on the bus that stopped in Benton at the drugstore. We didn't have Greyhound service; it was Cardinal or Blue Bird Lines, depending upon the day of the week. The trip to Dubuque was a really big deal for me. They had huge department stores, Roshek's and Stampfer's, with revolving doors and an elevator operated by an attendant in uniform. Dubuque was my first experience in a "big city" with the large, concrete buildings, traffic lights, and the crowds of people, all in a big hurry to get somewhere.

We had made a few trips to Beloit, Wisconsin, to visit my aunt and uncle, Tom and Arlene Ewing (my mother's sister), and their kids, Florence, Ben, and Jim. When Dad drove us to Beloit, however, it was usually there and back the same day, so we never saw much of the city. The Ewings had moved to Beloit after Tom decided to quit work in the mines around Benton, and he found factory work at Fairbanks & Morse. He had been working "below the grass" (underground) in the mines and felt the work down there was unhealthy. He was right about that. Years later, in his sixties, he would develop calcification in his lungs, requiring an oxygen breathing apparatus. His condition was caused by working below the grass those years in the Benton mines.

My mother had many friends in Benton. She would visit them, and they would come to our house for a visit. It was a good deal for me and my sisters because they usually served sweets like cookies or cake and ice cream. If we hung around for a while, we would get a treat. She also attended some formal club meetings like the Royal Neighbors Society and the Ladies' Aid Society in Leadmine, two miles east of town, where the women sewed quilts and other items for the needy (and caught up on idle gossip).

Benton was a small town, and local news traveled like wildfire through informal communication. There was no television and no home computers for e-mail in those days. At the supper table, Mom would tell Dad, "Maggie is in the Hazel Green Hospital with gall stones," or, "Frank Johnson's wife is pregnant again." The *Benton Advocate* was published just once a week, so the women in town usually had the news first. Dad got his news on Saturday night over a few beers with his friends at Rollie's Bar.

My dad lost his job when all the mines began to close down in the mid-1940s, and he took the job as hired hand on the Calvert farms. It only paid about forty dollars a week, so my mother helped out by working at the vegetable-canning factory in Cuba City during the summer and fall months when our family needed some extra money. She rode to and from work with some other ladies from Benton who worked there. She could then get some of the extras for the household and perhaps buy a piece or two of used furniture that we needed.

She always enjoyed music and would often hum and sing as she performed her tasks around the house. On Saturday nights, she would have the radio tuned in to "The Saturday Night Barn Dance" on WLS out of Chicago. Her favorites were Lula Belle and Scottie, Hank Snow, and the "Arkansas Wood Chopper." The radio was on most of the day. She would listen to the early soap operas while she did her housework: "Stella Dallas," "Ma Perkins," and "Just Plain Bill". I can remember those from when I was home from school with the winter flu or a bad head cold. At night she and I (and my sister Ruth when she got older) would sit and listen to the mystery shows on the radio. Her hero was Sam Spade because he reminded her of Humphrey Bogart. She also liked "The Shadow," though she would get all tensed up over some of the scary parts. The sound effects on those old radio shows were awesome!

There was no television in those early years of my childhood, and we would play cards and board games (or "parlor games," as they were sometimes called) for evening entertainment. We also spent a lot of time reading books that we borrowed from the public library in town.

Uncle Rip and Aunt Margaret Perkins would come up to our house for cards, coffee, and cake. (Aunt Margaret made the best cakes!) The card games were usually euchre, rummy, or seven-up. Grandpa Cook's favorite card game was seven-up (which was scored as high, low, jack, and the game), and he was always ready to play. There were times when we would have to wait until the Gabriel Heatter political commentary show ended before Grandpa could play cards, though. He listened to that show on the radio almost every evening.

We would get together with the Farrey, Ewing, or Cook families fairly often, as well, and those were happy times, especially during the long, cold Wisconsin winters. There was always lots of food, coffee for the adults, and pop for us kids. They never served alcoholic beverages at any of these family gatherings. My dad would bring home a bottle of cheap wine for the Thanksgiving or Christmas holiday meal, but that was about the only time. He also poured a small juice glass of wine for each of us children on those special occasions.

There was one parlor game my mother favored. I think she had picked up on this game at one of her Royal Neighbors meetings. It's played with everyone seated in a big circle around the room, and each has pencil and paper upon which humorous, disjointed stories are created. Every player is instructed to write the first line of the story in secret at the top of his or her piece of paper. This first line is the "who": "Frank and Jane," for example. It's best to use the names of two unrelated people in the room. The paper is then folded down at the top to cover the first line and is passed to the person on the right. All players write the second line, not knowing what was written on the first line. The second line is the "where": "in the backyard," for example, and the paper is folded down once again and passed to the right. This process is repeated with the third line, "when"; the fourth line, "how"; and the final and fifth line, "why." When the story is completed, the papers are passed to the right for the final time. Then each person in turn reads their story aloud for the rest of the group. The stories are hilarious (and sometimes, a bit "blue"). A parlor game such as this was typical family entertainment before the advent of television.

My mother was a sensitive person and was easily hurt. She wasn't one to be on the fence about an issue. It was either right or wrong, and you always knew where she stood. She didn't think it was right for women to be in bars or taverns, for instance, and she never, during her lifetime, entered one. She was tolerant of the behavior of others, though.

She was never prudish, never preached at anyone, and always tried to see the best side of a person. I believe that she was a good judge of character.

While my mother had definite opinions, she seldom meddled in my personal life, nor did she offer me unsolicited advice. Neither of my parents did that. They apparently felt that I had been raised to know right from wrong and that I was prepared to deal with life's problems as I grew older. If I made bad choices or if they sensed that I was having problems, they could read my feelings and seldom felt a need to preach at me.

Personal feelings weren't freely expressed in our family. I always knew that I was loved and could read it in my parents' eyes and happy smiles. My mother sometimes expressed her love for us with a big hug. She demonstrated her feelings more than my dad. I knew he loved us just as much, but he never expressed it in words—just with that sparkle in his eyes.

# CHAPTER 12

# THE TEENAGE YEARS

There was a four- to six-week period in July and August when hybrid seed corn was detasseled in southwestern Wisconsin. I was hired at seventy-five cents an hour to walk the rows of corn, pulling tassels. The seed companies transported us by bus to different farms in the area. I was tall enough as a teenager to reach the top of the cornstalks while others had to bend the stalk over to reach the tassel. One year, the company furnished motorized equipment where we stood in extended "buckets" and pulled tassels as we rode through the field. The machine straddled four rows at a time, so there were four of us on the machine, and we had to work much faster due to the rapid pace. Needless to say, this job guaranteed a healthy sunburn.

Also in the summertime, I really liked spending time at the Calvert farm where my dad worked. It was only a half mile from our home in Benton, and I spent most of my spare time there during the summer months. As the Calverts' son George and I got older, we had to take on more work: handling hay bales and shoveling corn instead of simply driving a tractor. When we put up hay, the neighboring farmers came over to help, and Mrs. Calvert would feed the whole crew at noon. Sometimes we would be served sandwiches, baked beans, potato salad, and lemonade. At other times, I can remember all of us sitting inside at their dining-room table, where we were served platters of pork chops with potatoes and gravy. At night I would come home tired, but I really felt good after putting in a good day's work. My dad, as foreman, laid out the work for us. Frank Calvert never performed any physical work. He was plagued with an upset stomach most of the time, known as the "gray sickness." My dad pretty much ran the day-to-day operation of the farm.

Because of my dad's long work schedule of six days a week and dairy chores every other Sunday, he didn't have a lot of home time with the family. He was seldom there for my ballgames or to take me fishing. We rarely took any long trips on Sundays because he would have to be back at the farm to do the milking and feed the livestock.

Fishing with Grandpa Cook

I often went fishing with my grandpa Cook, who lived with us. He liked to fish with a cane pole and bobber. I would take my rod and reel, and Grandpa would take his favorite old cane pole. Mom would pack us some sandwiches and wish us good luck, saying, "Now I'll be ready to fry fish when you two get back, but don't catch more than you can carry." I glanced over to see Grandpa grinning at her remark.

The two of us would hike down to the Fever River, about one and a half miles east of Benton. We would fish at different spots along the riverbank. Grandpa always looked for shade under a tree and a comfortable place to sit on the bank. Most fishermen will generally "read" the river for fish location, but not my grandpa. He read the river for a comfortable place to sit, sometimes hiking a quarter mile upriver to find a shade tree close to the bank—a tree that would support him just right when he leaned back. Over the years, he grew to know exactly where those trees were. It was not as important that that location on the river held fish. While Grandpa preferred catfish, I would work up and down the river seeking black bass.

During our time together, he would point out different tree species and tell me about them. Sometimes, when fishing was slow, we would stop to pick some gooseberries in a pasture or wild raspberries along a fence line. He always preferred cheese sandwiches for lunch, made with Mom's homemade bread. His thermos would hold coffee with cream and sugar. He dunked the sandwich into the coffee. I guess it made it easier for him to bite into the cheddar or Swiss cheese with his false teeth. Sometimes we would find a piece of pie or a raisin custard tart in our lunch.

Grandpa went prospecting frequently, and I remember one time when he had found indications of minerals in the lower end of Robson's pasture. He knew the different soil types and which ones indicated a potential for lead or zinc. He had been prospecting for most of his adult life, and in seeking a potential site, he would make a visual survey of the land surface. Good prospectors knew that the "Masonic weed," for example, grew up in shallow lead deposits many years earlier. Some prospectors would do some "dousing," or water witching, to locate mineral deposits, but I never saw my grandpa use that technique. Sometimes he would spot evidence of a previous digging and would investigate it further.

At Robson's place, he had done some hand drilling, and this yielded favorable indications at about ten feet down. He then proceeded to dig a small shaft with his round-mouth garden spade that had a sawed-off handle. He had struck water at about twelve feet, so he came home and spent one hot summer afternoon in our garage, building a hand pump. For this he used small limbs and branches of green wood. He carved, cut, and whittled on it, then sent me down to Mr. Larson's cobbler shop for a piece of leather to wrap the piston of the pump. He wrapped the leather tightly around the piston as he spat some tobacco juice on it. When I asked about that, he said the juice gave him a better grip on the leather so he could stretch it good and tight around the cylinder of wood. I remember that he always chewed Horseshoe plug tobacco and cut off each chew with the small blade of his pocketknife. The small blade was the sharpest, and it was reserved for that purpose.

The next day, he hoisted the pump over his shoulder and hiked out to the prospecting site in Robson's pasture. One of my cousins, Gordy Farrey, and I went along to pump out water while Grandpa did the digging down in the hole. I was amazed to find that the pump actually worked. I guess he had made more than one of these over the years.

Nothing ever came of the Robson test hole, but Grandpa must have made some minor discoveries of minerals in the past that gave him the incentive to keep on searching. One of his discoveries prompted him to form the Cook Mining Company. I found a stock certificate for Cook Mining in my mother's papers after she died in 1993.

Grandpa Cook was never one to sit around the whole day. In his retirement, he kept busy prospecting and gardening. Sometimes there would be some friction between him and my dad over the gardening methods. It wasn't easy for them to share work in the same garden because each took pride in his particular methods and gardening habits. While Dad would never admit it, I'm sure he appreciated Grandpa's help with the garden. I suppose his pride and independence prevented him from vocalizing it.

Grandpa, even in his late seventies, would hike out of town to a pasture somewhere and prospect for that elusive lead or zinc deposit. Sometimes during mid-July when the sun was hot, he would be working that hand-churn drill, a long, heavy, iron bar with a star bit at the business end. When he came home at night, he was bone tired but never discouraged. He knew it was unlikely that he would ever strike it rich, but he preserved his dream. My mother worried about her father, but his doctor told her, "Don't worry about it. He's in good health, and the exercise is good for him. A lot of men his age just sit around and wait to die. Besides, I doubt if you could talk him out of doing it." Grandpa was admired by all of us.

* * * * * *

We didn't have Little League baseball in Benton, so we would play sandlot pick-up games all summer long. We would "choose up" sides and play a series of games with the chosen roster for each team. My first baseball glove was a J. C. Higgins model from Sears Roebuck.

When I reached the age of thirteen, we played Pony League baseball in Benton. This was my first experience at an organized sport. We had some good baseball players in Benton over the years, and it had always been a popular sport in our town. The adult "town team" was one of the best in the area. The teams in this conference had to line up sponsors to pay for the equipment and uniforms. They also charged admission or passed the hat for donations at their games. The Monroe, Wisconsin, team was sponsored by the Huber Brewery. As a result, they could afford better equipment than the other town teams. They also hired some former college-level players to work at the brewery and always fielded a good team. Several small towns in southwestern Wisconsin sponsored teams, and there were one or two out of Dubuque, Iowa. Sunday afternoon ballgames were popular in Benton and the surrounding area. Benton won the regional championship several times and thereby qualified to play in the statewide tournament at County Stadium in Milwaukee. Three players from Benton had played professional baseball in the minor leagues during the early 1950s.

Our Pony League team was very competitive, and we won most of our games. Ray Swift was a good coach and taught me the finer points of playing first base. I was tall and could stretch way out for the close throws on an infield play. He taught me how to shift my feet when the throw was wide to my left or right. This technique came in handy when taking a throw from my cousin Duffy when he played second base. He was usually slow getting to the ball, and his off-balance throws could go anywhere. The coach had him playing second base as a substitute, and in one game he got hit right in the mouth by a ball thrown by our catcher. A runner was attempting to steal second. Duffy took his eye off the ball to watch the runner slide with his steel spikes up. He was trying to avoid being spiked in the shin. The ball hit him squarely and split his upper lip. It swelled badly, almost the size of his nose.

We gave Duffy a hard time over that incident, but a few games later, I took a nasty shot at first base and had to accept some ribbing as well. I was taking a long throw from third base when I was blinded by the sun, which set directly over third base. We were playing late in the day when my teammate Higgins backhanded a ground ball just inside third and made a perfect throw. Just before the ball arrived, it went directly into the sun, "ticked" the top of my mitt, and smacked me right between the eyes. It knocked me on my butt, and I was out cold for a few minutes. Fortunately, it didn't break my nose, but my two black eyes were a subject of conversation for a few days at school.

I was a good defensive ball player: I could snag those bad throws, stretch out to nail the runner, and backhand the hard-hit grounders. I was also a steady hitter—a steady .189! (I usually batted at the bottom of the order.) We didn't have good hitting coaches at Benton. There are techniques for hitting off-speed pitches, curveballs, sinkers, and sliders (which we called "drops" and "fast curves" in those days), but I didn't learn those techniques until much later in life when I was coaching Little League. We didn't get the same level of coaching as the bigger schools did. You had to be a natural hitter back then.

To me, athletics were a source of having fun, and while I played most sports, they were never all that important in my life. I never had that level of desire that most coaches look for in an athlete. I was just out there to have a good time. As a below-average performer, my self-esteem suffered during that period of my life.

I am reminded now of a humiliating experience during a particular baseball game in Galena when I was about thirteen. It was the first time that I had been spiked when playing first base. One of the opposing batters was thrown out by two steps when I took the throw from our shortstop, and I had foolishly left my foot on the center of the bag. In his frustration over being thrown out, he deliberately raked his steel spikes down my shinbone. I didn't feel much pain from it initially and chose to ignore the spiking so as not to give him any satisfaction. We played out the inning, and by the time I got to the bench, I was in severe pain. My shin was bleeding from a cut to the bone, and my sock was torn. As I sat there, the pain brought tears to my eyes. One of my teammates saw the torn sock and the bloody gash and asked, "What happened to you?" When I pulled down my sock to show him, it was worse than I had thought. Then when my teammates gathered around to sympathize with me, they cussed out that "bastard" on the other team and vowed to get even. Their sympathy caused me to openly sob, and that was a further embarrassment. That incident taught me a valuable lesson on playing first base, but the humiliation bothered me for years afterward. Why didn't I get angry when that happened and go after the guy instead of being so passive?

We learn a lot about ourselves during those formative years as our character is developed but don't fully understand what we've learned until we gain maturity later. As my grandpa Cook used to say, "Do you understand all you know about it?" He was referring to my studies at school, but his question applies to life's lessons as well.

As a teenager, I found that self-confidence can surge and wane, but earning the respect of peers is very important. Sometimes we put too much pressure on ourselves and suffer from self-criticism, especially during those formative years. I was tall and skinny in high school and about the youngest member of our class. Because of my rapid rate of growth and immaturity, I lacked coordination. I was always second or third string in basketball, but that didn't cause me to quit. I hung in there and enjoyed playing on the team, but I lacked that desire factor so necessary in organized sports. I didn't have that drive-to-the-hoop attitude. Sports to me were no more important than playing in the band or working on the school paper. My high school was small, with only about a hundred students in the entire high school, so everyone had a chance to play sports if they wanted to, and I was never cut from the teams.

I lacked the physique and competitive drive for football. It was foolish of me to try out for the team my senior year, but all of my friends talked me into it. My only experience with the game was those earlier games in Bill's backyard when I was twelve or thirteen years old. He had a big yard at the side of their house where we got together as kids to play tackle football on those autumn afternoons.

On the high-school football team, however, it was a year of misery, mentally as well as physically. As a senior, I was playing third string with the freshmen, and then developed two ingrown toenails and a misaligned hip, but I was too proud and stubborn to quit. I went to the chiropractor a couple of times to correct the hip injury. The toenails were more serious. I had inherited football shoes from a cousin, Ben Ewing, and they were a size too small, which caused the ingrown nails. The large nail on each foot grew worse each day. I applied salve, wrapped them in gauze bandaging, jammed them into those tight shoes, and tried my best to avoid being stepped on during the blocking assignments. Of course, that didn't work. When some player stomped on one of those injured toes, the throbbing reached all the way to my temples! The nails first turned black and green, then yellow, and then finally came off entirely. I stuck it out and finished that miserable season, mostly on the bench.

Many years later, I would read about former President Richard Nixon in Garry Willis's book, *Nixon Agonistes: The Crisis of the Self-Made Man*. According to the author, Nixon lacked athletic ability when he attended Whittier College in California, yet he went out for football. He was heavy and clumsy, so they positioned him in the offensive line where he was repeatedly stomped into the mud and run over by the opposing teams. In spite of his struggles, he never quit. That tenacity later paid dividends for him in the tough game of politics.

My lack of success in high-school athletics diminished my self-confidence at a sensitive time in my life, and, as a result, I was unduly hard on myself at times. I always seemed to have the respect of my peers, however, and I had a lot of close friends in school. I was never picked on. I suppose my classmates were less critical of me than I was of myself. They elected me vice president of the junior class and then president of our senior class. Had I read that Nixon book earlier, perhaps I would have chosen politics as a lifetime career.

Rock and roll emerged in the 1950s. It began as rockabilly music, an outgrowth of country and western with a strong beat. Then Elvis Presley arrived on the scene, blending the blues into this mix, with a singing style he'd picked up in Memphis. Most parents didn't like rock and roll, and some thought it was "the work of the devil." Elvis's hip movements were banned on television, and he was only viewed above the waist on those early variety shows.

We were anxious to get that important driver's license at age sixteen so we could cruise Main Street with the radio cranked up. Very few teenagers owned a car, so we borrowed the family sedan or the farm pickup truck. By keeping the family car washed and shined up (a necessity for cruising), our parents would normally consent to our use of the car as long as we honored the curfew.

The girls would stroll the downtown area on warm summer nights or hang out at the drugstore or café. We would invite them for a ride and cruise around Benton and the neighboring towns. The price of gasoline was about thirty cents per gallon. The riders would often pitch in their loose change, and we could ride around the entire evening on a couple of dollars. The guys would usually have enough pocket change left over to buy a Coke and french fries at the café, plus a quarter for the jukebox.

For the guys, beer and cigarettes were also in demand, and we found ways to obtain them. A gas station vending machine offered Lucky

Strikes, Camels, Phillip Morris, Chesterfield, Marvel, and a couple of other brands at twenty-three cents per pack. We paid with a quarter, and the two pennies in change were returned to us inside the cigarette wrapper. A sign on the machine was posted, "18 years and older," but that law was impossible to enforce on a vending machine.

The emboldened young smokers would tuck the pack of Luckies under the short sleeve of their white T-shirts and then roll the pack up in the sleeve to secure it. They would sometimes find it "neat" to tuck one cigarette behind their ear, let their hair grow longer, and then comb it back into a ducktail like Elvis. Others cut their hair short and, with the aid of Butch Wax, trained it to form a flat top, forerunner to the "brush cut."

Unlike neighboring states, Wisconsin had lowered the minimum age for beer to eighteen, and a great number of taverns were established to serve that younger market. We called them beer gardens. These places were licensed to serve beer only, on tap or by the bottle, but no wine or liquor. We could also buy cases of beer at a package store or some of the smaller mom-and-pop grocery stores in Wisconsin. We weren't eighteen during those high-school years, so we would have to seek out those businesses that wouldn't make an ID check. The military draft was in force, and all young men had to register with Selective Service when they turned eighteen. That became the ID card of choice for the beer vendors. My cousin Duffy was shaving at sixteen, and we would send him in to the store for the beer on a first-time visit to see if they would serve him. If he was successful, that store was rewarded with our repeat business. We were able to buy beer underage at very few stores, and one of them, at Prairie Corners, which had no cooler, sold warm cases of beer. Three of us sharing a case of twenty-four warm bottles of beer could get a pretty good buzz. In those days, it was common to drink and drive and to also drink while driving. We called them "road beers." We had to be especially careful when driving through Benton. If the coach saw us drinking or smoking, we'd be kicked off the team.

Howard and I enjoyed smoking a Crook brand cigar on occasion. They were dipped in rum and had a sweet taste and aroma. They were also crooked in shape, hence the name. One day our coach said he thought he may have seen Howard drive down the street while smoking a cigar. One of the varsity players said, "That wouldn't have been Howard, Coach. He's salutatorian of the senior class!"

During my junior year at Benton, I had a preference for math classes, especially geometry, and thought I would choose a career in drafting. During my senior year, however, I changed my mind when I took a class in business bookkeeping. I worked ahead in that class and finished the course before Christmas break. I was able to visualize all of the elements of business management and was very interested in how all of the components came together. The decision was made. It would be business for me, preferably in the manufacturing industry.

My family had no savings, and I wasn't aware of any scholarships available to me, so I chose to go to a two-year business college in Rockford, Illinois. Several recent graduates had chosen colleges in nearby Madison, and there was a well-known business college up there as well. I had decided that the party atmosphere in Madison would not be a wise choice for me. I had already acquired a fond taste for beer and had overimbibed on more than one occasion. No point in tempting fate.

A friend of the family, Clayton Ewing, arranged for me to obtain a low-interest student loan through his membership in the Masons, and he cosigned a note for me. My parents were proud of me for making the decision to go to college, but Dad was a bit apprehensive about me borrowing $5,000. He was always very conservative and had never borrowed money. Neither of my parents had tried to influence me one way or another and left the decision to me. They were confident that

I would do the right thing. Neither of my parents had gone to high school, and now they had a son going to college. I'm sure that they had mixed feelings of pride and apprehension.

The college loan covered tuition for the hundred-week program in business administration, three semesters each year. It turned out that I had chosen the same college that my great-aunt Lylia Cook attended years earlier, the Rockford School of Business. She was my grandpa's sister, and at the time she attended, it was known as Brown's Business College.

I had to find work after graduation from high school to save money for living expenses and books. I went to Beloit, Wisconsin, and lived with my aunt Melva and uncle Roy Shannon, but I found jobs to be scarce in 1957. I had no car, so Uncle Roy would drop me off in downtown Beloit on his way to work, where I could walk door to door looking for a job. Because I was only seventeen at the time, the only job I found was in a small neighborhood grocery. I took care of produce and swept the floor. I wasn't saving much money because the job didn't pay well, but my brief experience there landed me a job about a month later in the produce department of the big A&P supermarket in Beloit.

I postponed my entrance into college until January so I would have more money saved, then arranged for a job transfer to another A&P store in Rockford where I would be attending school. There was a problem, however. The store was about two miles, or eighteen city blocks, east of the college, while my rooming house was about a mile to the north. Since I had no car, it required a lot of walking every day. I worked three nights a week after classes and every Saturday at the A&P.

There were six guys in the rooming house owned by former city mayor Leo Waltz and his wife. Two of these guys were older Korean War veterans who were getting financial assistance through the GI Bill. My roommate was an Italian, a dark-haired guy who had just graduated from high school in the Chicago area. I stayed on his good side because he had an Oldsmobile that came in very handy despite it being a big, old "bomb."

One Sunday shortly after I started school, I took the Greyhound bus twenty miles north to Beloit to visit Aunt Melva and Uncle Roy. She asked me about my roommate at college, and I said, "He's an Italian kid from Chicago." Then she asked, "What's his name?" When I said, "His name is Jerry Anderson," she got a big hoot out of it. When she couldn't stop laughing, I suddenly realized how strange that sounded: an Italian named Anderson. Jerry's Italian mother had married a Scandinavian. With the black hair and dark eyes, he certainly looked Italian, and I never gave it a second thought until I got that reaction from Aunt Melva. She told that story over and over, and we always had a good laugh about it.

I enjoyed college, where I had all business classes and didn't have to deal with foreign languages, liberal arts, and other requirements of a four-year university. In 1958, we weren't allowed to use calculators in the early courses and tallied the columns of numbers the old-fashioned way. Our business math professor always had an exercise for us at the end of class. He would read off a string of two-digit numbers, and we were to add them in our head and then try to be the first in class to shout out the cumulative answer. He insisted on proficiency in mental math because it would be a "reasonableness check" against the calculator. He told us that we should have a reasonable result in our mind when the calculator comes up with the answer. It would help avoid keying errors.

All of the bookkeeping entries had to be made in pen and ink. A lot of us used cartridge-type fountain pens because ballpoint pens were of low quality in those days. They tended to skip and clot up, making a mess, especially when ruling off a line. We drew the lines with the fountain pen alongside a twelve- or sixteen-inch ruler with a metal edge. The ruler was placed upside down on the ledger sheet so as not to smear the ink. If a correction was to be made, you were to draw, with the assistance of the ruler, a single horizontal line through the incorrect entry and then enter the correct entry above it. We were told never to erase or "white out" an entry. The single line would allow you to still read the original entry for audit purposes. Some of our instructors were CPAs and were very fussy about obeying sound accounting principles. They absolutely hated ballpoint pens!

There was a heavy burden of homework with the accounting classes, and it was an especially tough schedule for me, working at the grocery store most evenings and all day on Saturday. The other guys in the rooming house had funding from their parents or from the GI Bill, so they didn't have to work. By the time I walked home from the job at A&P, it was nine o'clock or later. I would try to get about three hours of homework completed to keep up with my classes. Some nights I would be up much later, trying to get those debits and credits to balance.

It wasn't all work and no play. We found time for some beer and pool on the weekends. There were no girls or beer allowed in the rooming house, but we found we could hoist a six-pack of beer up over the front porch roof with a rope, then smuggle the empty cans out of the house the next morning. We never did find a way to get girls up there. They wouldn't climb the rope because most of them wore skirts in those days.

One of the girls at school was from Scales Mound, Illinois, and I finally got around to asking her for a date. We went to a movie one cold, wintry night. Of course I didn't have a car, so we walked about fifteen blocks from her rooming house to the movie theater. When we came out of the movie, it was snowing and blowing, with four inches already on the ground. That turned out to be a long walk to her place while facing the wind and snow. She never went out with me again.

Before I started college, and while I was working and living in Beloit with my aunt and uncle, I would wash dishes, clean their house, and help out with other chores to cover the cost of my room and board. One night, a Beloit Police sergeant came over to their house to visit with my uncle Roy. They had been friends for years. Over a few beers, Roy told him that I was going to attend business college in Rockford. The sergeant turned to me and said, "You ought to join the Naval Reserve down there. You can fulfill your military obligation while you're going to school." It turned out that he was a chief petty officer in the Naval Reserve, and he attended weekly drills in Rockford. He said, "You can do your military service and college at the same time."

I knew that I would have to serve in the military and would be drafted by the army within two years. His idea sounded pretty good to me, because I would rather serve in the navy than the army. Besides, if I enlisted, I would be able to choose my field of training. Most of the draftees went into the army infantry.

I thought about this for a week or two and then decided to join the Naval Reserve. I was sworn in about one month after starting college and began to attend drills once each week on Tuesday evenings. This was a six-year military commitment with a two-week cruise each summer aboard a ship off the East Coast. I would draw full pay for the two weeks, plus travel expenses. I would be paid a small stipend by Uncle Sam for the weekly drills that were held on Tuesdays at the Naval Training Center located on the south side of Rockford. It was beyond walking distance, but it was on a city bus route. After a couple of months, I was able to borrow Jerry's Oldsmobile to make the weekly trip by paying him some extra gas money or a six-pack of beer once in a while.

In May 1958, after just five months of college, I was called into the naval commanding officer's office and told that the navy was pulling reservists into active service because they were short of people. He said this didn't happen very often, only when there weren't enough voluntary enlistments to fill their needs. When I explained to him that I was going to college, he said, "In your case, you may be able to get a deferment. What college are you attending?"

When he learned that I was going to a private college, he said I could only qualify for deferment when attending a state-sponsored college or university. One month later, I was given orders and travel money to report to the Great Lakes Naval Training Center north of Chicago. I was to report for nine weeks of boot camp on July 8, 1958.

The college business manager said they couldn't refund my prepaid tuition, but I could apply it later if I returned to the school after completing my military service. I had prepaid the tuition with borrowed money but would not have to make any payments on the loan until after I finished school. Everything was put on hold while I served my country.

CHAPTER 13

# YOUNG AND SINGLE

In the spring of 1959, we cruised to the North Atlantic for a survey mission, mapping the floor of the Atlantic Ocean. We docked at Halifax, Nova Scotia, to install some new equipment and provide the crew with a couple of days of liberty before getting underway once again.

On July 4, to conform to navy custom, we were ordered into the nearest port to dress ship for the holiday. In this case, the nearest port happened to be Louisburg, Nova Scotia, a village just a bit larger than my hometown of Benton. When the order was given to "Dress ship!" we were required to fly all of our signal flags in a line, stem to stern, in a regulated manner. It is an impressive display of color.

The pier at Louisburg was in disrepair, so our captain was advised to anchor out in the harbor. We ran motor whaleboats to and from shore. When the captain went ashore, he was advised by the mayor that they would be hosting a street dance in the village square in our honor. They hadn't seen an American Navy ship in their little harbor since World War II, and they wanted us to join them in celebration. Needless to say, sailors in from the sea don't need much encouragement to party.

I walked a girl home after the dance and noticed a guy following us. She told me that the guy was her brother who was keeping a close watch on us. That's when I learned that she was only fourteen! She told me that young people leave Louisburg for the city after high school; therefore, all of the remaining kids here are younger. I bid her (and her brother) good night at the door and then joined my buddies who were gathered at the Canadian Legion Hall, the only establishment that served alcohol in this province of Canada.

In late December, we returned to our home port of Philadelphia, and then a week later, we cruised down the Delaware and put in at Davisville, Rhode Island, where the ship went into dry dock to have additional sounding equipment installed on the ship's bottom.

I was now well into my two-year active duty assignment with the navy aboard the USS *San Pablo* AGS30. We were performing our oceanography mission in the Atlantic Ocean, and I had gotten my sea legs. I never had the opportunity to transfer into electronics but was advanced to quartermaster third class, the equivalent of an army corporal. I thanked God that I was no longer chipping paint. My duties were now upgraded to include maintenance of the ship's log while underway, preparing weather reports on a regular basis, and updating navigational charts in the small chart room behind the pilothouse on the bridge. As quartermasters, we also took the helm during close-quarter maneuvers. Once the ship was in open seas, the deck crew took over duties on the wheel.

We had no signalmen on board, so the quartermasters on our ship also hoisted signal flags, transmitted and read flashing-light messages in Morse code, and were trained to use semaphore flags for visual signaling. One of the young ensigns on board, Mr. Edwards, was a recent college graduate. He asked me one day to teach him Morse code on the big signal light at the bridge deck. He was a bit slow to catch on but managed to learn the simplest four letters of the alphabet: H, I, S, and T. A few weeks later, we anchored in the harbor at Bermuda near a Canadian ASW Surface Group that included a cruiser with a Canadian admiral on board. The liberty parties from our ship went to shore by motor whaleboat and were required to return from liberty by midnight, popularly known as "Cinderella liberty." We had lashed a portable signal light to the pier, and our crew members, when arriving at the pier from their night on the town, were directed to flash our call sign, N B U K, and we would send the boat back to shore and pick them up. Of course most of the sailors had had a lot to drink, and in the last party to arrive at the pier prior to midnight, Ensign Edwards was the only one in the group of drunks to claim a working knowledge of Morse code. He was as "snockered" as the rest of them but anxious to show off his newly developed skill. Fortunately, I had the deck watch that night, and when I saw the shaky light beam flashing all around the skyline, I was able to recognize the four letters that Edwards had learned: S H I T—S H I T—S H I T. I immediately called down to the boat coxswain and told him to "get to that pier fast, or we will all be at Captain's Mast!"

The crew of the *San Pablo* cherished those liberty calls. We spent months at sea and, on certain occasions, would deep-sea anchor to the ocean bottom. On those assignments, we strung electronic gear out to several buoys arranged clockwise around the ship and then suspended instruments down to various depths to measure temperatures and ocean currents. We would also grab up samples from the ocean floor with a clamshell grapple that was powered by a winch on board. The civilian scientists on board would analyze the samples in our oceanography lab. While we were on station for this type of mission, we seldom saw another vessel. After months of isolation, we were ready for liberty whenever we made port.

We had been performing an assignment in early 1960 and had been deep-sea anchored north of Andros Island and the Bahamas, at the deepest part of the Atlantic, when a tropical storm swept through the area. The high winds tossed the ship severely, and one by one the huge anchor cables began snapping. The crew had been ordered below deck because a snapped two-inch cable could cut a man in half. By the time the storm subsided, all of our electronic gear was hanging by the one remaining cable. The navy sent out an LSD from the Seabee base on Andros Island to assist us. They attempted to hoist up our cable with all the gear attached, but after a few hours of effort, the remaining cable snapped, and all of the electronic gear was lost to Davy Jones's Locker. Our mission was scrapped for that trip.

The captain decided that we needed to take on more diesel fuel and that the crew had earned some liberty. Instead of cruising to the navy port at Jacksonville, he informed us that we were going to Miami. That announcement earned him a big cheer from the crew. It was a highly unusual destination because Miami was not a US Navy port. We would have to bring a civilian pilot on board to take our ship up the narrow channel at Miami Beach. Unlike the passenger cruisers, our ship had twin propellers, and our slowest speed was seven knots. The speed limit in that narrow channel was five knots, so we had to alternate between "one-third ahead" and "all engines stop" in order to maintain a slower speed yet maintain steerage. All commands had to be given by the civilian pilot while we were going in and out of Miami. He, in effect, took temporary command of the ship.

We finally tied up at a pier, and within an hour the first liberty party hit the beach. Our ship spent a couple of days there, and that was long enough because we had spent our savings and poker winnings by that time. Miami was pretty expensive for a sailor's wage.

Aboard the *San Pablo*, we were spending most of our time at sea, so I was able to send a portion of my modest pay home every month. There was no way to spend much money aboard ship. My mother had opened a savings account for me at the Benton State Bank.

When we visited foreign ports, food and alcohol was cheap, with the exception of popular tourist destinations like Bermuda, Nassau, and Halifax in Nova Scotia. Like many sailors, I was a pretty heavy drinker by now. I had started as a teenager, drinking beer whenever we could find an opportunity. Now in the navy, it was no problem to obtain alcohol at age eighteen to twenty, and I took advantage of those opportunities. I remember, for example, drinking rum and Coke in the Dominican Republic capital of Santo Domingo where we paid only $1.50 for a half liter of rum. The rum was of low quality. When we held the bottle up to the sunlight, we could see solid particles floating in the liquid, but sailors enjoying their first liberty in months don't worry about details such as that. We simply mixed it with the Coke, squeezed in some fresh lime, and enjoyed the sunshine in the heart of the city.

In the city's central square, a bunch of us gathered in the park to mix our rum and Coke while the Republic's government soldiers had taken up positions on the street corners with loaded weapons. The country was under the control of dictator Trujillo at the time we were there, and rebel forces were preparing to overthrow the government. We were advised not to discuss any politics with the locals because there was no way of knowing whether they were loyal to the government or the rebel forces. We simply made the best of the situation and had a good time. It was a dangerous situation, however, and the day could have ended badly. Alcohol in a revolutionary setting can be risky business.

We escaped Ciudad Trujillo unscathed and returned to our ship at the pier. When we finally got underway in Miami, an hour and a half late due to rounding up some stray crewmembers, I was assigned the duty of keeping the ship's log, and the other QM3, Howard, was on the helm. The new civilian pilot who came on board to guide us out of the Port of Miami said he had never commanded a twin-screw ship, and I could see he was visibly nervous about the situation as he talked to our captain. My job was to record the exact time of when the pilot took the "conn" and then write down every command given, along with the time of each of those commands. The civilian pilot was now in temporary command of the vessel until we reached open sea.

As we eased away from the pier and into the narrow channel, the pilot's commands were coming fast: "All engines back one-third; left standard rudder; all engines stop; left full rudder; starboard engine back one-third; all engines stop; right standard rudder; all engines ahead one-third."

We were in the narrow channel and attempting to maintain the required maximum speed of only five knots. As we headed down the narrow channel, the pilot continued: "All engines ahead one-third; all engines stop; all engines ahead one-third; all engines stop." The ship would drift while the engines were stopped, and then as we began to lose steerage, the ship would begin to swing to port or starboard, and he would kick in the engines for a minute to regain steerage. The pilot stood next to me in the pilothouse, and he appeared to be sweating profusely. There was a four-lane causeway close to our port side. It was merely a stone toss away, and we could clearly see the passengers in the vehicles that streamed along the road. This channel was extremely tight, and while we had been underway for a half hour, it was still a long way to open sea.

Then all of a sudden, my buddy Howard yelled out, "Lost steerage, sir." All of the officers in the pilothouse came to rapt attention and stared at Howard. He repeated, "Lost steerage, sir," louder this time, and was spinning the wheel back and forth with no effect. He spun it all the way hard to port, then to starboard; still no response from the rudder, and we could see the bow of the ship swinging slowly toward the shoreline!

The captain yelled, "Drop the anchors!" The officer of the deck reminded the captain that he didn't have the conn. The captain then ran over to the pilot and yelled in his ear, "Give the order to drop the anchors!" I glanced at the pilot. With white knuckles, he was firmly gripping the rail in front of him, staring straight ahead, obviously in shock.

Within those two or three minutes, the *San Pablo* "thumped" up onto the beach with a firm stop. At about the same time, the pilot finally gave the command to drop the anchors. Both of them plopped needlessly onto the sandy beach. In the radio room, two sailors spilled to the deck when their chairs tipped over from the impact. Food in the galley spilled out of the pots, and the cooks were bounced off the bulkheads.

From the wing bridge on the port side, we could almost reach out and touch the palm trees on the shore. Much of the traffic had come to a stop on the causeway, and people were out of their cars, snapping photographs of a US Navy ship resting on the beach next to the highway. It would be something to show the folks back home!

The captain knew there would be a big investigation over this fiasco, and he rushed over to me to verify my written entries in the ship's log. "Show me the entry where the pilot took command," he ordered. When I showed him all of the entries, with times noted, he was satisfied that he would be spared most of the blame. He grabbed up the ship's log and went off to lock it up in the safe.

Howard and I went out on the wing deck. It was weird to look down over the side and see the sandy beach beneath us. A crowd of people had gathered to get a close-up view of such a rare sight. We heard the sound of a helicopter and looked up to see a television news chopper circling overhead. Evidently, we would be on the evening news.

It took about an hour for three civilian tugboats to reach us. With towlines connected to our stern and starboard side, they managed to pull us off the beach. Fortunately there was minimal damage to our ship, but we were sure there would be some major damage to the pride of the US Navy. This would certainly be unwelcome news in Washington.

It was the next day before the crew learned the full story. Apparently the chief of the engine room, like many of the crew, was severely hung over following liberty in Miami and fell asleep in his bunk. This left a young EM3 from Michigan in charge of the engine room. After being underway for twenty minutes, the port generator was acting up, and the young engineman, stationed below deck, decided to switch the electrical load to the starboard generator. Had he followed procedure and contacted the bridge to get permission, it would have been denied because we were still in the narrow channel. Thinking we were out in the bay by this time, he began the step-by-step procedure in his manual and threw the lever to switch the electrical load. He must have skipped a step or two because electrical power was lost throughout the ship. The steering system was electro-hydraulic, which meant that without electricity, the rudder couldn't respond no matter how many times Howard spun the wheel.

We had other misadventures aboard the *San Pablo*, but they didn't merit the glare of publicity that the Miami Beach incident generated. Because the military conducts its investigations privately, we never heard the outcome, so I don't know if the captain's career was later affected by this unplanned beach landing.

\* \* \* \* \* \*

I was released from active duty in July of 1960 and was assigned to inactive Naval Reserve for three more years to fulfill my six-year military obligation. Military service was obligatory, and three other guys from Benton were discharged at about the same time. Two of them were cousins of mine, Gordy Farrey and Ron Robbins. There were four or five of us hanging out around Benton during the summer and fall of 1960. We each lived at home, spent the daytime looking for work and evenings drinking beer and shooting pool. We were enjoying the civilian life, and drinking had become a central part of our social life. It was common then to drink beer in the car, and we would place a cooler of beer in the trunk and drive from Benton to Shullsburg, Cuba City, or the other towns within a few miles of one another. Sometimes we would pick up some girls and have a beer party down at Horseshoe Bend on the Fever River, or stop at a couple of bars. There were a lot of bars in the Wisconsin towns and a few "roadhouses" along the highway. After the bars closed at two in the morning, we would sometimes go to the after-hours clubs in East Dubuque, Illinois. I was usually one of the guys there when they announced "last call" at closing time.

Gordy and I both landed jobs at the John Deere factory in Dubuque, Iowa, seventeen miles west of Benton. A lot of men from Benton worked there, and they offered good jobs with good pay. We were represented by the United Auto Workers. My job was in building F, where I drilled oil holes in the crankshafts on the third shift. There were five of us who carpooled to and from work and took turns driving. When I got home at eight in the morning, my mother would cook me a big breakfast of four fried eggs, potatoes, and a half pound of bacon. Then I would go to bed. Sometimes I didn't sleep well because of the heartburn. At other times, it would be due to the noisy kids in the neighborhood when there was no school.

One of my friends, Royce McNett, was dating a girl from Shullsburg, a mining town eight miles east of Benton, and he told me about a friend of his girlfriend, LuAnn. Her name was Sharon O'Flahrity, and the two girls were seniors at Shullsburg High School. I had met Sharon briefly during my high-school days when I was cruising Main Street in Shullsburg with three of my buddies from Benton. We had picked up a couple of girls, and they rode around town with us for a while. One of the girls was Sharon. She was good looking and seemed to have lots of spunk. She talked and acted pretty boldly at the time, had an outgoing personality, and had a good sense of humor. All of these traits appealed to me, but since I was a senior in high school, I felt she was too young at that time. I hadn't thought any more about her until Royce brought up her name three years later. When Royce mentioned, right out of the blue one night, that Sharon wasn't dating anyone, I got the impression that Sharon, through her girlfriend, LuAnn, must have put him up to approaching me. Of course, women would never admit such a thing.

After Royce urged me on a couple more times, I phoned Sharon and arranged a date for the Community Picnic at Cuba City, Wisconsin. She said she would be staying at a girlfriend's house in Cuba City and asked that I pick her up there. When she came out of that house, I was surprised to see her carrying a suitcase. I said, "What the hell is going on? Aren't you rushing things a bit?" She got a little flustered and explained that she would be returning to her house in Shullsburg after our date and asked if I would be willing to drive her there with her luggage. I told her, "No problem."

I knew right then that we were going to get along just fine. We laughed about that for years afterward, and I always enjoyed telling our friends about my first date with Sharon.

We were pretty much a steady item from day one. She was a good "necker" and enjoyed drinking beer with me, so that was also a plus on the balance sheet. Sharon seldom drank very much, but I made up for it. I had become a pretty heavy drinker by that time, and most of our social life centered around drinking; we associated mostly with other couples who drank. We liked to play euchre and hearts with friends, and we would sometimes pick up a six-pack of beer after seeing a movie and just drive around. We called it "road tripping." There were four of us guys from Benton who were dating Shullsburg girls, so we double-dated quite often. In the middle of the week when we weren't dating the girls, we would mostly hang out in the taverns, drinking beer and shooting pool. We often talked about our future plans, as well as sports and women. As the night wore on, we would get into the "beer philosophy" that was seldom remembered the next day.

Back in my high-school years, I would often daydream about a house with a white picket fence, a loving wife (brunette with medium-length hair like a certain cheerleader from Cassville), and a bunch of kids playing ball in the yard—maybe a half dozen or so. I had been raised up in a close, loving environment based upon sound family values. Even at this early age, I wanted to build on that foundation by pursuing a business career and raising a family. I suppose this type of planning at an early age was fairly common in the fifties.

As our relationship grew, it was apparent that Sharon and I shared the same dream, except for the six kids. Although she was a practicing Catholic, she preferred a smaller number. We grew madly in love, and I couldn't wait to get to Shullsburg to see her. I wanted her to become my wife and didn't know how much longer I could wait. I was twenty-one years old and had gone back to the Rockford School of Business following the navy tour, but went home every weekend, primarily to see Sharon. I had more than a year of school remaining, and Sharon wanted to attend a four-year college. She was working on obtaining a financial grant so she could attend the university. We spent hours discussing our future and how we could work things out. Our backgrounds were similar: we were raised in poverty but with moral and conservative values. Sharon could get no financial help from other family members because the O'Flahritys didn't get along with one another. An uncle had the means of helping her, but she never approached him for help because her dad and his two brothers had fought for years over the family farm inheritance in Montfort.

My plans had been made earlier. They were interrupted by a tour in the navy, but I was back on track again. I wanted to focus on business courses that would support a career in the manufacturing industry. In the late 1950s and early 1960s, young people were serious about planning their life's career. That attitude changed a few years later with the advent of the hippies and "peaceniks." In early 1961, my mind was made up. I wanted to hire on with a blue-chip company and work my way up the corporate ladder. In the meantime, I was enrolled at the college and working part-time at a truck terminal five nights a week. I was mastering the courses at school, and I could clearly see my future in business. My confidence was further bolstered by my uncle Tom Ewing. He said, "You'll do just fine, Gary; you've got a good head on your shoulders, and you've got the necessary drive and ambition."

I was one of the first of the Perkins grandchildren to attend college. My cousin Kay had attended Platteville State College and was now employed as a music teacher.

Kay's father, my uncle Clary Perkins, was the only member of the family still working in the mines. Most of the smaller mines had closed down by 1961, but two large operations near Shullsburg were still operating, and another near Scales Mound, Illinois. Clary, like my father and grandfather, worked "above the grass." None of the Perkinses of my father's generation, to my knowledge, ever worked below ground during their years of employment in the mines.

While my family had a history in mining, and my great-grandfather James was one of the Cousin Jacks who emigrated to the mines in America during the Civil War, there would be no miners in my generation. I would be seeking inside office work, an unusual occupation for a Perkins. My father and his brothers had taken up farming, carpentry, masonry—mostly outdoor employment—after the mines closed.

My plans had been made, and I was anxious about finishing college and beginning a career in business. Sharon had made some initial plans for college, and we had a lot of serious discussion about our future together. We were crazy about each other, and I wanted to share my life with her. I drove home on weekends from Rockford and phoned her three or four times a week. I would leave classes by three o'clock each afternoon, grab a sandwich and fries, and report for work as a nightshift rate clerk for a trucking company, Dohrn Transfer. I had some difficult courses in corporate accounting and advanced cost accounting, so I had to find time for homework. Fortunately the courses in business law, mathematics, and psychology required no homework, so I was able to keep up with my coursework. It was a tough schedule, but I maintained a 3.7 grade point average.

Then, like a Midwestern thunderbolt, came the news that brought our life into a sharper focus. Sharon was pregnant. We had made all our plans through a logical step-by-step process, planning for the fall college term, visualizing our future in the years ahead, and living our dream. The one thing that defies logic, however, is love. Love is an emotion, and as any psychologist will tell you, "Emotions don't make sense."

When she first told me that we were going to have a baby, she broke down and cried, and as I held her and tried to soothe her, I knew immediately that we could work through this somehow. I told her that our dreams weren't shattered, merely accelerated. I think she was surprised that I could remain calm at a time like that. A man generally copes with a crisis through logic. (A sense of humor helps too.) I was already planning what we would do. I was ready for marriage and had been for some time. The thought of presenting Sharon with an engagement ring the previous Christmas had crossed my mind, but that was only a brief thought, and I had dropped it immediately. I had felt that I wasn't ready to support a family until I finished college and obtained gainful employment.

But now, two things were certain at this point: she was pregnant, and we were madly in love. We would get married, but we wouldn't go into this blindly with a "love conquers all" attitude. We were young, and the odds were against us. We had no money saved, and our parents were distraught over the situation, and they couldn't help us much financially. I would have to find a better-paying job, and Sharon would have to scrap her plans for college. We discussed all of these things for most of the next night, and I made a formal proposal of marriage. When I say that this was one of the happiest moments of my life, to most people it probably sounds, at best, illogical. But like the man said, emotions don't make sense. I was excited about our future together.

Sharon's parents, Bob and Florence O'Flahrity, couldn't afford a big church wedding, and my folks had no money, either, so we decided to elope. Our parents knew of our plans, but none of our friends knew about them. My mother knew that our relationship had been serious for almost a year, so I wouldn't say she was shocked by the news of our wedding plans. She expressed disappointment, however, that I had not yet finished college. She was also concerned, and Florence, too, was worried about our future because we were so young.

I don't believe Florence had confidence in our abilities to be venturing out on our own. She overruled our selection of an apartment in the north end of Rockford and dragged Bob all around the city until they found one near the business district that they felt was more suitable. The one we had selected was on a street lined on both sides with large elm trees, and Florence felt that place would be too dark. She didn't want Sharon to be alone all day on a dark street in the "big city." The apartment they selected for us was on the third floor of the building. It was small but newly decorated. It had a Murphy bed that folded out into the living room and a small porch on the back. The building had no elevator, so we would have to carry groceries and laundry up three flights of stairs. It had lots of windows to let in light, and we would have neighbors close by, so Florence felt better about us living there, near the center of town.

We were married in July 1961 by the justice of the peace in Rockford and then left immediately for a brief honeymoon at Lake Ripley in Wisconsin. We stayed at the big lodge where Aunt Melva and Uncle Roy Shannon had spent their honeymoon years earlier. It was a beautiful setting, with a large lawn stretching down to the water. The lodge kept rowboats at the dock. Sharon wasn't fond of boating, but I talked her into a boat and rowed her around, keeping close to the shore until she felt more comfortable on the water. We were assigned a room on the second floor of the lodge with windows that looked out over the large lake. On our wedding night, we learned that the bedsprings creaked. When we came down to the dining room for breakfast each morning, an older couple would display a knowing grin as we took our seats at the dining-room table. We were a bit embarrassed, but after a couple of days of sunburn, it no longer showed. I also burned the tops of my feet while rowing the boat. When it came time to leave, it was too painful for me to wear shoes, so I drove back to Rockford in my bare feet.

We were cozy in our new apartment. There was a large walk-through closet that led to the bathroom with its new fixtures. The kitchen was large enough to accommodate a table and chairs. We were disappointed, though, to learn that the rear porch had rotten joists and we couldn't use it. The landlord told us to keep the French doors locked for safety. That porch would have been ideal for grilling our brats and keeping the beer on ice. Sharon soon made friends with some of our neighbors in the building, and I had to admit that her mother was right. This apartment was the best choice.

It turned out that I had had more cooking experience than Sharon. She could cook a roast, but I had to show her how to make gravy. I also fried pork chops while she prepared the salad and vegetables. We decided one weekend to roast a chicken in the oven while we went to church, so on Saturday I went to the grocery next door to buy a roasting hen. On Sunday morning, I prepared the stuffing, Sharon put the chicken in the oven, and we went off to church. When we got home, she pulled the pan out of the oven and found it to be almost half full of grease, so we ladled it out of the pan and put the chicken back in the oven. Thirty minutes later, the pan was once again full of grease. It turned out that I had brought home a big, fat stewing hen instead of a roasting chicken. She never let me forget that mistake and told that story to at least a hundred people over the years.

We got married once more for good measure, this time in the Roman Catholic Church, St. Peter's in Rockford. I had taken Catholic inquiry classes and had been "rebaptized" a Catholic. I told the priest that I had been baptized as a child in the Primitive Methodist faith, but he said, "Well, we're going to do it again in case the first one didn't take." Father Knott was a Jesuit priest with a great sense of humor, and I enjoyed taking the class with him as the instructor. For us to be married in the Catholic Church, we had to agree to raise our children as Catholics and sign a written agreement to that effect. I told Sharon that I would convert so that we would be a Catholic family. I hadn't been going to church as a Protestant, so what's the harm?

The wedding ceremony was held at St. Peter's Cathedral in August. Royce and LuAnn McNett stood up with us. We had a formal wedding reception the next day in Sharon's hometown of Shullsburg at the American Legion Hall. I bought a half barrel of beer at Mike's Bar in Shullsburg and set up another one at McCarthy's Pub in Benton. Sharon said, "You'll have every freeloader in town sucking down your beer!" I didn't know if she meant the drunks in Shullsburg or those in Benton. Both towns had their share.

One of Florence's neighbors baked a four-tier wedding cake for the reception, and it was still warm from the oven when she brought it to the hall. Several of the women were putting up decorations, and the men were setting up chairs and tables. My dad was close by the table where the lady had placed the cake. He was maybe ten feet away when he noticed that the cake had begun to tilt. In his typical fashion, he said calmly, "Say, what's the matter with that cake?" The women looked over, then screamed and ran to the table just in time to save it from tipping onto the floor. I think it was a friend of my dad's who once said, "If you Perkinses were any more laid back, you'd be in reverse!"

Sharon and I had a lot of friends, and I had a lot of relatives with all of those Perkins and Cook family members, so there must have been a couple hundred people at the reception. The cake had a bit of a list to the port side, but it tasted really good, so no one minded.

Our marriage got off to a good start despite my limited time at home. I continued to attend classes during the daytime but had to find a better-paying job to make ends meet. I managed to land a job at the Weyerhaeuser corrugated box plant in Rockford, but it meant working a full eight-hour shift from three to eleven at night. It was a factory job, and I had to be there by three o'clock to punch the time clock. It was a tight schedule that required me to leave school in the middle of a math class every afternoon. I was grateful to have the weekends off.

On my first day of employment with Weyerhaeuser, I drove into the plant parking lot on Twenty-Fourth Avenue in a 1953 Plymouth sedan with a wrinkled top. I had wrecked this car about six months earlier after a night of drinking with my friends. They were all ready to quit when the bars closed in Benton, but I insisted on going to East Dubuque where the bars were open until four in the morning. My cousin Gordy and I had had plenty to drink, and he tried to talk me into going home, but when I insisted on making the seventeen-mile trip to East Dubuque, he decided to follow me. He knew that I was in no condition to drive.

I only drove two miles down the road before nodding off at the wheel. There was a jolt that caused me to awaken as the Plymouth ran onto the right-hand shoulder of the road. When I overcorrected, the car slid on the gravel shoulder, performed a 180-degree turn, slid off the left side of the road, rolled over, and bounced up onto a farmer's fence on the opposite side of the road.

I remember sitting at the wheel with the car facing back toward Benton. I restarted the engine and put the car in gear, but the rear wheels simply spun. Thinking I was stuck in some mud, I opened the door and looked back to discover that the left rear wheel was two feet off the ground! I was on top of a fence post that had wedged under the left rear fender.

Gordy made sure that I wasn't injured and then promptly left when a state trooper arrived on the scene. Fortunately, the trooper was a friend of my dad. He put me in the police car, radioed for a tow truck, and drove me back to Benton while lecturing to me the whole time. He said, "Haggens isn't going to be proud of you for this adventure!" He then wrote me a ticket for inattentive driving.

This was one of three cars that I wrecked as a result of drinking. In each case, I felt guilty and stupid the next morning. I gave serious thought about what might have happened had I collided with another vehicle and silently vowed that I would never do that again. In this particular case, it was my dad's Plymouth that I had wrecked, and I felt especially guilty and remorseful about it. I had found this "cherry" Plymouth that had been owned by a spinster schoolteacher, and I bought it for my dad. It was his car that I had wrecked. He didn't say much the next day but gave me one of his "dark looks" that made me feel even worse about what I had done. I knew that I had hurt him and felt bad about it for years afterward.

I bought him another car, a blue-and-white 1953 Buick, and kept the Plymouth for myself, dents and all. I made quite an impression when I parked it at the Weyerhaeuser plant on my first day of employment. My first job at the box plant was second-shift quality control inspector. I walked around the plant floor with a stack of inspection forms on a clipboard and checked the production orders at each machine. This was done at frequent intervals throughout the night to ensure proper quality as specified by the customer, including dimensions and graphics. I also cut samples of corrugated paper as each run was made and performed crush and compression tests in the plant laboratory. There were a variety of duties, which made my job interesting and provided an opportunity for me to learn the manufacturing process from start to finish.

My boss knew I was studying accounting, so when a job opened in the office a few months later, he told me about the opening. The raw material clerk had quit her job to raise a family. I was hired in the office as her replacement at $325 per month. This would be a salaried job that provided medical insurance. Since Sharon was already pregnant, the maternity coverage wouldn't apply in our case. We would have to pay those costs out of pocket, so I took a second job as a part-time employee at the Sears store in Rockford. I worked some evenings and Saturdays in their credit department. That brought in extra money that we would need, but I would no longer be able to attend college classes at night. We didn't feel that to be important because I had completed almost all of the accounting courses, leaving economics and a couple others remaining. In any case, I didn't feel that an associate degree was all that important. I could now put my training in accounting to use with this job at Weyerhaeuser.

My career began to pick up speed right away. After only two months as raw materials clerk, the office manager fired the cost accountant, so I applied for his job and was accepted with a one-hundred-dollar pay raise. With this new assignment, I was able to put my brief work experience in the factory and my formal education in cost accounting to good use. Things were working out okay for us.

Sharon was expecting the baby in February, near my mother's birthday. With the part-time income from Sears, we were able to put some money aside for the upcoming doctor and hospital bills, but I would soon have to begin paying back the student loan of $5,000. As luck would have it, Weyerhaeuser implemented a new standard cost system at year's end and wanted it to be fully implemented by the end of January. This required extralong work hours, and the overtime money was a welcome bonus. I had to cut back my hours at Sears, but I was bringing home more money in December and January. The credit manager at Sears wasn't happy about my reduced hours at the store. He was impressed with my work and also disappointed when I refused his offer to train me as a future Sears credit manager.

Sharon hadn't gained a lot of weight during pregnancy, and most people didn't know we were expecting. Her health was good, although certain foods would upset her stomach and she had some bouts with morning sickness. Her pediatrician, Dr. Heinemeyer, was up in years now. He had delivered Sharon when she was born at the same Rockford Memorial Hospital nineteen years earlier. On one of her office visits, he happened to mention that a lot of babies are born during storms when atmospheric pressure is low.

On January 7, a month before the baby was due, I was working that Saturday morning at the plant when a blizzard struck Rockford. It was snowing, blowing, and drifting with more than twelve inches on the ground by noon. The phone rang at the office, and it was Sharon, telling me her bag of water had broken and that the doctor told her to come to the hospital. He told her there was no need to rush but that she should try to get there within an hour or so.

I was not expecting this, and my mind was racing as I rushed out to the car. It took a while to get all the snow off the windows, and then I managed to get stuck in the parking lot! I got down on my knees and scooped the light, fluffy snow with my hands and then worked the old Plymouth back and forth until I finally broke free and roared out onto the plowed street. I pulled the car up in front of our apartment building (it was still snowing and blowing), put the car keys in my jacket pocket, and trotted up the sidewalk and then up the three flights of stairs to our apartment. Sharon was waiting for me at the door: "What took you so long?"

We were both getting a bit tense by now, but I told her not to worry; we still had plenty of time. She had her bag packed with personal items for the trip to the hospital but said she needed toothpaste. I clambered back down the three flights of stairs, ran to the grocery store next door, bought the toothpaste, and then ran back up the three flights of stairs one more time.

When we finally got down to the car, I helped her inside with snow blowing and swirling around in the wind and then reached in my pocket for the car keys. They weren't there! Baseball jackets have those slash-style pockets, and the keys must have fallen out when I was jogging between the car and the building. I got down on my knees and swept the snow off the sidewalk with my gloved hands. When I didn't find them right away, I told her I was going to have to retrace my steps to the store and back. I suggested that she wait inside, so I helped her up the three flights of stairs and then went back down to continue sweeping along the sidewalk on my hands and knees.

That was when this big Irish cop walked up to me and asked me what I was looking for. After I explained, he said, "Well, you better forget about the keys. With this weather, it would be best to stay off the roads."

I said, "I have to take my wife to the hospital."

"Is she sick?"

"She's going to have a baby."

"Jesus, Mary, and Joseph! I'll call a police ambulance! Let's get inside!"

When Sharon answered the door this time, she was surprised to see the big Irish cop standing next to me. We came inside the apartment, where he placed a phone call for the ambulance, and we were soon on our way. There were two cops with the ambulance, and one sat in the back with Sharon. I had to sit up front with my feet on a big medical kit and my knees under my chin. The cop in back kept asking, "You doin' okay there, Mom? If things start happening, tell us right away, okay?" Then, on top of everything else, we had to stop and wait for a long freight train to cross North Rockton Avenue. Finally, we made it to Rockford Memorial.

The doctor was mad as a wet hen. They didn't have time to prep Sharon, and she went into hard labor a few minutes after we arrived. Our first child, a beautiful little baby girl, arrived a month early in the middle of a blizzard and got her dad pretty rattled. But that's only one reason why she's always been so special.

Pamela Jane only weighed five pounds, fifteen ounces, and we couldn't bring her home right away. When Sharon's mom, Florence, saw her for the first time, she said, "Oh, Sharon, you can't possibly care for a baby that small!" So my mother, Jeanette, came down to Rockford and stayed for a couple of weeks to assist her daughter-in-law with the new baby. Thank God for my mother's calming influence.

As for me, the proud father, I went to work on Monday morning with my daughter's photo taken just after she was born. I placed it on my desk at work and accepted congratulations all around. I didn't tell my coworkers all the details about the snowstorm, the lost keys and ambulance ride, or that I had to walk home from the hospital on Sunday morning. It was several miles from the northwest side of Rockford to the east side where we lived. Along the way, I stopped at St. Peter's Cathedral, kneeled down, and gave a prayer of thanks.

Within the next six months, we moved into a four-unit apartment building that had a second bedroom. I bought Sharon a used wringer washing machine for seventy dollars, and we put it in the basement. That put an end to the weekly trips to and from the Laundromat. We had the only washing machine in the building, so we would rent it out to our neighbors. We sometimes used this extra cash to buy beer for our Friday night euchre games with the Duffys, who lived upstairs. We could buy the quart bottles of beer for fifty cents each.

When we first moved into the apartment, we noticed a sour odor and thought it might have been a diaper smell from the previous tenants. We scrubbed and then painted the entire place, floors and walls, but the odor remained. Later on, a neighbor told us that the previous couple had a stuffed hawk hanging over the dining room table. Apparently they hadn't cleaned it properly before stuffing it for display. An application of shellac primer and another coat of paint finally masked the smell of that dead hawk.

In 1964, Sharon went full term with Peter John. He was born on September 26 and was of average weight, about seven and a half pounds. After we brought him home from the hospital, he had trouble keeping his formula down. He was often constipated, and his little tummy would become distended. We took him back and forth to the pediatrician, and a number of tests were inconclusive. Everything seemed normal. The problem continued for two months more, and he was getting very little nourishment. A surgeon performed a colostomy just to keep him alive. We had a good pediatrician who had interned at the Mayo Clinic, but he was unable to determine the cause of the problem and told us so. Sharon and I were in his office when he asked if we wanted him to contact another specialist. We had heard of a Japanese doctor in Milwaukee who had treated an infant that was born with a bowel defect. Our pediatrician looked this doctor up in his directory and phoned him while we were there in his office. Over the telephone, Dr. Suribachi suggested that Peter may have been born with Hirschprung's disease, a rare defect where a portion of the large intestine has no nerve cells. He suggested that we get in touch with Dr. Orvar Svenson at Children's Memorial Hospital in Chicago. Our pediatrician then phoned Dr. Svenson and arranged to transfer Peter to Chicago by ambulance.

At this same time, my father was in the University Hospital at Madison, Wisconsin, with what they diagnosed as cirrhosis of the liver. We were traveling the ninety miles to Chicago, where Peter was confined, and then, from Rockford, I went north to Madison, Wisconsin, a couple of times a week to see my dad, shave his whiskers, and try to lift his spirits. He was severely sick and was yellow in color with jaundice, but he never voiced a complaint. His eyes lacked their normal sparkle. He knew that he was close to death. It was a particularly stressful time for all of us. While in Chicago, I often drove to a nearby

Roman Catholic Church, lit candles for my son and my father, and then kneeled and prayed.

Peter had more surgeries before the problem with his large colon was corrected, and he was less than six months old. The diagnosis of Hirschprung's had been correct, and Dr. Svenson told us that while the disease is rare, it tends to be genetic and affects male children primarily.

My dad wasn't so fortunate. He died on January 25, 1965, at sixty-two years of age. He had drawn just one Social Security check after his many years of labor. We would learn years later that my father's problem was with the bile ducts in his liver, and it was also a genetic malady. Years later, my sisters were both diagnosed with primary biliary cirrhosis. The doctors in Madison were not aware of that type of cirrhosis at the time of my father's death.

It's normally an uphill battle for couples who marry at a young age, but I believe the extraordinary difficulties made our marriage stronger. Sharon was a good mother and wife. She was a driving force in our marriage and remained highly supportive of me in my career. We had many long talks about our future as our family grew, and we were making our marriage work; as she once said, we were "dirt-poor but happy." We knew that there would be better times ahead of us, and we appreciated this opportunity to raise our children while we were still young.

As in any marriage, we had our disagreements at times but were able to overcome them. Often it was a case of financial pressure. She had the spunk and quick temper of the Irish. Her bloodlines included the O'Flahritys, Dailys, Morgans, Egans, and Gallaghers. I had the stubborn and independent characteristics of the Cornish with a bit of an Irish mix, so there would be some minor fireworks at times. We both came from rather poor families and were raised in a small-town environment. Religion wasn't a problem between us because I had converted to the Roman Catholic faith, and we attended Mass every Sunday as a family. That kept us centered.

We did experience a major flare-up during the first year of our marriage, and I believe it was mostly due to our family differences, in the way we were raised. Sharon was an only child, and her mother was a dominant parent, typical in many Irish families. Her father was an alcoholic, a binge drinker who couldn't hold a job for long. Bob was very intelligent, and I liked him when he was sober, but every few months he would go on a two- or three-week drunk. His many talents were wasted because of the booze, so his primary source of income when I knew him was from painting. The Murphy brothers would always hire him back again and again because he could paint church interiors like no one else. He could do all of the fancy gilded work inside the Catholic churches. The Murphys painted many of these churches throughout Wisconsin, and when Bob was working for them, he brought home a good wage. His check, however, went to Florence because she handled the finances as well as the rest of the family responsibilities. She also worked outside the home because she couldn't count on Bob to have a paycheck every week.

While I was raised by my folks to be independent and was given freedom to make my own choices, Sharon's mother was very involved in her life, perhaps to an extreme degree. Florence was overprotective and a controlling type of person, and I had sensed, long before we had married, that there may be some fireworks down the road. It turned out to be a pretty short road.

After Pam was born, we were struggling financially even though I was working two jobs. There would be some additional stress over my spending money on beer while she was made to wait until the next payday for some items she needed. In a phone call to her mother, Sharon would tell her how poor we were, and Florence would secretly send her money. Then when we would have an argument over finances, she would say, "Well, if it hadn't been for my mother, I wouldn't have these shoes!" or something such as that, to hurt my pride. Her frustration built up one day over finances, and we really had it out. We said some hurtful things to each other, and the hurt turned to anger. When she brought up her mother again, I became resentful and probably said the wrong thing.

The next day, she packed some clothes, took Pam, and went home to her mother. We only had the one car, which I had driven to work, so she took the bus to Shullsburg. After work on Friday, I drove up to Shullsburg, and we all three had it out in Florence's kitchen. It was Florence and I doing most of the talking, and we got everything out on the table, so to speak. I told her that she was going to have to let go, that she wasn't doing Sharon any favors by keeping her tied that way. As things heated up, I sensed that, in their discussions before I arrived, Florence had convinced Sharon that a trial separation might be in order. Then I said something like, "So you don't need me around? You just needed a name for the baby? Is that what this is about?" That led to another hot round of debate, and then all got quiet. I admitted to Florence that we were having money problems, but I was confident that we would work through these difficulties. It was just going to take some time; there were better days ahead.

After more discussion, things calmed down, and I turned to Sharon and said, "I'm going back home. I love you, and I want you and Pam to come with me." Our family of three then got into the car, waved good-bye to Florence, and left for home. Florence and I never again had a major disagreement like that. We had reached an understanding.

Shortly after Peter was born, I received a raise in salary, and our family finances were somewhat improved. There was now less stress in that regard. We enjoyed going to church on Sunday. Sharon liked to get

Pam and Peter all dressed up, she would put a roast in the oven, and we would all go to St. Peter's for Sunday Mass. Church for me was a time of healing, often physically as well as spiritually. I often drank too much on the weekends and went to church with a hangover. Sometimes it would be a Saturday night card party with the neighbors or downtown shooting pool with the guys, always with the beer. Most of my buddies drank, and many of them, like me, often drank to excess. In later life, I would learn that I subconsciously chose friends who drank because that was my preference. My alcoholic characteristics were surfacing, and they would get worse because the disease is progressive. However, at this point I wasn't able to recognize my drinking as a disease. In my mind, I was a hard worker and a hard drinker, and simply had to work harder at controlling my drinking habits just as I had worked hard to control the other aspects of my life. When I attended church on Sunday, it was an opportunity for me to ask the Lord for help, to give me strength, because I often felt guilty about abusing alcohol. Sharon said on more than one occasion that I was a better Catholic than she was, but maybe I just had a stronger need to be there.

My career was on a fast track at Weyerhaeuser. I had learned most of the office jobs at the Rockford plant, and by the time Patrick Jay was born in 1968, I had been promoted to office manager. At the age of twenty-eight, I was the youngest manager in the Container Division. My strengths lay in manufacturing cost accounting, and I learned a great deal more about the business by spending as much time as possible out on the production floor.

I was the office manager for only six months when I was impacted for the first time by office politics. An employee with no accounting experience had been "dumped" into my accounting department prior to my promotion to manager. The production manager persuaded my predecessor to take him after he had failed as a shipping clerk. It was obvious to me that he wasn't going to work out in my department because he had no aptitude for the job. When I described the situation to my boss, the general manager, he said, "Well, Gary, if he's not working out, you'll just have to fire him."

Knowing the employee was in his midforties with five kids to support, I felt bad about having to do this deed and also resentful because of the politics that put the employee in this position in the first place. I was going to have to call him into the office the next morning, and I didn't sleep well the night before.

Surprisingly, it went well. We had a long talk about his strengths and weaknesses, his interests and concerns about his future. He thanked me for being honest with him and said he felt I was doing him a favor because he knew that he wasn't fit for this job in accounting. I told him he could stay on until he found another job and that we would pay him severance because he had been with us for almost five years.

George Rehfield was the general manager at Rockford. We got along just fine, and I admired his style of management. He had been the sales manager at Chicago and had been promoted to the Rockford position about the same time that I was promoted to office manager. In addition to sales, George had an accounting background, which was quite unusual in the packaging industry. In our first few months together, I found that we could communicate well, and early on, he said, "Gary, I want you to tell me where we can improve the profit. We need to do much better."

My analysis of the Rockford plant indicated a need for change in product mix. I told him that we had sold some business that didn't fit well in the plant, was labor-intensive, and absorbed way too much cost burden. We could "throw out" some of these accounts but would get a lot of resistance from the sales department.

He said, "Don't worry, I can handle that problem. I want you to give me a complete analysis. Crunch some numbers. Look at our product mix, make a machine-by-machine analysis in production, and show me where we can make the biggest improvements. We need to get on this right away. You set up the targets, Gary, and I'll knock 'em down!"

I understood exactly what he wanted from me and thought this to be the opportune time to bring up my dissatisfaction with my present salary. I had been promoted to office manager with an increase in base salary, but the new pay didn't reflect much of an increase in net pay because I had been earning a lot of overtime pay as the plant cost accountant prior to this promotion. This new position would be exempt of any overtime pay. He of course argued that overtime shouldn't be included in base salary adjustments, but I argued that it made a big difference in my take-home pay. I had to support a family, buy milk for the kids. I was now taking on much greater responsibility and was justified in demanding a higher take-home pay, overtime or no overtime; it didn't matter. He said he would look into it and see what he could do.

Throughout the next year, I had regular meetings with George where I outlined the targets for profit improvement, backed up with a lot of numbers. True to his word, he executed the necessary changes and directed the sales department to sell products that matched up with our plant needs. This meant that the sales staff had to be more selective in what they sold. If certain sales accounts didn't fit, they would be thrown out. George also got me another one hundred dollars a month in salary, so things were going smoothly. Of the thirty plants in the Container Division, Rockford was named "Most Improved" the following year. That brought another pay raise for some of us.

Sharon and I would have talks in the evening after the kids went to bed. I told her that I was really impressed with George Rehfield's management style and that maybe someday I would have an opportunity to reach the position of general manager. This would become my dream, my career goal. I was able to put my college education to good use as office manager, and the company was sending me to Chicago for additional outside training. The corporate executives from Chicago and Tacoma, Washington, were visiting the Rockford plant on a frequent basis now, and we were being singled out as an above-average plant operation. Some of the profit-improvement procedures that George and I had implemented in Rockford were applied at other plants in our division. This was providing me with good visibility, and the big executives were taking notice.

# CHAPTER 14

# IN MY THIRTIES

In the mid-1960s, Weyerhaeuser Company invested heavily in state-of-the-art electronic data processing throughout the company. They embarked on a five-year feasibility study for the Packaging Group with a staff of about two hundred, which was located in leased office space on Wacker Drive in the Chicago Loop. Almost half of these employees were hired from outside the company—IBM, General Electric, Western Electric, Sperry Rand, and Honeywell—and included one former executive from the US Atomic Energy Commission. The remaining staff was transferred into Chicago from within the company. These were primarily midlevel managers of various specialties within the Packaging Group's three divisions: Shipping Container, Folding Carton, and Milk Carton. There were a total of about fifty plants in the Packaging Group. A few of the managers were also brought in from Weyerhaeuser's paper mills from their Containerboard Division. The members of this new MIS (Management Information Systems) Group had a broad range of business experience, and their new job assignments in Chicago would be for a term of five years, the life of the feasibility study.

Manufacturing businesses in the 1960s had to develop their own application software for processing sales orders, estimating costs and selling prices, scheduling production, and virtually all other business applications, including payroll and general accounting records. There were no software "shelf items" available for purchase during this time. If a manufacturer wanted to convert manual office applications to electronic processes, the systems had to be designed in detail, written into program language, and repeatedly tested and "debugged" until a pilot system was finally operational. Weyerhaeuser had made a full commitment to this project with a tremendous investment in data-processing hardware and in salaried payroll to support such an ambitious project. The purpose of the five-year feasibility study was to analyze the present manual applications within the Packaging Group, develop a variety of computerized systems to replace or augment them, and then implement these new systems in a half dozen pilot plants selected from four regions of the United States. At the end of the five-year program, senior management would evaluate the results at the pilot plants and arrive at a "go" or "no-go" decision for implementing these systems at the remaining forty or so manufacturing plants in the group.

By early 1966, the company was about two years into the feasibility study and had chosen the Rockford plant as one of the five pilot plants within the Shipping Container Division. The others were Rochester, New York; New Orleans; Los Angeles; and Olympia, Washington. As the office manager in Rockford, it was my responsibility to coordinate with the MIS staff as they conducted studies at our plant location in preparation for some preliminary design of the new systems. I spent a considerable amount of time with these people, explaining the fundamental steps in manual procedures for cost estimating, selling-price calculation, production scheduling, sales order entry, and invoicing of shipments. The MIS staff of systems designers provided me with insight as to how the computer would play a major role in these functions. They described the future benefits we could expect at the plant level. This was some amazing stuff! It would be a major leap in technology because in the 1960s computers were at an infant stage in American industry. Government agencies and the military had been using computers for years, but the manufacturing industry was using manual methods that hadn't changed in twenty years or more. Their most recent upgrade had been the advent of the electronic calculator in 1965. This bold new computer venture would put Weyerhaeuser Company on the cutting edge of a new business technology.

The MIS project really piqued my interest, and as the studies progressed at Rockford, I eagerly became more and more involved. My accounting staff at Rockford was well-experienced by now, and the office was running smoothly, so I was able to hang out with the MIS guys when they visited the plant. Sometimes we would gather at a bar after work, and they invited me to have dinner with them on occasion. By talking with these guys, I began to see the big picture, the major role that computer technology would play in the future of this business. I wanted to board this train!

Sharon and I would often discuss the MIS project, and she could tell that I was excited about this new opportunity. It would be a new frontier for the manufacturing industry, and any experience that I could gain in a venture such as this would definitely bolster my chances for reaching a career goal as a general manager. Most of the veteran managers opposed change. They were disinterested or actively opposed this "computer stuff." I was much younger (at twenty-eight, the youngest office manager in the division) and felt that this would be an important tool for future managers.

Sharon and I talked more and more about it, and she was very encouraging. I was looking beyond a career in accounting, and the office manager position was merely a means toward an end. I had no interest in pursuing accounting any further. My predecessor at Rockford had been promoted to the Division Accounting Office, but I couldn't see myself as a "fixed-asset specialist" or something along that line. I wanted to be in the thick of things and maintain a high profile. I didn't want to get swallowed up by this big corporation. Weyerhaeuser employed some thirty thousand people at the time, and it was my intention to stay above the grass and maintain visibility. Others undoubtedly felt more secure by blending into the work force. To them, high visibility, rising above the grass, was akin to placing one's head in the line of fire: "Make one mistake and your career is finished." I was more risk-tolerant and willing to maintain a high profile as a means of advancement in the corporate world.

As an example, I had caused a stir at the Division Office when I took it upon myself to change the month-end reporting procedure, in violation of the Standard Procedure Manual, the corporation's Bible. Tom Holland, the division accounting supervisor, called me and said, "Gary, why do I get twenty-nine reports at the end of each month from the other plants that conform with the procedure manual, but from Rockford I get this thirteen-column, handwritten worksheet? Can you please answer that?"

"Because," I told him, "I found a better way to account for inventory. It's now more accurate and saves the company over four hundred dollars a month in clerical cost."

After some heated discussion, he finally agreed to accept my numbers if I would send him a memo that detailed the savings to the company. What he was requesting, of course, was a PYA memo that he would have in his file to protect his ass. Sharon and I shared a big laugh over that story.

In the fall of 1966, I registered at Rockford College for a two-semester course in systems design. Again, because computer technology was a new science for business at that time, the classes were taught by outside businessmen with some experience in the field. In this course, we were taught to analyze manual office systems, break them down into basic steps, and then put the steps down on paper as detailed flow charts. In the more complex jobs, these flow sheets would cover an entire desktop. These detailed designs would then be turned over to a computer programmer who would write the COBOL or FORTRAN language required for a large-scale "second-generation" computer. I attended these classes in the evenings. Meanwhile, back at the office, I would break away from my tasks as office manager whenever I had the opportunity, to pump more information from the Chicago MIS group about progress with the feasibility study. I finished my course in the summer of 1967 and phoned one of the MIS managers in Chicago, telling him, "I have a certificate in my hand that says I'm a systems designer, and I would like to come in for a job interview."

With the blessing of my boss, George Rehfield, I accepted a job transfer, at a higher salary, to Chicago, where I would join the Order Entry/Cost Estimating development design team. While Sharon and I had realized that we would possibly have to relocate our family to the Chicago area, she was now having some misgivings about the idea, when this prospect became a reality. We had lived in Rockford for our entire married life of six years, and the move to the Chicago area was going to be stressful. I also had some second thoughts but kept them to myself while putting on a brave face. I had developed a good track record at Rockford and had received annual merit increases in salary as a result of my hard work. When Rehfield had come to Rockford as the new general manager, the plant had not been performing well. I had just been promoted to office manager, and he had come to rely on me as the "numbers guy." We had worked together to improve profit at the plant. In addition, Rockford was the first plant in the division to successfully install the new standard cost system. The new system had become a tool to further enhance profits by highlighting cost variances that required corrective action. It was like improving your golf score by first getting rid of the double bogeys. Rehfield fully supported the new management practice of MBO, or management by objective. We had accomplished a lot at Rockford, and my position as office manager was rock-solid. It would have been comfortable for me to simply cruise along at this job, but I remembered what Bob Ringwood, the division controller, had told my boss a couple of years earlier: "It's good to know that Gary is doing such a good job for you, but don't let him get comfortable. Keep the water level at his chin." I've never forgotten his words in all these years, and I applied that advice to subordinates who worked for me in later years. Unlike many managers, I have never been afraid to delegate responsibility and authority. If you "grow" people, it strengthens you as a manager and benefits the organization as a whole.

When I made the big leap to MIS in Chicago, the water was definitely "at my chin." Any new job can be intimidating at first, and this one was certainly no exception. The staff in Chicago was bright and talented, but what really impressed me was their ability to deal with abstract concepts. This was blue-sky development, and we were cooking from scratch. Nothing like this had been done before, and Weyerhaeuser Company was pouring a lot of money and talent into this project. The computer room alone took up half of the eleventh floor in the big office building on Wacker Drive. The department staff was located all around the perimeter of the eleventh floor. There were three levels of management in the MIS department of about two hundred people. There were project leaders at the midlevel positions who directed a staff consisting of systems analysts, designers, and computer programmers.

There were a couple dozen people in Operations, which was responsible for hardware and operating-system maintenance as well as supervising dozens of keypunch operators. All computer programs were keyed in Hollerith code onto punch cards.

Each project had a monetary budget, and a time chart was drawn up with a target date for completion. The projects were broken down into rough concepts, and the designers detailed the process step by step on huge, hand-drawn flow charts. The charts were then backed up with pages of written documentation. Once the design was completed, a programmer wrote the computer language to perform the steps, and the coded language was punched into cards. The huge stack of cards was then fed into the computer, where it was compiled into a "program." Because most of these programs were very complex, they often failed in an initial trial run, so the processes of testing, rewriting, recompiling, testing, and debugging would often repeat over several cycles before it would be ready for a full test run at one of the pilot plants. We would occasionally be required to go back to the drawing board and perform major changes in design. This was cause to begin the processes from the beginning once again. When we finally got the design project implemented at the first pilot plant, some minor glitches or bugs would often crop up, or we would discover a business situation that hadn't been anticipated in the original design. That's why the pilot plants were selected as a method of testing the design. It gave us an opportunity to clean up the system and make minor changes before it was implemented at the remaining plants.

There were times when the plant personnel wondered if we actually knew what the hell we were doing. The problems that cropped up during the test stage at the pilot plants could be very frustrating to the plant office staff. I once told Martha at Rockford, "This is why you are the pilot plant."

She responded, "You mean guinea pigs?"

"You could say that."

Delays and snags were commonplace as we worked on these projects, and there were frequent meetings to keep all of the MIS teams coordinated because the data from these projects was interrelated to others through a software process called IDS, or Integrated Data Store, a cutting-edge technology developed by Honeywell. A single piece of data, say customer number, was stored in just one location of a particular disk but could be accessed by any number of systems: order entry, estimating, plant scheduling, invoicing, sales reporting, and so on. With this type of integrated file, a change in one system project affected the others, so we had to keep all of these projects coordinated and all of the design teams on the same page. Frequent updates of written documentation were a required aggravation. No one liked to write documentation after the design was completed because it seemed so mundane.

I was assigned to the Order Entry/Cost Estimating design project. After a prior two-year effort by an eight-person team, their design had been scrapped because it didn't meet the requirements of the division controller. Therefore, the former team members had been reassigned, and now—with a staff of only three people—we were to start over with a new design. I was the system designer, Ed Swarthout was the programmer, and Nick Strauss was the program analyst. None of us had met previously, but I learned that both Ed and Nick had considerable computer experience. They were also very sharp guys. They knew very little about business applications, such as sales order processing or cost estimating, but I was amazed by how quickly they were able to grasp these processes as we went along. I had virtually no technical experience at this point, but I had a thorough knowledge of the manual business processes, so we would soon form a well-balanced team: three "hot shots."

I have to be honest: the MIS assignment was a bit intimidating at first, and for the first couple of weeks, I wasn't sure that I would be up to the task. I had transitioned from being a competent office manager to a floundering systems designer at a big office with over a hundred employees. At the same time, I was trying to convince Sharon that a move to Chicago was in the best interest of our family. To relieve the stress, I told her that we didn't have to move immediately, that I could commute the ninety miles on the weekends for a while.

I was now working with some really sharp people with superb verbal skills, dealing with abstracts (a unique experience for me), learning new acronyms and technical phrases, a whole new jargon. Obviously I had trouble keeping up to speed in those early meetings, but as time went on, I became more confident. My six years of experience at the Rockford plant began to pay off, and I knew a heck of a lot more about the packaging business than I had realized. The three of us dived into the details, and as we improved upon our ability to communicate with one another, the design began to take form. The cost system was primarily a math problem, and Nick had the aptitude for that. He loved math problems. Ed was a bit introverted, a detail guy who constantly questioned my designs and made sure that he thoroughly understood what I was trying to accomplish in my design flow charts. I would lose patience with him at times but had to admit that his questions resulted in an efficient, more accurate design. As a result, his programs were clean, and we didn't have to waste a lot of extra time debugging and recompiling despite the complexity of these systems.

I taught them the box business, they taught me the computer business, and I was now able to do some "tech-speak." We had a prototype up and running in a mere six months. Two months later, the division controller approved our design for the cost-estimating system, and we were taking it to the pilot plants. We implemented it first at Rockford, then at New Orleans, Rochester, Olympia, and Los Angeles. The director of MIS suggested that I take charge of the implementation at these plants because of my prior experience at the manufacturing plant. The employees at the plants would have to be trained on the new system, and our technical personnel in the past had experienced difficulty in communicating with the plant staff. It was assumed that they would be more comfortable, and thereby more cooperative, with me out there. That proved to be true.

We were able to get the cost system on line in the space of eight months whereas our predecessors had struggled with the design for two full years only to have it rejected. There were a couple of reasons for our success. As a three-man staff, Ed, Nick, and I were more efficient, the communication was improved, and these two guys were brilliant. The other reason was that I had come up with a simpler design concept.

Months earlier, I had the occasion to spend time with the previous design team over a few beers. They told me that they had taken a scientific approach to the problem and had gone from COBOL to FORTRAN in an attempt to carry each calculation out to the nth degree using sophisticated formulas in mathematics. They felt that they were coming up with accurate results, but the controller rejected their design because their results didn't match up with the manual cost system. The former team member told me they had argued that their results were more accurate, but the controller wouldn't budge. He wanted identical results to the old manual system.

Once I learned that we had to please the controller, I simply loaded matrix tables from the manual cost book, inaccuracies and all, into my design and thereby ensured that we would come up with identical results to the plant's cost manual worksheet. Nick, with his math background, balked at my approach because he didn't cotton to the idea of compromising accuracy by rounding decimals to whole numbers in the application software. After further debate, I convinced him that while the plants wouldn't gain accuracy with our system, they wouldn't lose any either, when comparing it to the manual system. It would be a win-win situation. If the division controller wanted identical results, we would be more than happy to provide them.

The implementation phase had begun at the Rockford plant because it was the closest to our Chicago office. It was decided to implement both cost estimating and order entry at the same time because we had completed both designs, and the two were closely related. It would be a fairly smooth implementation at Rockford because I was well-acquainted with the staff, and the general manager at Rockford, George Rehfield, gave me his full cooperation.

I had designed these systems, and I also had intimate knowledge of the various clerical jobs at the plant, so I was confident of a successful implementation. The primary problem was that in the late 1960s, the plant personnel had zero computer experience. The personal computer in that era had very little memory and was only suitable for games and simple word processing: a typewriter with memory. None of the office staff at Rockford had any computer experience whatsoever, so fear was their biggest hurdle.

There was also a great deal of pressure on me to get this system up and running because this was the first to be implemented by MIS. For two years, the plants had heard all the talk about these blue-sky systems that would offer them such great benefits; now it was time to fish or cut bait. We had to walk the talk. The top managers at MIS were anxious about this first project at Rockford because the corporate office in Tacoma was pressuring them to get something going. They were spending millions of dollars and had yet to see any results from our development group. And of course, the other plants were glad that Rockford had been selected as the first guinea pig because, coming from "corporate," they just knew that it would probably be a messed-up venture. The general managers out there in the field didn't want any part of a big project that would sap valuable man-hours away from their primary business of custom packaging. Since I was in charge of implementing the very first online computer project in the field, I was once again above the grass, in a high-visibility position, and all levels of management would have their sights on the Rockford project. I wasn't worried because I had full confidence in the system and in the office staff at the Rockford plant. I was grateful to have the opportunity to crank this baby up and was eager to get started.

Right off the bat, there was the expected resistance to change when I explained the new order entry process to the Sales Service staff at Rockford. This group was reluctant to go on a "real time" basis and wanted to enter each sales order twice: once by their current manual method and once again on the new computer system, "in case something goes wrong." Martha, especially, was nervous about having real sales orders processed by a central computer in Chicago and then transmitted back to her office in Rockford. She thought we should continue the manual system as backup. I responded, "No way! We're not going to go with parallel systems. It's twice as much work, and you will give priority to a manual system that you're familiar with while backsliding on the new process. We'll never get fully online that way. We've got to go real time on this. With this steady volume of sales orders, it's the only way it will work!"

She continued to complain to her boss, who in turn took the issue to Rehfield, the general manager. George called us all into his office, whereupon I fully explained my reasoning for implementing order entry on a "real time" basis.

George said, "Isn't that like flying without a parachute, Gary?"

"No," I said, "it's more like high-flying without a net. But remember that we have made countless dry runs in Chicago before I came out here. Now we can expect some minor glitches here and there as we process your sales orders, but if a major problem erupts in a worst-case scenario, we'll simply shut it down and go back to the manual method."

Since we had all worked together as a team when I was the office manager at Rockford, I was able to get their cooperation. George made it clear, however, that I would have to take the blame if the project proved detrimental to his plant operation. On that note, we cranked up the new order-entry/cost-estimating system.

Martha began filling out briefly coded input sheets for each sales order of corrugated boxes and passed them to Margaret who punched them into paper tape on a teletype machine. She then transmitted the tape for each batch of orders over the teletype to Chicago where the Honeywell 435 computer accessed our new order-entry program and determined the product specifications of basic sheet size and scoring dimensions, calculated the standard cost, filed the details on the disk drives, and returned a finished production order to the teletype machine at the Rockford office. The turnaround time that first day was less than two minutes. Since the production order was printed on multicopy paper, all Martha had to do was distribute the copies. Our form was close in design to the former handwritten production order that the production department had been using for some years. This made it more acceptable to the Scheduling and Production Departments. After the order had been produced in the plant and loaded for shipment, the invoicing was even simpler. Martha sent the order number and quantity of shipment via teletype to Chicago, and the invoices were printed and mailed to the customer from there. A daily sales report was transmitted back to Rockford at the end of the day.

In the late 1960s, we didn't have the technology of sending data over telephone lines and there were no space satellites, so we were required to use teletype transmissions between the plants and the central offices. Today this method of communication would seem extremely cumbersome, but at that time it was high-tech. The plant personnel saved countless hours of clerical time each day and eliminated month-end reports that were now captured by the computer. In a matter of just a few weeks, the Sales Service staff in Rockford forgot all about the old manual order-entry system that had been in effect since the 1940s.

During the implementation project at Rockford, Sharon and I were wrestling with the subject of a move to Chicago. She was dragging her feet about moving the family. I was spending much of my time at the Rockford plant and, therefore, more time at home. We had done some preliminary house hunting in some of the Chicago suburbs, but finding a house to lease similar to the house we were renting in Rockford was a difficult task. There were lots of apartments and townhouses available but very few single-family houses for rent. We wanted to be well out into the suburbs, away from the Chicago metropolitan area, and near a commuter train line so I could conveniently get to the Loop every day.

Sharon was a bit overwhelmed by this move and really didn't have her heart into house hunting. Her friends and her mother were not very supportive, either, because people raised in a small town were naturally quite apprehensive about moving to Chicago. I was left with the responsibility of finding a house for us while deeply involved in the new job. We didn't make much progress on house hunting over the first six months.

Because of the size of the feasibility study at MIS and the fact that so many employees were moving into Chicago at this time, Weyerhaeuser Company decided to rent two adjoining apartments on the Near North Side. This would serve as temporary quarters while employees were house hunting in the area. The company apartments on West Elm would accommodate six to eight guys, and I was a "resident" there for quite a long time, about nine months. Another employee, a former production manager who had joined the MIS group, was there for over a year because his daughter needed special medical care back in Michigan, and for that reason he couldn't relocate his family. He and I held the longevity records at the company apartments. When it came time for me to move out, they threw a special party for me. Kevin Welch flew in some live lobsters and a peck of clams from his hometown of Boston, which we washed down with a few cases of beer. The party ran into the wee hours, and a couple of guys who missed their last commuter train to the suburbs were forced to bunk with us at the apartment. I loaned one of the guys clean socks and jockey shorts.

It was in July of 1968 that our family finally moved into a leased three-bedroom home in Orland Park. I bought a second car, an old 1958 Ford sedan, to drive the ten miles to and from the commuter train station. It was a forty-minute ride to work on the Rock Island Line. The passengers sat in the same seats every day, four guys playing pinochle, two pairs playing cribbage, the rest of us reading the *Chicago Sun-Times* or working out of a briefcase. I preferred the *Sun-Times* because it was a tabloid paper and much easier to handle on the crowded train. Some guys read the *Chicago Tribune* by folding it a certain way, but I could never get the hang of it. From the downtown train station, it was a fifteen-minute walk to the office. Riverside Plaza was a brand-new building in the Loop on Wacker Drive, next to the Chicago River. Our MIS group had the top two floors plus a few other offices at scattered locations in the same building.

Gary Perkins's family, 1969

Our life in the suburbs was okay. We had young neighbors next door with children of preschool age, so our three had playmates. Orland Park wasn't much of a town. It was a residential community with few places to shop, but there were large shopping malls in some of the adjoining suburbs. We had a large yard for the kids. The backyards had no fences, so they had the run of the entire block. We had a concrete patio for cookouts.

We found that first relocation of our family to be somewhat difficult because we had lived six years in Rockford, where all three children had been born. Our youngest, Patrick, was just three months old when we moved. We had grown comfortable in Rockford and enjoyed times there with friends and neighbors. The move to a big metropolitan area was a major challenge for us. During this time, most families like ours had just one breadwinner, and wives normally were home with the children, especially while they were young. Our kids were less affected by the relocation because children of preschool age are quite carefree and make friends easily. I had the excitement of the new job and could readily see the progress that I was making. In Sharon's case, it was difficult for her to make a new home in a strange place with her husband gone for ten hours a day. Fortunately, she is outgoing and made new friends, primarily through our children, but it was hard for her to see any immediate benefit in moving. In spite of my bringing home a much larger paycheck, higher expenses in the city chewed up most of it.

The young mother next door stayed home with her four boys while her husband worked in the city, so she and Sharon grew to become close friends. There were some periods of friction between Sharon and a couple of the other women in the neighborhood, but she got along well with most of them. There would be times when I would catch a later train home at night because of extra work or after having a few drinks with the boys, and that would also cause some friction at home.

The MIS group in Chicago was bright and talented, but there were a lot of heavy drinkers in that group. In that regard, I had no trouble fitting in with those guys. It was common to have alcohol at lunch, and we were supported by liberal expense accounts. There were occasions when I got home after the kids had been put to bed.

By the summer of 1969, I had been authorized to hire an assistant to help implement the pilot plants. Rockford, New Orleans, and Rochester were now online. Jon Bial was brought on board, and he assisted me on the Rochester implementation. He could now work on his own to get the rest of the plants on the system. The five-year feasibility study had been completed at Chicago, and the decision was made to relocate the MIS group to the corporate offices in Tacoma, Washington. While most Chicago employees turned down the opportunity to relocate, there were about fifty of us who agreed to make the move. At age thirty, I was offered the management job of project leader for development, Container Division. I would have eight people, designers and programmers, working for me and would be given a big raise in salary. The company would also pay the expenses to move the family and would provide an interest-free loan for the down payment of a new home in the Tacoma area. I couldn't wait to break this great news to Sharon!

I knew that this would really heap stress on her if I didn't handle it just right. Fortunately, we had only lived in Orland Park for a year, and she didn't really like the place. I decided to point out all of the positives of moving the family 2,200 miles. It would be a great promotion with a big salary. We could now afford to buy our first home, and we could take our time to locate in a good community with a good school system. We would be making the move with others from Chicago, so we would be among friends out there. The winters are mild in Washington, and the area offers lots of outdoor recreation for family activities.

There really wasn't much of an alternative to making the move. I knew that my successor in Rockford wasn't making the grade, and I could have gone back there at my old job as office manager. I didn't mention that to her because it would have been a dead-end job for me. I didn't have enough experience yet in computer technology to land a comparable job for another company in Chicago or Rockford, so I stuck to the positives and convinced her that this move would be good for our family and good for my career. We would be foolish to pass this up when all expenses were going to be paid.

Another career opportunity had come up a year earlier. I turned it down. A former coworker of mine from the Rockford plant had taken a position with a pizzeria supply outfit in Chicago. It was rumored that the business had ties to the Mafia. He had been set up in an executive position, and when we met for lunch in Chicago one afternoon, he described a pizza box plant that they had bought (probably by some "strong-arm" method) and said they were in need of a plant manager. I offended my friend by replying that I didn't like his employer's business connections. He denied any Mafia affiliation, but I still had an uncomfortable feeling about the deal, and there was no way that I would work for the underground, no matter what salary they would be willing to offer. My Perkins forefathers had refused to work underground at the mines, and I was no different. I had to be above the grass, maintaining my independence. When I turned him down, that pretty much cooled our friendship.

Sharon was never definite in any major decision. She would discuss with me all of the pros and cons, but it was always my decision to make. She would always have a wait-and-see attitude, and it was no different in the move to Tacoma. This left me with the feeling that if things didn't work out, she would say, "I knew it," or, "We shouldn't have done it. It was your idea." After all the worry and negotiation was over, things always seemed to work out favorably for us in those early days. In one sense, there was a balance between my optimism and her reservation. I suppose she kept me grounded. The Man Upstairs may have had something to do with it too. He was looking out for us. With his help, gentle persuasion from me and from some of my coworkers at Weyerhaeuser, she finally agreed to make a house-hunting trip with me in July 1969 to Tacoma, Washington.

We looked for houses along with five other Chicago couples during a record heat wave where the temperatures were in the midnineties, a rare event in the Puget Sound area. After touring homes with a Realtor, all six couples would gather at the motel in late afternoon, break out the beer, laugh about our house-hunting adventures, then go out to dinner with all expenses paid by Weyerhaeuser. After traipsing through about six houses on the hottest day of all, Sharon's stress level had reached its peak. I made a wrong turn on the way back to the motel in Lakewood, and we were lost for a few minutes. We joined the others in one of the motel rooms, and after I walked down to the recreation room with a couple of the guys to shoot pool, Sharon suddenly broke down and began bawling. One of the other wives asked her what was wrong. She said, "Gary made a wrong turn!" For Sharon, the stress had been building for months over this relocation, and this one minor incident had obviously broken the dam. She had a real come-apart. We learned to laugh about it later and retold that story a number of times to family and friends.

Looking way, way back, I wonder if my great-grandfather James Perkins had encountered similar difficulties when he moved his family around this country a hundred years earlier. As a young lead miner, he had gone from Wisconsin to Colorado, to northern Michigan, then to Pennsylvania and back to Wisconsin. Some of these trips were close to a thousand miles by horse and wagon, and he was most certainly concerned for the safety of his wife and young children. Perhaps his young wife, Eliza Jane, thought that he, too, was chasing a dream. I wonder if she had broken down emotionally and bawled her eyes out like my Sharon had done. He must have been a persuasive man with a sense of optimism, willing to take risks to secure a future for his growing family. I was fortunate to inherit his genes. Sharon and I would relocate twice more before settling down for good while our three children finished high school. James, too, had finally returned to Benton, Wisconsin, to raise his family of nine children.

Perkins family in Puyallup, 1970

Sharon and I bought our very first home just south of Puyallup, Washington. It was newly built, surrounded by fir trees, and nestled into a country development with large lots. Weyerhaeuser Company advanced us $6,500 for use as a down payment, and we later learned that we were one of the few employees who repaid the interest-free note on schedule. Another couple from Chicago bought a house nearby. Ron Reid and I worked at MIS. His wife, Kathleen, and Sharon became close, and this turned out to be a long-term friendship.

Years later, in 1984, Ron would become my sponsor when I began treatment for alcoholism, but during those early years, we were good drinking buddies, along with five or six other coworkers who also liked their beer. Whether golfing, fishing, outdoor cooking, or just hanging out, we usually had a beer in hand. He and I made an attempt to quit drinking in 1970. Deep inside, we both knew that we had a drinking problem, but, typical of the alcoholic, we couldn't admit it to others, so we disguised our intentions by setting up a game where we abstained from drinking. Ron and I paid fifteen dollars a week into a pot, assuming that to be a conservative estimate of what we spent each week on booze. This was an honor system, and if we slipped or relapsed while on a business trip, for example, we had to pay a five-dollar penalty for each occurrence. We made sure that everyone in the office knew about this venture by drawing up a formal contract that we each signed and then posted on the office bulletin board for all to see. Our secretary opened a savings account at a local bank, and she deposited our contributions each week. She also posted a bar chart indicating the amount of penalties paid by each of us. We ended the contest after four months and split up just over $600. One of our coworkers at Weyerhaeuser asked, "What are you guys going to do with the money ... go out and get drunk?" We said, "Sure!"

We didn't drink it all up. Ron bought a new lawnmower with his share, and I bought a tent, sleeping bags, and camping gear that our family used for many years afterward.

We were no different from any other alcoholics. Most can't get past the stage of denial. Subconsciously we were reaching out, burdened with guilt and remorse, and wanting to get off the merry-go-round. While our drinking caused serious family problems and an occasional run-in with the cops, we hadn't reached bottom yet. The drinking hadn't yet become a serious detriment to our job performance (many alcoholics are also workaholics and overachievers), and those close to us never really confronted us about the drinking. Our wives complained to us and criticized our drinking habits but never served us with an ultimatum, nor did they attempt to force us into a treatment program. So at this stage, I still felt that I could do a better job of controlling my drinking. I continued to drive forward with my career, an overachiever who outperformed the competition as I took on more and more responsibility.

Because of adverse economic conditions during the latter part of 1970, top management at Weyerhaeuser was considering a major cut in our operating budget for systems development. They wanted to know precisely what further benefits could be expected by continuing the blue-sky development projects and, conversely, what harm would come from cutting back on this future development. Their subsequent decision would have a direct impact on my department, so I was chosen to make a presentation to the two senior vice presidents, explaining what we were doing and why. My two immediate bosses stood behind me while I flipped through the charts that I had prepared for the presentation. Whenever it appeared that certain parts of my talk were gaining positive acceptance, my bosses quickly stepped forward to take credit; when the reaction of the two vice presidents appeared questionable, they would hang back. That's the way of corporate politics.

A week later, the decision was made to downsize the entire MIS Department by one-third. Bill Hoss, the MIS department manager, chose Bill Waples and me to prepare a cut list for downsizing the department. Assigning this task to two midlevel managers was highly unusual. The department head would normally prepare the personnel severance list, but in this case he felt that Bill and I could be objective and that we would come up with a fair and impartial list of personnel to be cut from the department. He assigned us the responsibility on a Friday, and it was to be completed and submitted to him on Monday morning. He said no one would know who had prepared the cut list—"It will be our secret"—and he wanted it done over a weekend to "prevent any accidental leaks" prior to the announcement. He further stated that no one in the department was exempt from the cut list, including himself. To cut one-third of the MIS staff meant that our list would total thirty-three people, and Bill and I were to have it done by Monday!

Needless to say, this was a most difficult assignment. We had to choose the people to be terminated when the unemployment rate at this time was very high: 20 percent in the greater Seattle area. Some of our employees were in their forties with families and had relocated here from Chicago and points east. Bill and I spent the entire weekend in the corporate conference room with the shades pulled for privacy.

For the first few minutes Saturday morning, we just sat there and looked at each other, dumbfounded. We didn't know where to begin. We discussed some potential approaches to the problem but couldn't get a grasp on a method that would work out to our satisfaction. After an hour or two, we found ourselves just sitting and staring at a blank wall. That was when one of us decided that perhaps the best thing would be to walk away from it for a while. We drove over to a local bar, drank a couple of beers, and shot a game of pool.

Back at the conference room at noon, we hit upon a solution. Instead of considering people and personalities, we would first concentrate on the projects and determine which of those could be placed on a cut list to meet the one-third reduction. That approach would temporarily postpone the emotional aspect of the chore. Once we determined the list of projects remaining, we then determined the job skills required to support those projects. The third step then was to list all ninety-nine employees in the department and identify the skills of each person. It was late Sunday afternoon when we completed the final step of matching people skills to project requirements, an impersonal process that was similar to staffing a new business. The people who didn't match up to the needed skills wound up on the cut list. There were no politics involved, and we both felt that this was as fair as we could make it. To this day, only a handful of people know that Bill Waples and I prepared that cut list for the MIS Department.

In a letter to my mother on February 3, 1971, from Puyallup, Washington, I wrote:

*Dear Mom,*

*I hope this letter finds you in good health since it has been so long since we've heard from you. Have you been sick during the winter? It seems you've had a lot of snow in Wisconsin this year.*

*Judy said you've spent quite a lot of time in Benton to take care of the house. I'm addressing this to Madison as I assume you've returned by now.*

*We've had two or three inches of snow out here twice, and people had a lot of trouble driving when they aren't used to it. It's also quite wet here when it snows so the roads are pretty slippery. Of course, we "Easterners" don't have too much trouble with two to three inches of snow.*

*Our family has stayed healthy all winter except for a few colds. Patrick is coming down with chicken pox right now.*

*Peter and his buddy Mike up the street got a big applause when they sang a duet for their kindergarten class. The way he told it to us, he and Mike had been practicing one of the new hits: "I Think I Love You." So one day last week they simply volunteered to sing it for the class, and everybody stood up and clapped. Pete likes school and hates to miss a day (which is different from the way I used to be!). During one of our two snowfalls, I had a tough time talking Pete into skipping school so we could all go sleigh riding in the mountains. I had to promise him that I would write a note to his teacher.*

*Pam has been selling mint candy for the Campfire Girls. She's a "Bluebird," which is like the Brownie Scouts, and she goes to den meetings on Wednesdays. We can't believe she's nine already. She has quite a few girlfriends, and we're forever hauling her somewhere. On her birthday, we took Pam, three of her girlfriends, and our two boys to Shakey's for pizza. They gave away balloons and candy and played "Happy Birthday" for her. That gang sure ate a lot of pizza! It cost me fourteen dollars!*

*Both Pam and Peter are coming and going with their school friends and also to and from our neighbors'. Patrick spends most of his time around the house, and he's a real "bugger." He never shuts up! When he's talking, (which is all the time), you had better pay attention! He shadows you from one end of the house to the other. Sometimes we can talk him into going downstairs and playing in the family room. Ten minutes later, he's right back with a few more things to say. When he grows up, he'll probably be a salesman, maybe for baby photos. Remember your encounter, Mom, with that photo salesman in Rockford about eight years ago?*

*I had a friend from the office at the house one night who had never met our kids. This was about two weeks before Christmas, and Patrick came up to him and said, "Will you give me fifteen dollars?" Joe asked him what he wanted the money for, and Patrick said, "I need some Hot Wheels!"*

*Well, he later got five or six little Hot Wheels cars from Santa, and he now carries them around with him all the time; even takes them to bed!*

*Sharon has been spending whatever free time she can manage at the sewing machine. She has a whole closet full of dresses, pant suits, robes, etc.*

*My latest project was building cabinets in the garage. One section has a countertop with a hole in it and a garbage can underneath to catch waste board scraps, sawdust, etc. I found an old toilet seat, painted it bright yellow, and put it over the hole in the countertop. We're hoping that, during one of our parties, someone will refrain from using it for the wrong purpose!*

*Well, it's about midnight, so I guess I'll hit the sack. Take good care of yourself and let us know when you want to come out for a visit.*

*Happy Birthday, Mom!*

*/ Gary*

\* \* \* \* \* \*

My entire project of future systems development was one of the first to be cut. Had we not taken a fair and nonpolitical approach, I could have saved part of it, but it wouldn't have been the right thing to do when people's careers were at stake. Most of my people had the skills required to be reassigned to other projects; others were put on the cut list, including myself.

The company wanted me to join the Containerboard Division and head up computer applications for their data-processing department at the new paper mill in Enid, Oklahoma. In this midlevel management position, I wouldn't have the challenge of designing and implementing new systems but would be charged with administering the support and maintenance of routine systems for accounting, production, and sales. When this offer was made to me, I assured Sharon that we wouldn't consider moving the family to Oklahoma and that this type of job in a different division of the company didn't appeal to me.

This was to become an important turning point in my career at Weyerhaeuser. It was early 1971. A few months earlier, I had graduated from Weyerhaeuser Management School, class number fourteen. The company accepted twelve nominees at a time for this school, beginning with George Weyerhaeuser and his senior management team as class number one. As a member of the fourteenth group of twelve managers, one could assume that I was in the top 170 of 40,000 employees. At any rate, I was extremely honored to have been nominated and chosen for this opportunity. My class included midlevel managers from saw mills, paper mills, plywood plants, and other operations within Weyerhaeuser, including a member of the Corporate Public Relations Department. The school was held offsite, an intensive four-week program where we were locked up in a hotel night and day. In addition to the Manpower Development staff, the company contracted a dozen outside experts to conduct the various classes. They had us engaged for about sixteen hours each day.

One segment of the school dealt with self-analysis, where they encouraged each of us to take a personal inventory of our skills and interests. We broke down into groups of four and critiqued each other as managers. It was during this process that I realized that over the last few years I had transitioned into staff or a supporting type of manager as opposed to "line management" responsibilities. My career goal, which Sharon and I had discussed years earlier at the kitchen table in Rockford, had been to become a plant general manager, and I now knew that this would be an ideal time for me to get back into the "infantry," closer to the direct operating end of the business and line management.

Further thought led me to decide that a move into the sales area would be a wise choice because no one in the packaging industry could become a general manager if they lacked direct sales experience. The corrugated box business was very competitive, and a strong sales and marketing effort was central to the success of a plant operation. Sharon and I had more serious conversations about the current situation. We were at a major crossroads in my career in the packaging industry. My job was being eliminated at the corporate office, and we had to explore options. As a family, we wanted to remain in the Pacific Northwest if possible because we had made a lot of close friends and the kids were at school age. Pam was in the third grade, and Peter had just entered kindergarten. Quality of life was good in the Puget Sound region. I would try to land a sales job there in the Northwest.

# CHAPTER 15

# CHICAGO ONE MORE TIME

When I told my boss at MIS that I wasn't willing to take the management position in Oklahoma and had plans to reenter the corrugated container business, this time in the sales field, he offered his support by suggesting that I talk to the personnel department about finding a sales position in the Pacific Northwest. I didn't have a lot of faith in personnel people. During my nine years with Weyerhaeuser, I had gained an unusually broad work experience and felt that I had a good track record, so I got on the phone and took advantage of my network of contacts within the company.

The Container Division vice president, a former sales manager, said he was glad to hear that I had chosen sales as my next career step and suggested that I talk to the Western Region vice president. I did meet with him, but nothing materialized. The aerospace industry on the West Coast was hard hit by the loss of federal contracts, and there was a 20 percent unemployment rate in the Seattle area. He said it wasn't much better in California. Furthermore, Boeing, the largest employer in Seattle, had laid off a great number of their employees, and they were applying for work here at Weyerhaeuser with little success. The Western Region boss admired my decision to go into sales but said, "Your timing is bad for this move. Maybe you should wait for a better time." He also pointed out to me that I would have to accept an entry-level position in sales despite having worked nine years for the company, four of those in management. The move into sales would force me to accept a major cut in salary, and he wanted me to be aware of that.

Sharon and I talked it over some more. She wanted me to be happy in my work and to be able to pursue my long-range plans, but she also hated the thought of having to move once again. She left the decision up to me. I knew she wanted to stay in the Northwest, just as I did, and there was a chance that I could land a lower-level job in MIS, such as in the payroll or accounting EDP systems, but taking a backward step can be disastrous to a career. If I remained in MIS, I would be forever cast as a computer guy and, in a company of that size, would be lost in the shuffle. If I wanted to pursue my goal to become a general manager, I would have to make the move out of MIS. It was now or never, in my mind.

I made more phone calls to contacts within Weyerhaeuser Company and was tentatively offered sales positions at three locations: New Orleans, New York City, and the Upper Midwest. This North Central Region would be my best opportunity because the market is very provincial in the South. A "Yankee" would have a tough sell in that part of the country, and it would be unlikely for me to be successful in that "good, old boys" network. Neither Sharon nor I wanted any part of the Big Apple, so we focused on the nine plants in the North Central Region with headquarters in Chicago. The vice president there was Ed Grain, a former Baltimore Colts linesman who had been the boss at MIS in Chicago when I was there a couple of years back. He knew me well, was pleased to know that I had decided to get into sales, and said he had opportunities for me in Wisconsin, Iowa, Minnesota, and Chicago. "Go visit these plants and take your pick," he said. "Once you make a decision, we will have to work out something on your moving expenses." That seemed to me his major concern, so I immediately phoned my boss in MIS and asked if he would be willing to pick up my moving expenses of about $11,000.

When MIS agreed to pay for my move, I arranged to make my first plant visit to Manitowoc, Wisconsin. After the visit, I phoned Sharon and told her that the market there was very stagnant, the operation was quite provincial, and the general manager was a throwback from the 1950s. I was sorry that our first choice of Wisconsin wasn't going to work out. We weren't too keen on Minnesota or Iowa, either.

Chicago appeared to be the best opportunity. It was a fast-paced, highly competitive market, and since I was going into direct sales for the first time, this would be an opportunity to very quickly determine whether I was cut out for sales. If I was going to fall flat on my face, I wanted to do it sooner rather than later. When I informed Ed of my decision, he said, "I was hoping that you would decide on Chicago. You won't regret this move. You can close sales deals faster here than anywhere else. If you lose an account, there are three more just down the street."

Back in Puyallup, Sharon and I had to face the consequences of making yet another move. We had only been in our new home for a year and a half. I promised her that we would return to the Seattle/ Tacoma area within a few short years. We both liked that area. But now we had to put our home on the market and find another place to live in the suburbs of Chicago with good schools for the kids. "That wasn't the half of it," as my father would say. We also had to absorb a 30 percent reduction in salary while spending far more for a home in the more expensive Chicago suburbs. I was very apprehensive because any number of things could go wrong in this venture, not the least of which could be my failure in the sales field. I tried my best to maintain a positive attitude around Sharon and the kids. In truth, the kids weren't bothered at all about moving to Chicago. It was just another childhood adventure for them. On our trip back there, we planned to make side trips to visit San Francisco and Reno. That kept the spirits up.

One more complication cropped up unexpectedly when Sharon had to have surgery a couple of weeks prior to our planned house-hunting trip to Chicago. The doctor forbade her to fly, so I had to take on the task of finding a house. She and I sat down together and went through the Kepner-Tregoe decision analysis method where we listed all of the "musts" and "wants" in a home, school, and neighborhood environment, then ranked them by priority. I commuted from Puyallup to Chicago every other weekend. After spending a full day on my new job where I was making cold calls in the Chicago market, I would then drive out to the suburbs, meet with a real estate agent, and look at a couple of houses. The Kepner-Tregoe list made the search much more efficient because we could zero in on just the homes that met the criteria. I took a lot of photos of homes that met our needs and brought them home to Sharon. After a couple of weeks, she chose the tri-level in Woodridge with the open kitchen, formal dining room, and large recreation room. I liked it because it offered an opportunity for cosmetic improvements and had been on the market for over a year, which allowed us to make a much lower offer. We decided to put in an extremely low offer and hope for the best. The house had been on the market for over a year due primarily to the homeowners' poor choice of colors: olive carpet with salmon walls upstairs and turquoise walls with pink bath fixtures in the lower bath. We saw this as an easy fix. Our low offer was accepted.

I had also visited the elementary school in Woodridge and was favorably impressed. The schools in DuPage County were highly ranked, but, of course, that meant higher-than-average real estate taxes.

Our friends gave us a farewell party in Tacoma, and over a few beers my coworkers at Weyerhaeuser said that they really envied us for having the guts to leave the protective cocoon of the corporate office, accept a big cut in pay, and begin a new career challenge. Some of them felt that, following the cutback at the corporate office, they were stuck in jobs that were no longer exciting. It was years later that a couple of these friends confided in me that they were disappointed in their jobs during the final ten years before retirement but felt that they couldn't change employment because of the high level of pay and benefits that they were receiving.

I suppose my great-grandfather James, the lead miner, would describe my move into sales as going "below the grass," taking an underground job. It was dangerous in some sense and perhaps could prove to be an unpleasant work environment, but I was hopeful that it would pay off in the long run and gain me the sales experience I needed to fulfill my lifelong goal. Somehow I was confident that I would someday get back on top, above the grass, and regain that high visibility that I felt was necessary to succeed within the broad scope of a large corporation.

While it appeared to some of my colleagues that my action displayed courage, I didn't see it that way. My decision to venture into the sales field and further pursue my chosen career goal was based upon my need to gain personal satisfaction. I wanted to be happy in my work, not stuck in a rut somewhere, simply going through the motions and living with a sense of regret.

I suppose one could call this decision a demonstration of my independence, perhaps rooted in my Cornish heritage. Those "tinners" and lead miners from Britain were a stubborn, independent lot. My father displayed those characteristics when the mines closed at the end of World War II. He passed up opportunities to take higher-paying jobs in the Dubuque factories because he didn't like that type of work. He enjoyed outdoor work like farming and aboveground jobs at the mines. He took the farmhand job in the middle 1940s instead of a factory job despite the big difference in wages. Some men went into debt at that time to purchase their own dairy farms, but not my dad. He didn't want to go into debt and become tied to some banker. He was satisfied to work for wages, as long as he did what he enjoyed and could remain somewhat independent. His father and brothers demonstrated these same characteristics, so the Cornish heritage was quite apparent in the Perkins family, one generation after another.

In April 1971, we made the move and spent four years in the Chicago suburb of Woodridge, southwest of the city. It was a good neighborhood, next to an elementary school, and there were a lot of families of our age living there. During the first two years, I sold a lot of new business in Chicago and won back the huge M&M Mars candy account that had been lost by my predecessor. I'll never forget the first sales call I made to the purchasing manager and his boss at their Chicago office. When we first met, the director of purchasing said to me, "We've got nothing against you, Gary, but as far as we're concerned, Weyerhaeuser is out of here!" That set me back, but not for long. "Can I buy you guys a cup of coffee? I'd like to at least learn why you feel that way." He agreed that they owed me that, and the three of us had a half-hour discussion in their company cafeteria where they specified their problems with us as a supplier. After a few minutes, the conversation took a more casual turn, and the director asked me if Weyerhaeuser manufactured "beauty bark." I told him that yes, it's a byproduct from our sawmills in the Northwest and that I had purchased it in the past for my lawn. He said, "I was thinking about applying some in my yard. I'll bet it's a lot cheaper out there than it is in Chicago." I responded, "Yeah, I suppose so." Nothing more was said about the subject. I told them that we had valued their business in the past and that I would review their problems with us and report back to them soon.

I hadn't moved my family to Chicago yet, so two weeks later when the moving van arrived at our home in Puyallup, Washington, I loaded twelve bags of beauty bark in the back of the trailer. A couple of days after we moved into our new home in Woodridge, I made a sales call at M&M Mars and asked the director of purchasing, "Where do you want the beauty bark delivered?" I delivered the bark to his house in the northwest suburbs the following Saturday with a borrowed pickup truck. I kept out two bags for myself. I was learning something about "Chicago sales techniques."

The Mars account maintained five suppliers of corrugated boxes and bought five semitruck loads per day. It was a very big account. Over the next twelve-month period, our volume gradually increased to reach a 20 percent share at $330,000 per year. At that point, we were ranked at number one in service to Mars. I was learning the sales game, and this victory played a great part in my gaining some high visibility within Weyerhaeuser. I was well on the way to selling a million dollars of product. Once again, I was working above the grass.

A year later, I nailed the Keebler Biscuit account, following six months of hard work. Don Anderson, the purchasing agent, was a tough sell, and I had to remain persistent to finally get my foot in the door. It was less than three days after writing my first order from Keebler that I found a note on my desk. Our Chicago sales manager instructed me to surrender Keebler to our National Accounts Division. When questioned, he pointed out that Keebler had eight locations around the country, and that fact alone qualified them as a national account. I argued that the National Accounts team hadn't sold any of the other locations, so this one should remain as my Chicago account. We had a big go-round over this. He knew that I had been working hard on this for six months, and we had discussed strategy on this project. I had kept him apprised of my progress throughout this time. Now he was caving in to the National Accounts manager. He knew that I was right about this, and he should have backed me up. I was working for a weak sales manager who didn't want me to rock the boat. He said, "Take it easy, Gary. You're selling enough business. Besides, you're on straight salary with no commission, so this isn't going to cost you anything. Just take it easy; enjoy yourself; play more golf." I told him that I was far too young for semiretirement!

I was getting impatient in Chicago. Ed Grain had moved up to the corporate office, and with this weak sales manager who preferred to play politics, my sales position here was likely to become a dead end. I could see that I would be lost in the shuffle here in Chicago. I made some phone calls to the Pacific Northwest, but Weyerhaeuser offered no sales opportunities out there. Economic conditions remained depressed. After some weeks of continued mental anguish, I concluded that while I had gained some success in the sales field with less than three years of experience, I would have to make a job change. A man has to be happy in his work.

It would not be an easy decision to leave Weyerhaeuser because they had been a good employer. Over the past eleven years, they had treated me well and invested in me by sending me to a number of outside classes and seminars: a number of computer classes, a project management seminar called Critical Path Method, the prestigious Weyerhaeuser Management School, and, most recently, a sales training seminar when I took the job in Chicago. The sales training was beneficial, but I learned much more by breaking into the dynamic Chicago market. It had been the right decision because Chicago gave me the opportunity to learn sales techniques in a short period of time.

Going into sales for the first time, I didn't have the greatest respect for salesmen. To my mind, they were a bunch of "good-time Charlies" with a line of bull and a fat expense account—a bunch of prostitutes who lowballed prices and bought the business by wining and dining the customers. I soon learned that there was much more to this profession than I had imagined. There are important techniques to be learned in a sales seminar, but in the real world you have to establish a relationship with a customer before you attempt to sell them. These buyers are professional purchasing agents, and when you meet one for the first time, they are quite skeptical of you and the company you represent. In repeated calls on the prospect, you try to move them from skepticism to the quizzical stage and then, finally, to a level of commitment where they are ready to buy from you. They won't write out a purchase order unless they have full confidence that you and your company will provide the service and quality they require. These purchasing agents can be very selective because, in Chicago especially, it is a buyer's market. There are six or eight competitors vying for the business. A study in 1972 revealed that corrugated boxes were the third most competitive product in the Chicago market following steel and chemicals.

I soon learned that if you rush the sale by lowballing a price to get a quick order, it will be a short-term victory because you will lose that business when the next guy comes in and does the same thing. You cause the price level to drop and end up with no business, which is a cardinal sin in sales. Conversely, when you spend some time to establish a relationship with the buyer over several personal sales calls at his place of business, he will be at the "commitment" level and will protect your interest because he wants you as his supplier. When you take the time, you will detect his particular problem with his current supplier: service or quality, for example. This is crucial because you can then convince him that you and your company can offer improvement in those specific areas. This information is not easy to obtain. He won't freely divulge his problems; you've got to dig for them. Observation is the key. Get out into his plant and see what's going on; talk to plant employees; get to know other key people at his plant. Most buyers are willing to oblige you with a plant tour. They enjoy showing off their operation, and it shows that you are truly interested in their business operation. A box salesman can learn a lot by walking around a sales prospect's production floor if you stay alert for opportunities. Once you determine his business problem or an idea for process improvement, you can ask for a trial order, a chance to make him a hero with his employer. If he has confidence in you at this stage, he will ask you to quote a price.

I learned the hard way never to quote prices too soon. When I had asked to quote some items on my first or second sales call, the buyer always had a list of items handy in his desk drawer: "Here, quote these." When I came back with prices, I never got an order because he would always tell me my prices were too high. I hadn't taken the time to build a relationship, so even if my prices were lower, I had no chance of getting the business. He would simply show my prices to his current supplier and tell him, "Here, look at these prices from Weyerhaeuser. If they can sell boxes cheaper, so can you." I committed the cardinal sin of lowering the customer's price without getting the business.

The professional salesman will learn to feel out the price. Ideally, you want to be as close as possible to his current price level, and if he has serious problems with his current supplier, you may get the business at a percent or two higher. I found that if a buyer was serious about changing suppliers, he would often provide me with his current price because he had a genuine need for my help and was willing to "guide me in." One method was to leave his supplier's price list on his desk while he left the room or turned away to talk to someone. I became quite proficient at reading numbers upside down from across his desk.

My years of experience in the Rockford plant had given me a leg up in sales because I had a thorough knowledge of the corrugated box plant operation. After making a few calls on a new prospect, I would offer to redesign his packaging or propose a change in the printing or artwork on the package. Sometimes he would have a new product that would require a packaging design. My plant experience would enable me to find a less expensive way to produce the boxes, saving the prospective customer a few cents per item. There were several instances where my box design saved packing labor in the plant, another benefit of taking the time for a tour of his production department.

The Chicago market had been good to me, and I was able to open a good number of new accounts for Weyerhaeuser. After just two years, I had gained confidence in my ability to sell packaging and considered myself a professional salesman, but I had already reached a plateau in Chicago with the company because of a weak sales manager. He had gotten his job due to politics (his father was a general manager in New England), and I didn't want to be coasting along in a dead-end position. I wanted to open up a lot more business and build on my sales experience. I couldn't do that with Weyerhaeuser in Chicago. I felt confident about finding a sales job with a competitor, so, reluctantly, I turned in my resignation and left Weyerhaeuser Company after twelve years of employment. Sharon and I took the kids up to Wisconsin, where we relaxed and spent a few days camping and fishing. I needed to unwind. I would look for a job later.

The Chicago economy was strong, and I soon landed a sales job with Hoerner-Waldorf, a subsidiary of Champion International, another Fortune 500 company. Their plant in Waukegan, Illinois, manufactured custom corrugated boxes, the same as Weyerhaeuser, but this plant was much larger than most. They preferred manufacturing large double-wall boxes for bulky products that were difficult to package. One of their largest accounts was OMC Corp, makers of Johnson and Evinrude boat motors. Bob was Hoerner's talented packaging engineer, and we got along fine. He was a country boy from Fort Dodge, Iowa, and could solve most any packaging design challenge.

One of my top sales prospects was Tru-Value Hardware. Their Carpentersville plant manufactured lawn mowers, and they bought large volumes of corrugated boxes, presently supplied by four of our competitors. I had quoted some prices, but we had yet to land our first order.

In October 1974, they introduced a rototiller for the first time. When I found out about it, they had already selected a box design from among proposals by five other companies. Reluctantly, they agreed to allow me to make a last-minute design proposal, but they had only one prototype, and it was due to be shipped to K-Mart in Detroit the next day. I couldn't take it out of the plant, so I took a number of key measurements of the tiller as their engineers looked amusingly over my shoulder. When I had finished, one of them said, "You're going to come up with a packaging design for this machine based on that pencil sketch you just made?" I know they were laughing among themselves after I left.

That afternoon and evening, I drove to several hardware and department store outlets to look for a rototiller with a similar shape to the Tru-Value prototype. After three stops, I found a Toro machine at a J.C. Penney store that looked like a good candidate. I purchased it using Sharon's J.C. Penney credit card and told them to leave it in the box. The next morning, I lugged the Toro tiller into the Waukegan plant and set it on one of the benches in the design lab. I worked alongside Bob, our designer, as we carefully unpacked the tiller and inspected the package it came in. He then took my rough sketch and key measurements and designed a new box with a simplified yet stronger inner packing that required less material than the existing pack. By reducing the material required, we could sell the package at a lower price. Bob did an amazing job.

After Tru-Value received the prototype returned from Detroit, I drove out to the Carpentersville plant with our newly designed package. The purchasing agent and I met with those same engineers in their lab where they slipped the tiller into our package. With a minor modification here and there, it fit perfectly. Those engineers were amazed.

We drop-tested the product, and our design held up well. When I presented the price quotation, we came in lower than the other competitors, and I was rewarded with the order for the first shipment. Bill Eustice, the sales manager at Hoerner, joined Bob and me that evening for a few beers in celebration. He put them on his expense account. The next day, I returned the Toro tiller to Penney's and was granted full credit on Sharon's charge account. I told her about it later.

I enjoyed making cold calls on new prospects; not many salesmen did. Most were more comfortable when calling on the buyers they had known for some time and were reluctant to find new business. Bill Eustice and I were talking about that one day in his office. He appreciated my efforts in bringing new accounts into the Waukegan plant. I told him about a young salesman I had worked with at Weyerhaeuser. He was just out of college and found sales to be a lonely business. He was always asking me to make joint calls with him where we would both call on some of his new prospects for the first time. We would make these calls together a couple of times a week until I told him that I was too busy with my own accounts and wouldn't be able to join up with him that often. He told me that he didn't like working alone, was having no success in opening up new business, and spent most of the day just driving around with the radio cranked up. I told him that a salesman has to be self-motivated. Granted, it can be a lonely feeling when you've had a bad day in sales. Getting turned down time after time can make you feel depressed, but just like the football player who feels all beat up after a loss on Sunday, he has to pick himself up and get motivated for the next game. We've all had those bad days, but there were times when the last sales call of the day turned out to be a winner. That would charge you up where you wanted to make another call, but it was too late in the day. At times like that, you wanted to work all night. He wasn't convinced; he left Weyerhaeuser after a few months and returned home to Oklahoma. He phoned me a few months later and told me he was selling real estate there. He liked it better because he had clients in the car with him when they looked at homes. I guess he was more successful when he had people around him.

The Hoerner-Waldorf plant in Waukegan was designed to produce corrugated boxes for large bulky products, so I concentrated my sales efforts accordingly. I sold an account in the Chicago suburbs that manufactured riding lawn mowers. They built the mowers on an assembly line, and the mower came off the line mounted on a wooden base pallet. We furnished a large double-wall box with two-color printing that slipped down over the top of the mower and then was stapled to the wooden base pallet. They bought a couple of truckloads of boxes each month, so it was a good account.

In addition to the purchasing agent, I developed a good relationship with the two engineers who designed the mowers. Mike and Joe were from Nebraska, graduated from the university there, and had all the Cornhuskers gear to prove it: red coffee cups, sweatshirts, and hats. They liked their beer, and we often had a couple when I took them out for lunch. Sometimes I would wind up my workday in their area and arrange to meet them after work at a neighborhood bar, where we would shoot pool and drink a few pitchers. They could really put the beer away. Mike told me that they never drank during the month of

February, however. I assumed that they gave it up for Lent each year, but he said, "No, we just want to assure ourselves that we're not alcoholics by abstaining from alcohol for a full month."

I invited Mike to the annual fishing trip sponsored by Hoerner-Waldorf. Dick Hoerner, the founder of the business, owned a couple of cottages on an island on Lake Vermillion in northern Minnesota. The Hoerner sales force drove up there each spring with a dozen customer clients to enjoy three days of fishing for walleye pike. The cottages had running water and indoor plumbing, but we had to do our own cooking. The customers were required to pitch in with the cooking and other chores as well. Anyone who couldn't cook was assigned to dishwashing detail. It was a great way to unwind for a few days and get the purchasing agents away from their high-stress jobs in the city.

Mike and I shared a boat that was equipped with an outboard motor, and we would start fishing with the rest of the party just after daybreak each day. We were close to the Canadian border, and it was cold up there in May. Ice remained along the shoreline in places. We caught a few walleyes the first day, then limited on the second. On the third day, it was cold and breezy with a light rain falling. Mike and I were hunched down in the boat with our fishing poles set in pole holders. Mike's parka was Nebraska red, of course. He told me that he was raised in Yahoo, Nebraska, and his fishing experience was limited to the riverbank variety. He was really enjoying this lake fishing in spite of the weather.

After an hour and a half of pure boredom and chill-to-the-bone dampness, my fishing rod jerked, and the reel began to sing as the line went streaming out. I had a big fish on there! I worked with it for about a half hour in the misting rain until I finally got it up near the boat. It was a big northern pike that looked to be over two feet long, and when it saw the boat and Mike's red parka, it took off again. It ran and ran; the line was disappearing on my reel, and I cautiously and gently tightened the drag, hoping it wouldn't break the light eight-pound test line.

Somehow I managed to get this monster up toward the boat without snapping the line and yelled at Mike to grab the net. All we had was a small net for walleye. "That fish will never fit in this net," he said. I told him our only hope was for him to make one quick swipe, capture its head, and sweep it up and into the boat. He said he had never netted a fish, so I told him to hold the net in the water so it would be invisible to the fish and get ready. "Does it have teeth?" he asked. "Yeah, but don't worry. Just get the net on its head and throw it in the boat!"

Mike was a hero. He made one big sweep, and the big pike landed in the boat right in front of me. It started thrashing around as I tried to hold on and keep it from jumping out of the shallow lake boat. We had no gaff on board, so I grabbed an oar and tried to beat it on the head, with little success. Then I remembered reading an article in *Field & Stream* that described a method of paralyzing a fish by grabbing its eyeballs with your thumb and middle finger. As soon as I did that, the fish went limp.

We cranked up the motor and headed back to camp, certain that we had won a prize for the largest fish. We measured the length at forty-two inches. It was a female and had just come off spawn because her belly was flabby. She weighed in at twenty-two pounds, ten ounces. I was later notified in September that I had come in second for the season's largest fish, so I didn't win the canoe and electric motor. We stopped near Duluth on the way home, where I left the fish with a taxidermist. I just had to have that one mounted!

The new business that I sold fit well in the Waukegan plant because I got to know the needs of their operation. I spent time with the guys in production and made sure I sold "to the plant." When the business ran well in the plant and they made a good profit, then I was assured that my customer would get good quality and service from us. It became a win-win situation: good for our plant and good for the customer. It's important to sell the plant as well as the customer. I spent time with the plant personnel at a local watering hole after work and sometimes made the long drive home to Woodridge with a few beers under my belt. That posed a problem one winter evening during a snowstorm. I rear-ended a taxicab in Chicago when it stopped in the middle of the street to pick up a fare. The Chicago cops detected alcohol on my breath and told me to leave the car there and take a ride with them to the police station. They sat me down on a bench at the station and brought me cup after cup of black coffee. After a couple of hours, they drove me back to my car with the smashed grille and told me, "Merry Christmas. Drive safely." No ticket was written. I was lucky this time. In a depressed state of remorse, I knew that I had to control my drinking and vowed not to let this happen again. Of course, it would happen again because I hadn't come to that stage yet where I could admit that I was powerless over alcohol.

I worked for Hoerner for a couple of years and throughout that time maintained contact with potential employers in the Pacific Northwest. I had made the promise to Sharon that we would return to the Northwest, and neither of us could forget it. She made sure of that. To be honest, I missed that area as much as she did.

Finally, during the summer of 1975, I had gotten some positive feedback from three different packaging companies in the Seattle/Tacoma region. They were willing to interview me if I could get out there. I bought an airline ticket and then told Bob Conrad, the general manager at Hoerner-Waldorf, that I would be interviewing for a potential job out there. I told him that I would give him a month's notice if I accepted a position. This was a risky thing to do, but I wanted to be up front with him; besides, word travels fast in the box business. Bob wished me good luck and said, "I know your family wants to return to Seattle. I like that area myself. If you don't land a job, Gary, you still have one here."

Menasha Corporation needed a sales representative for their corrugated box plant in Tacoma, Washington, and of the three opportunities out there, it was the best offer.

Fibreboard Corporation had made me an interesting offer, but it would have required relocating our family to Phoenix. I would be selling mostly in New Mexico and west Texas, and when I had sold a suitable market share, Fibreboard would build a new plant in El Paso, whereupon I would be named general manager.

I told Sharon that I wouldn't pursue this opportunity any further, however. As a family, we preferred to locate in the Pacific Northwest. We agreed that the Menasha offer in Tacoma was our best bet.

Before the Menasha sales manager could put me on the payroll, however, I would have to visit their corporate office in Neenah, Wisconsin, and meet the upper management—"just as a formality," he said. They would pay my expenses for the trip.

A few days after returning home to Woodridge, I drove up to Neenah and met Len Tweedie, the senior vice president of their Container Division. After a brief interview and tour of the offices, he asked me to spend a half hour with their industrial psychologist, Dr. Bud Green.

When I walked into Dr. Green's office, I expected that he would want me to fill out one of those psychology forms, look at puddles of ink on a sheet of paper and describe what I saw, or something of that nature. Instead, he gestured toward a lone chair in the center of his spacious office, sat down on a chair opposite me, and said, "Tell me about yourself."

I was caught speechless for a moment, then quickly responded, "Well, I was born at an early age …" With that, he broke up. We both had a good laugh, and the interview went smoothly from there.

I accepted the sales job with Menasha, and in August 1975, we were finally on our way back to the Northwest. While this was our family's fourth relocation, these moves are always traumatic in many ways. We had made a lot of close friends in Woodridge, and our families in Wisconsin were close enough for weekend visits. My promise four years earlier of getting the family back to the Northwest had now lost some of its luster as far as Sharon was concerned. Now that the time had come, she had gradually grown negative about the thought of having to pull up roots again. We got into some heated arguments, which led first to hurt feelings, then anger, and at one point I told her, "You're always a move behind." That comment added more fuel to the fire.

Some ten years later, I would learn that an alcoholic person such as I would often be manipulative, and perhaps that was the case in this instance. While we had had a series of discussions prior to my job change and the subsequent decision to move back to the Northwest, I had been persuasive throughout these conversations, and I suppose I may have been manipulative in some sense. I also determined later on that I had workaholic tendencies because alcoholics are often overachievers as well. I was never satisfied to remain in one career position for long. I had to climb the next mountain. During a therapy session much later, in 1984, I told how my career promotions provided only a brief personal satisfaction for me. I felt that rather than having climbed the mountain, the mountain came down to meet me. In other words, the job wasn't as big as I had thought it would be, and soon I would be looking around for the next one. In this move back to the Northwest, I felt that I was fulfilling a promise to the family, but in all reality I may have been manipulating the family so that I could push on toward my long-range career goal. I'm not sure of my motives. It may have been a combination of the two, but in any regard, I was certain that the family would benefit from this move. I would make sure of that.

My mother-in-law, Florence O'Flahrity, was also upset about our family once again leaving the Midwest. She and Bob had been suffering through a disappointing marriage for years, and Florence's whole world revolved around her only three grandchildren. Whenever we had gone to Wisconsin for a weekend, we always stayed overnight at Florence's, never at my folks' home in Benton. I would go to Benton by myself on Sunday afternoon, or maybe take one or two of the kids with me if they wanted to go. My mother was disappointed if she didn't see her grandchildren, and she always asked, "And how is Sharon?"

As we approached the time to pack up and leave Woodridge, we decided to take Florence with us. To make peace in the family, I said, "We will be driving the station wagon out to Seattle. She can ride along, then stay with us for a while." It didn't require much coaxing for her to make the trip, but she worried about Bob getting drunk and burning the house down while she was away.

After the moving crew came and packed up our household furnishings and the van pulled away, we drove up to Wisconsin and picked up Grandma Florence. We then drove eight miles west to Benton to say good-bye to my mother and sisters, and made another stop near Boscobel for a brief visit with my uncle Bill Perkins and his two boys before getting on Interstate 90 for the trip west.

We had made this trip three years earlier to the Seattle area during a family vacation and visited friends out there. At that time, we took the tent and camping gear that I had bought with my "booze prohibition" fund that Ron and I had accumulated during the wager. That trip was one of the happiest family experiences of all our years together. With no television or telephones for those three weeks, it brought our family much closer. We had loaded up the station wagon with my custom-made rack on the roof and left Woodridge with an open plan. We stayed at a campground in Minnesota the first night but were kept awake by hundreds of drunken fishermen. We weren't aware of the opening of the walleye season in Minnesota.

In Medora, North Dakota, we stayed in a campground near the Badlands. When Pam noticed a "Horses for Rent" sign along a nearby road, she urged us to stay an extra day so we could take a trail ride in the scenic Badlands. I don't believe Sharon had ever ridden before, and she needed a bit of help from the trail guide. Pat was only four years old, so they put him aboard a short-legged pony. That led to his getting his feet wet when we forded a stream. Pat was really fond of the little pony and wanted to take it home with us. "Where would you keep it?" Sharon asked. "We could tie it to the kitchen table," he responded.

Now, four years later in 1975, we were following this same route. On this trip, we stayed in motels instead of tent camping because we had to be at our new home in Redmond by the time the moving van arrived with our household goods. Grandma Florence enjoyed the trip. She was able to spend a few days with her grandchildren and saw a lot of the West for the first time. She kept a journal, and as we traveled through the Rocky Mountain states, she made entries describing again and again: "The deep blue sky and majestic mountains ... the deep blue sky and majestic mountains ..." We had a lot of fun when she read it aloud to us and realized how redundant it was.

The selection of the house in Redmond had been typical of our prior experiences where the final decision was always left up to me. Sharon would tell me what she wanted; I would make a list and then ask her to rank musts and wants as we had done prior to the move to Woodridge, near Chicago. As we reviewed the listings, we could then eliminate those that didn't match up, and this process kept our number of choices to a minimum. When we had purchased our very first home in 1969 near Puyallup, we had looked at far too many houses, and all of that confusion and stress was tiring. That ordeal caused Sharon to finally break down and cry at the end of the day. In Woodridge, I was forced to select the house because Sharon had had cancer surgery and couldn't make the flight. I always treated the purchase of a house as an investment opportunity. I could make most improvements myself and then sell it at a profit to build up our equity. We were able to roll the equity forward as we went from one home to another. After making improvements over a four-year period at Woodridge, for example, we were able to sell the house in three days with a nice gain in capital. Upon the return to the Northwest in 1975, Sharon wanted a level-entry, ranch-style home with a full basement. As a rule, they don't build homes in that area with a basement, but I managed to find three of them scattered among the communities of Bellevue, Edmonds, and Redmond. A week later, we had flown out there and signed the papers for the home in Redmond.

As we drove the highway west, I noticed that Sharon was rather subdued at times, and it was apparent she was once again struggling with "movers' lament." The kids' excitement during the trip plus the accompaniment of her mother made the journey more tolerable for her. I felt badly about her trepidation, and during lunch at a Montana restaurant, I vowed to the family that this would be our last move: "You kids will finish school in Redmond."

Moving when the kids are young can be a good experience for them in many ways, but that's not the case after they reach the upper grades in school. At the junior high level in particular, they can experience extreme levels of peer pressure, and it can be difficult for preteens to blend into the student body at a new school. All three of our kids were into sports and extracurricular activities, so we were confident that they would gain valued friendships once we got settled. Pam would be going into ninth grade, and she would have the most difficult transition to a new school. I was serious about making this the last move until they all finished high school.

Our new home in Redmond was up on the east side, overlooking the business area just a few blocks downhill from there. It was within walking distance of all of the public schools, and there were six youth baseball fields just a few blocks away. The house was brand new, with a lot of square footage and a full, unfinished basement. Because of a sluggish housing market, it had a very attractive price. The unfinished basement gave me the opportunity to finish it to increase its value. It seemed to match our needs perfectly.

I had the basement plans in mind before we moved in, so I soon began building a large bedroom down there for the two boys to share. It had built-in shelves and storage for their baseball gear. The house had three bedrooms upstairs, and Grandma Florence took one of those. The boys "helped" me apply drywall to the stud walls as I worked on the family-room area. I patched up all of their mistakes: hammer holes, bent-over nails, and other "whoopses." Peter was ten, and Patrick was seven years old at the time. We later added a bathroom, a small den, a laundry utility room, and a small workshop. My workshop really got squeezed down in size after framing out Sharon's utility room, which included custom-built cabinets and a sewing space (which she never used).

The boys stayed by my side during the basement construction. I told them we could be partners and call this business "Hit and Miss Construction." As with any other construction crew, we ran into a couple of problems. After erecting the walls, we found that we couldn't get the large fiberglass shower stall past the furnace in the hallway. It was an inch too large, so I removed a big window in the den, and the boys helped me shove the shower unit through the window space. Then

Pam said she thought the wall by the den looked to be cockeyed. I told her it was just an optical illusion.

I insisted that our recreation room have a wet bar, just as we had in the Woodridge home, so I built one in the corner at the base of the stairway. Sharon didn't like the basement stairs coming directly to the bar, so after further discussion, I tore out part of the stairs, added a landing, and put a ninety-degree turn in the stairway. That change set us back about three days, because the boys and I only worked on a part-time basis.

We had a lot of drinking parties at that bar with friends and neighbors. Our basement could accommodate a large crowd, and it became the traditional location for the annual New Year's Day open house. Our Irish priest, Father Lovett, showed up every year for that party. He mixed in well with everyone and would join us for a drink or two and bum cigarettes from me. He told me that he only smoked when he drank.

# CHAPTER 16

# A FINAL SETTLEMENT IN THE NORTHWEST

The Redmond home was almost perfect for us. Our kids were active in sports and school activities, and we soon made a lot of new friends, primarily through our kids' activities. I made it to almost all of the boys' baseball games and took up coaching Little League baseball and soccer. Pam joined the high-school tennis team. We got into soccer for the first time just after moving to Redmond. Pat wanted a soccer ball for his birthday and then asked me to teach him the fundamentals. I had spent hours and hours with the boys, teaching them the fundamentals of baseball, and he assumed that I could also teach him about soccer. I knew nothing of the game, but we went up to the park on a Saturday and kicked the ball around. I made some inquiries the following week and located the president of the Redmond Soccer League. Jerry invited me to his home for coffee and explained that the kids entered the soccer program at the age of six. He said they were putting a team of eight-year-olds together who were new to the game, and Pat could join that team.

"There is one problem, however. We don't yet have a coach for this new team. Would you be interested?" he asked. I told him that I knew nothing of soccer. He countered that it was much easier to coach youngsters in soccer than it was in baseball. "It's less boring for the kids of this age, and you could all learn the game together! Have another cup of coffee."

A while later, Patrick and I left his house with three practice balls and a whistle. I was now the coach of the Redmond Rounders, a team of eight-year-old beginners in what was popularly known as the "bumblebee league." I soon learned how this age group earned the nickname: the kids found it difficult to maintain their positions on the field, and the whole team chased the ball everywhere, like a swarm of bees. I had to find a way to get this team organized, so I went to the Redmond library and checked out four books on soccer, one of which provided clues on practice drills for young players. That book saved my bacon. As we ran some of these drills, I found that Jerry was right. Soccer was easier to coach because I was able to form the players into several working groups and kept them all on the move. They were all participating in drills at the same time, burning up that excess energy, with no time for boredom.

My sales job at Menasha Corporation was off to a good beginning, and I felt comfortable with the sales team at Tacoma. Sales Manager Don Foote and I were both of Cornish heritage, and we talked about that over a few beers on a couple of occasions. Sharon and I did a lot of entertaining, and our large home in Redmond accommodated frequent house parties. We maintained a comfortable and hospitable environment at our new home. Our kids' friends were always welcome at our house and sometimes shared a meal with our family. These were good times, and the future looked positive for us.

Sharon and I made many friends through the kids' activities. The boys were in the Yankee system of Little League baseball, and Pam was on the high-school tennis team. We were invited to a lot of house parties, and we reciprocated in kind. We became especially close to some of the other Yankee parents. They were a fun-loving group, and we often partied after the games.

Sharon's mother, Florence O'Flahrity, spent most of her time at our Redmond home. We had provided the spare bedroom for her, and she enjoyed being near her active grandchildren as they grew up. She relied upon her husband, Bob, to look after things at their home in Shullsburg, but I know it worried her somewhat because he was in the advanced stages of alcoholism and not in good health.

Pat had his first lesson in sales as a nine-year-old when he and his soccer teammates were each given a case of candy to sell as a fundraiser. When I came home from work one evening, I could tell he was depressed. He told me that he had only sold a few bars of candy to the next-door neighbors, and none of the strangers down the street would buy. He said he was going to quit and turn in the remaining candy.

I said, "Pat, I suppose you're asking them if they would like to buy a candy bar, and they're saying 'No!' Is that right?"

He said, "Yeah, they're all a bunch of cheapskates!"

"The secret to sales is to avoid the questions that have a yes or no answer. Don't give them an opportunity to say no. First, you should introduce yourself. Tell them who you are, that you live just up the street, and that you're raising money for your soccer team. While you're talking, take a bar of candy out of the box and hand it to them. Make sure you get the candy bar in their hand. If they don't grab it at first, poke them in the belly with it. They'll grab hold of it in a natural reaction. Go on to tell them how good the candy is and then close the deal by asking them how many bars they want. They'll buy the bar that they're holding in their hand and maybe a couple more." He went on to sell that case of candy and a good part of a second one.

Despite our Rounders team opponents having two years experience on us, we managed to win one game that first season. Then that following spring, Pat managed to sell another two cases of candy bars. Nothing lifts a kid's confidence like winning a ballgame or selling more candy than the next guy.

As the kids reached the upper grades and high school, their activities were more and more outside the home, so we tried to work in some weekend camping and fishing trips whenever possible. We found it difficult to schedule family activities because of weekend baseball tournaments and my home-improvement projects around the house. Our family life was now more fragmented because of the kids' activity schedule, but they were beginning to gain some independence, and that was a good thing.

While we now spent less time together in family activities, it was quality time. On one occasion, the boys and I traveled over Stevens Pass to eastern Washington to fish for rainbow trout at Jamison Lake. We had gone there a couple of times before, but this particular trip was a memorable one. It was a rainy weekend in May, and we had towed my old utility trailer behind the Suburban, fully loaded with our fishing and camping gear and an outboard motor, and my fourteen-foot aluminum boat was lashed to the top.

The trailer was purchased from a local man in Issaquah. It had been home-built in Sand Point, Idaho, and mounted on an old car axle with fifteen-inch wheels. The builder had designed it to haul a snowmobile. It was heavy-duty, four feet wide, with a steel deck and four-foot-high sidewalls. Because he owned an Arctic Cat snowmobile, he had painted it a deep purple and pink, the popular colors of the time.

Sharon hated the looks of it when it was parked in front of our house, so I agreed to repaint it. The boys were eager to help. I parked it in front of the garage, and we applied two coats of white as the base color. The boys were learning painting technique and were doing well until some of Pat's friends decided to pitch in and "help." From that point, workmanship suffered to some degree, and they managed to make a bit of a mess in the driveway and also spattered the cedar siding in a few places.

I managed to paint a close imitation of the Seattle Seahawks logo on each side in blue and green, and then attempted to clean up the work area as best I could. The trailer became well-known around Redmond. When I made my weekly trip to the city dump, some people would ask, "Is that one of the Seahawks football players?" That alone made the boys and me proud of our handiwork.

We pulled out of the driveway on a Friday night, and by the time we crossed Stevens Pass in the Cascade Mountains, the rain had diminished, but it had grown quite dark. After we crossed over the pass at 4,500 feet and had traveled most of the way down the eastern slope on the two-lane highway, I felt the Suburban lurch and sway a bit, and I thought it might have been caught by a sudden gust of wind. The big, sure-footed Suburban just wasn't handling right, so I slowed down a bit.

Then, in the darkness of night, I saw something pass us on the left side and then caught a glimpse of it in the beam of the headlights as it went cruising past. Pat said, "Look, Dad, there goes a wheel!" Sure enough, a wheel had come off the old "Seahawks" trailer, passed us in the oncoming lane, and then disappeared in the darkness as it rolled ahead of us, down the mountain slope. As I slowed the Suburban, the handling became more erratic, and the axle of the trailer finally dropped to the pavement. In the rearview mirror, I could see sparks flying like a rooster tail behind a speedboat. I brought the rig to a stop on the right-hand shoulder of the road, the trailer tilted severely to the port side.

After getting out and inspecting the trailer with a flashlight, we found that the entire hub had come off the axle. There was no way to repair it, so we unloaded the trailer and managed to stuff everything into the back of the Suburban, including the fourteen-foot boat, with five feet of it hanging out over the tailgate.

Pete asked, "What are we gonna do with the trailer, Dad?"

"We're gonna leave it right here. It's off the road. Let's go fishin'. We'll deal with it on the way back. I'll figure something out."

The boys and I spent a great weekend, tent camping and fishing at Jamison Lake. We gathered around the campfire on Saturday night and recounted our adventure with the trailer, laughed about it, and had a great time. We also caught our limit in trout, but that was just a bonus to a great weekend.

We stopped on our way home on Sunday and looked for that trailer wheel but couldn't find it. A nearby farmer agreed to cart the trailer off the road and keep it as salvage. We had a story to tell when we got home Sunday night, and I knew right then that this would be one for the memory bank. The boys would be telling this story on me for years to come.

With Pam getting ready for college and Pete in high school, Sharon decided she wanted to work outside the home. She attended a bookkeeping class in the evenings and landed a job at a travel agency. After about six months, she advanced from bookkeeping into sales as a travel agent. She was successful in sales because she had an outgoing personality and enjoyed meeting and mixing with people. As her sales increased, she qualified for "fam trips" (familiarization trips) in the United States and abroad. She had found a rewarding career in the travel industry. This opened up a new life for her and gave her a sense of independence. She now had money of her own.

It was around this time that our marriage began to suffer more serious stress cracks, but neither she nor I fully recognized a downward tilt in our relationship. We had always had our differences, as many married couples do, and much of that was due to our conflict in personalities. I had always been independent, a "self-made man" with a logical life plan, and she had been raised in a much different family environment. Her mother was dominant, and her father an unreliable alcoholic. Florence had managed the family affairs throughout her marriage to Bob, and Sharon, the only child, had been totally dependent upon her mother.

Now Sharon, an adult child of an alcoholic, was married to a man who drank heavily, and although I had maintained a successful career path, she could take advantage of my burden of guilt and remorse following a late night of drinking. I was often in the doghouse, and I think she enjoyed that feeling of having the upper hand, just as her mother did with Bob. I wasn't as submissive as Bob, however, so the sparks would fly. I wouldn't call ours a love/hate relationship because it wasn't that extreme. We did really love and care for each other, and it was always fun to make up afterward. Each time, I sincerely promised to cut back on the drinking, but it was foolish to think that I could control it.

Some of the stress cracks began to open up further as our bickering and disagreements were becoming more frequent, weakening the foundation of our marriage. She had gained a new independence with the travel career and really pushed the envelope. I could no longer manipulate her as I subconsciously had done in the past. She demonstrated her independence when she went out on her own, or with a girlfriend, and bought her own car, a pre-owned Toyota. As I now look back, that was the first time in our married life that she had taken a serious step on her own, and I know she was justifiably proud of herself. I felt hurt that I wasn't consulted because she had always avoided serious decisions in the past and had left them up to me. This time I wasn't informed until after the deed was done. She knew that it hurt my pride and took some satisfaction from that. She never did inform me like, "Look, honey, I bought a car!" She simply parked it in the driveway and waited for me to discover it. In my mind, there was a certain spitefulness about what she did, like a dog crapping on the carpet, then waiting for someone to step in it.

The car incident could have been humorous under different circumstances, but, unfortunately, it was typical of our relationship, which further deteriorated in later years. She no longer liked my Suburban, the "gas guzzler," and I criticized her "rice burner." She knew that I disliked foreign cars and preferred to "buy American." There was no humor in these barbs, and the fractures in our marriage were opening wider. She spent more time with her girlfriends and with coworkers. My work and my drinking buddies occupied most of my time.

I was promoted to sales manager after four years at the Tacoma plant. Menasha's plant was one of the smaller corrugated box plants in the Pacific Northwest market area, and we had an uphill battle against the bigger operations. Our plant had a critical need for increased sales, a bigger share of the market. Our sales force had grown complacent, so soon after taking over the Sales Department, I announced that we were "going to the mattresses!" I had to explain to them that this was a Chicago term that was used by the Mafia when they were about to embark on a gang war. The Mafia families would move into abandoned buildings, away from their biological families, and conduct their warfare from these temporary quarters while their wives and families would be safe at home. These gangsters would be holed up sometimes for weeks and would sleep on mattresses thrown on the floor.

I chose the Portland, Oregon, market as our soft-target area. We would blitz the area and target some new business prospects. I took all five salesmen down there, rented motel rooms, and had extra telephones installed in a suite. We then literally tore the Portland industrial guide into six sections, and each of us got on a phone and performed a "market study." I gave the salesmen five scripted questions to gain necessary information from each prospective customer. It was an early form of telemarketing, and it really worked out well. When the prospect was told on the phone that Menasha Corporation was considering a new plant to be located in Portland, they opened up to us. To them, a new supplier in the market would mean that price levels would fall, and they could buy their boxes at lower cost.

A couple of our guys questioned the ethics of lying to these people about the plan for a new plant. "We're not really lying," I said. "If this market study indicates a high business potential, who knows? Menasha may decide to build a plant down here at some time in the future. The board of directors simply isn't aware of it yet."

We got great results from the phone work. Within the first hour, we not only had pages of prospects but also the volume of their purchases, the names of their current suppliers, future needs of their business, and names of contacts at their company for follow-up. Joe Jenkins got so excited about some of the prospects that he wanted to run out right then and make personal calls on those people. I told him to hold his water and to keep on dialing more numbers. We had to first finish all of these lists by Friday, and then we would follow up with the personal sales calls. By the time we left town, he and Ed Dorn, our other Portland-area salesman, had all of the new sales prospects that they could handle. This team project not only helped them open some new accounts but also charged up the entire sales force. The rest of the sales team returned to Tacoma with a higher motivation, and they were successful in opening new accounts in their market area as well. They had shed that complacent attitude.

About six months later, in February 1980, my boss, the general manager of the Tacoma plant, was told to take an early retirement. The plant had lost money for seven years running, and this latest upsurge in sales volume didn't save his butt. The division vice president then offered me his job, and I jumped at it! Finally, after some twenty years, I was to reach my lifelong goal! General manager was the best position in the packaging industry. While he had to follow some general guidelines and policy from corporate, the GM of each plant was granted broad responsibility and the authority to support that responsibility. In a sense, it was the equivalent of having your own business with a lot of financial support. This financial support was provided by Menasha, so of course one had to be accountable.

Sharon and I were elated with this important promotion. We recalled the early days in Rockford when I had the dream and she had encouraged me to follow it. The cost to get here had been significant. We had moved four times, and there were pay cuts and sacrifice. Now it was all coming to fruition. We had more serious talks during this time of our lives than we had had in years. Our relationship should certainly improve from here on, shouldn't it? Would we be able to patch up those cracks in our relationship?

I relished the challenge of taking over a plant that had lost money for seven years. It couldn't possibly get worse, and, having worked there for five years, I was pretty sure I could turn things around. I felt like the baseball manager taking over the last-place team with nowhere to go but up.

The first thing I did was gather all 150 employees in the factory lunchroom for a pep talk. I wanted to tackle the primary problem of low morale among the employees. I told them we had the skills and experience to turn this operation around. I talked baseball: team effort; no more separation of management and factory; we're in this together; work as a team, but everybody play your position; be accountable; we can do it!

I promoted Gene York to plant manager, the "head coach" in charge of production. I had confidence in Gene. He was of good Midwestern stock, from southern Indiana, and well-experienced in production. He had been a foreman on the plant floor, but I felt that the previous general manager had unfairly restricted him from further promotion. Gene was a bit rough around the edges, and I suppose my predecessor didn't see the potential in him that I did. When I named him the new plant manager, it surprised many people at the plant. Some were skeptical, but that would soon change.

He and I worked closely together: we met every day to gauge the progress, identify the problems, and develop a plan to get them resolved, one after another. We had to make some personnel changes, deal with the labor union that had our production workers under contract, and keep the sales cranked up. We spent some long hours at the plant, including some work on the weekends.

Service to our customers was improving, and plant productivity was increasing. By the month of May, we had made a small profit, and in June we made more. The team was fired up just as we were headed into the most favorable summer months for this market area. We had the ship pointed in the right direction and were mildly optimistic of making a profit in 1980. We had this baby above the grass!

I felt that I was embarking on a bright new phase in my career with the packaging industry and couldn't help reflecting on my past twenty years in the business. It had been an amazing trip. I had begun my career as a factory worker at Weyerhaeuser in 1961. That first job paid a mere $1.50 an hour as Sharon and I were struggling to make ends meet. We had rented out our wringer washer to provide beer money for the Friday-night euchre games and thereby avoided a budget deficit. Five years later, I was elevated to office manager at the age of twenty-seven. That was when I had set my sights on the prize position of a plant general manager. I lacked a four-year college degree but felt confident that I could overcome that deficit with hard work.

A subsequent four years in computer systems development had broadened my work experience and gave me an opportunity to work closely with upper management at Weyerhaeuser. That exposure proved valuable, and my performance was rewarded with a management position within the MIS Department and the opportunity to attend the prestigious Weyerhaeuser Management School.

If I were to reach my career goal as a general manager, however, I would need some experience in direct sales to complete my qualifications. So in 1971, I made the risky decision to enter sales. It required a temporary reduction in income and a third relocation for my family, but the subsequent six years in sales and sales management filled out my resume. Few candidates could match my broad range of business experience over these nineteen years.

Now, in 1980, I had snatched up the top job at Menasha Corporation's Tacoma plant. As general manager, I had not only complete responsibility for the plant operation, including sales, marketing, and production but also the opportunity to turn a loser into a winner at Tacoma. I was more than ready for this challenge.

I spent long hours at the plant, analyzing the operation and planning changes. The plant employees were at first skeptical of my management style. I created a motivational climate by delegating responsibility and authority. My approach was to lead rather than push. I replaced the autocratic style of my predecessor with a team concept where every employee was able to contribute and gain personal recognition for his or her effort. I convinced the office manager that we would share profit-and-loss results with the employees. At the Tacoma plant, that had not been done before. My predecessor had kept the financial records confidential. That practice, along with his unwillingness to spend time with employees on the plant floor, created a general climate of distrust between employees and management. The result had been low productivity and repeated operating losses.

It took a while for the labor force to gain confidence in this new work environment, and I made it a point to call them together on a regular basis to share progress results as we began to show steady improvement. When we began to make modest profits for the first time in years, I passed out recognition and encouraged the department supervisors to follow my example. Within a few weeks, we noticed that the employees were actually encouraging one another to do a better job and were willing to "rat out" the guy who was bringing down performance within a department. People were now happier to be at work, and the environment was much more positive. As I took my regular tours around the plant floor, employees would come up to me and ask, "How did we do last week?" They were eager for recognition. We still had to deal with the labor union, but when we took the same open and honest approach with the union representatives, we were able to develop a degree of trust in those negotiations as well.

When the more positive results at Tacoma were submitted to Menasha's corporate office, they were pleasantly surprised. The region vice president phoned me on a weekly basis to confirm results. He wanted to know how we were able to accomplish this turnaround after seven years of operating losses in Tacoma. Although our profits were modest at this early stage, the progress made him and his superior, the division vice president, both look good. Winning will boost everyone's confidence, and at Tacoma, we felt we were real heroes.

Yet something was nagging at me. We had needed some major repairs on a printer/folder-gluer machine, and there had been an unexpected delay in getting the funds approved by the corporate office. We had waited three months, and they were continuing to stall for some unknown reason. Their excuses were flimsy, and their answers evasive on other issues as well.

Then in July we had an unannounced visit by the region and division vice presidents. They phoned me from the airport, requested that I come there and pick them up, and instructed me to come alone. This was highly irregular. Instead of taking them directly to the plant, they asked me to take them to the nearby Holiday Inn at Tacoma, where we took seats at a booth in the coffee shop. That's when they told me that the Tacoma plant was to be shut down!

"But don't worry, Gary," they hastened to say, "you're going to take over a much bigger plant in Wisconsin, and we have a job for Gene as production manager in another Midwestern plant."

When they got no response from me, the division VP said, "We'll do the best we can to find jobs for your people."

My head was spinning at this point, and a lot of thoughts came and went, all fighting for space in my brain. For one thing, why would they be shutting down a plant that was making money for the first time in seven years? What about all of my plant employees to whom I had promised a winning season? They were motivated and proud of what we had accomplished in Tacoma as a team. How would I explain this devastating crisis to them? And how would they receive this news? This was 1980, and the national recession was especially critical in the Pacific Northwest with 20 percent of the regional workforce unemployed. How were we going to find jobs for our people at a time like this? None of this made sense to me, and I felt the anger rising as I sat there listening to my two superiors droning on and on with detail plans for the shutdown.

When I finally got past the initial shock, I questioned them about the sensibility of this decision to close down Tacoma. After some hedging, they finally told me that Menasha Corporation had made a deal to sell all of their West Coast holdings to Weyerhaeuser, my former employer. There was one snag in the deal, however. The US Justice Department would not allow the Tacoma plant to be included in the sale because Weyerhaeuser already had two similar plants in Washington State, and they would be unfair competition with a third plant in the state. Therefore, Menasha felt that since they did not own the building where the Tacoma plant was located, they would simply shut down the operation and sell off all of the machinery, equipment, and inventory. Following this action, they would then be permitted to proceed with the sale of their remaining West Coast assets in Oregon and California.

These VPs further intimated that the board of directors had made this decision the past December, and then promoted me to general manager the following February after the decision had been made! The division VP, Len Tweedie, told me that they had done that so I would be at the top position in order to make the lateral transfer to the larger plant in Wisconsin as general manager. They had anticipated most of my questions and had brought along the director of personnel, who was going to stick around a few days to help find jobs for our employees. He explained that they would pay a healthy severance to those who could not be placed in other jobs and would extend their medical coverage for a period of time.

I was still mentally wrestling with all this information as we got back in the car and drove to the plant. They said they realized that this was an emotional time for me, and, if I wished, they would make the announcement to the plant and office personnel. I immediately responded, "No, I don't want a group from corporate to come in here and announce a sudden plant shutdown. I will talk first to Gene, then he and I will make the announcement to all of the employees."

The production workers were all members of a labor union, and I had managed to develop a level of trust with them since I took over the operation. I had often spent time on the plant floor, remaining visible and approachable. I had personally kept them informed about how we were doing on a week-to-week basis. I acknowledged their good performance and was quick to pass out recognition in front of the whole group whenever it was warranted. Because they had gained confidence in me, I felt that I should be the one to break this news to them. I told Gene that the factory crew might feel like they had been betrayed, so I didn't know how this announcement was going to be received by them.

I asked one of our foremen to assemble the production workers in the plant lunchroom. While Gene made the announcement to the office staff, I somehow managed a strong, steady voice as I told the entire production workforce that our venture had come to a sudden end. I couldn't offer an adequate explanation. It was an extremely unfair situation.

It was about the toughest thing I had ever done because the company did not allow me to tell the real reason as to why they were closing. The sale to Weyerhaeuser would not take place until the Tacoma plant was out of the picture, and upper management didn't want any premature news leaks. Therefore, the announcement to the employees cost me a great deal of personal credibility. When you have your ball team turned around and going in the right direction, then the rug is suddenly snapped out from under them ... it leaves you with an empty feeling that's hard to describe. I felt devastation, then hurt, anger, resignation, sorrow, back to anger, and round and round. My mind was overloaded, and it was impossible for me to mentally digest all of this. I was certainly in some form of shock. It didn't fully sink in until days afterward.

A friend of mine, Joe Eaves, told me that when he cut off his finger in a table-saw accident, he heard a *zing* when it happened, then heard his severed finger *thump* against the wall behind him. He didn't feel a thing for a while, and then the pain came on with a fury. That pretty well describes my initial state of shock over the plant closure.

This crisis at the plant and my having to announce it to the employees was bad enough, but this was an even bigger issue for me personally. My family life was about to enter a period of crisis. I was concerned about my employees, but what about me and my family! I couldn't accept that transfer back to Wisconsin because the Northwest was to remain our home. This had been our last move. I had made that promise to the family. There was no way that I was going to promote the idea of pulling up stakes and moving once again. Sharon and I were experiencing an upturn in our relationship, the kids were happy in Redmond, the boys were approaching their high-school years, and we all enjoyed life in the Pacific Northwest. The position in Wisconsin was intriguing because it was the premier plant of the corporation. It was the "showplace" plant at Hartford, with $8 million worth of new, state-of-the-art equipment. It was within thirty miles of the corporate offices, with high visibility. I knew something about the plant too. I was fairly certain of the cause of its operating losses despite the investment in new equipment, and I felt that I could probably turn it around. Their management problem was similar to the one I had overcome in Tacoma. The opportunity to turn around the Hartford operation could lead me to an upper-management position and, who knows, maybe a vice presidency if I got the required results.

There were many things going through my mind. By the second or third day, the reality of the plant closing finally began to sink in. Like my friend Joe, my "finger" was beginning to throb. I was kept busy with planning the plant shutdown, getting the final orders run for our customers, deciding the sequence of employee terminations, and determining the length of time for which we would need maintenance personnel and office staff. Who would be turning off the lights as the last one of us went out the door?

CHAPTER 17

# THE NEW BUSINESS VENTURE

On the third day following the announced plant shutdown, the initial shock had eased, so Gene and I went out and got "snot-flying drunk." It was at some point that evening that we first discussed the possibility of restarting the Tacoma corrugated box plant as an independent operation. Gene brought up the idea. It was obviously a dream. We both laughed about it. I thought he was joking but soon realized that he was halfway serious about it and was hoping for a positive response. We had another beer and talked some more. The more we talked, the better it sounded, and the better it sounded, the more beer we drank.

After we sobered up the next day, we realized that his idea merited more thought. "Just when did you first begin thinking about restarting the plant?"

Without hesitation, he responded, "From the first day of the announcement!"

We began to put a plan on paper, jotted notes about business strategy, and did some preliminary number crunching. The deeper we got into it, the more sense it made. Menasha had many good employees, but we would have to avoid the labor union. A labor contract like Menasha had with the United Furniture Workers would be too restrictive for a start-up operation. It would be a difficult financial challenge to get a new business off the ground during this recessionary business climate. The prime lending rate was around 18 percent. With a union out of the picture, we could cherry-pick the best employees from Menasha because jobs were scarce with unemployment at 19 percent. Still, it wouldn't be an easy task to convince them to accept a job with a new business during the recession. They might not want to accept the risk when they had a family to support. We knew we would have to maintain a modest hourly rate but felt we could provide first-rate medical benefits as an incentive. The employees wouldn't have to worry about "Mom and the kids"; they would be protected with good medical and dental insurance. Then as business improved, we could bump up the wages and perhaps consider a profit-sharing program. Having a good employee base was critical in a new business, and we would have to really concentrate in that area. We both felt that people would be our most important asset.

From a marketing standpoint, we would be the only independent box operation north of San Francisco. As the "local guys," or underdog, we would have an advantage over the competition. The provincial businesses in the Puget Sound area would readily identify with us as an independent, locally owned operation: "one of their own," so to speak.

Gene was concerned about raw material supply. We would be competing against the big Fortune 500 forest products companies and would have to buy our containerboard from these same people, corporations like Weyerhaeuser, Georgia-Pacific, Boise Cascade, Willamette Industries, and Longview Fiber. These were fully integrated companies that had corrugated box operations that were supplied by their own paper mills. They were the Goliaths, and we would be David.

I told Gene, "Don't worry about getting paper. These guys will have to sell us some of their containerboard. The US Justice Department is scrutinizing these big boys, and sales of some of their product to an independent competitor would make points with the feds. They wouldn't dare turn down our request for paper."

We felt confident that we could clear the three major hurdles: employee workforce, customers, and raw material availability. Once we got these components set up, the new operation would be positioned to compete for a required share of regional business despite a nationwide recession. We could be "lean and mean." We kept working on the three-year business plan, making modifications here and there, until we came up with a "best-case" and "worst-case" scenario that we could present to a banker. We didn't have the luxury of a computer in those days, so I made hundreds and hundreds of entries on thirteen-column accounting paper.

Sharon thought this was a pipe dream. She assumed that I would eventually give it up and settle for a regular job in the Seattle/Tacoma area. I explained to her that I couldn't just walk down the street and get another job as a general manager or sales manager. In the packaging industry, appointments at that level are made within the company. It's an extremely competitive business, and the plant management must have an intimate knowledge of their market and the company business strategy and how to marry the two. There are significant differences in business philosophy between one company and another. That's why the position of general manager is such a plum—a once-in-a-lifetime opportunity.

For the previous twenty years, I had worked hard to build a base of experience and achieve my goal as a GM, only to have Menasha mess up my plan. It made me angry and deeply disappointed. I knew that after turning down the promotion in Wisconsin, my career plan with them was over. There was no way that I would push the family into leaving Redmond unless it was absolutely the last straw.

Forming a new business operation of this size would be a major undertaking and especially difficult during a national recession, but as Gene said, "Perk, if we don't at least try this, we'll regret it for the rest of our life. We'll ask ourselves, 'What if we had pulled this off back in 1980?'" I agreed with him. Gene and I were going to go as far as we could with this proposal despite a nagging feeling in the back of our minds that Sharon could be right: it's a pipe dream.

We put the phone call through to Menasha's corporate office in Neenah, Wisconsin, and advised Richard Johnson, the CEO, that we wanted first right of refusal on the purchase of the Tacoma plant assets. There was no immediate response from him, just silence on the other end of the line. He wasn't expecting this turn of events. Finally he said, "Do you think you can raise that type of money?"

"Yeah, we have some possible sources."

"You know we've already made overtures to sell off many of the plant assets. Boise Cascade will be there Friday to look at the folder-gluer, and there are some others that are interested in the trucks and rolling stock. We wouldn't have much time to work this out with you guys."

He further reminded Gene and me that if we didn't accept the positions in the Midwest, we would be terminating our employment with Menasha, and if we pursued this course, we would have to waive our rights to any severance pay. Dick was trying to discourage us. While he didn't welcome this complication, he demonstrated a sense of loyalty to his employees. Fortunately, that was an admirable trait at Menasha and common since their founding back in 1842. Old man

Smith, in those early days, would invite his employees to his home for Thanksgiving dinner. The company was unique in its fair treatment of employees.

"We're concerned about the plant lease, Gary. There are five years remaining on the seven-year lease agreement with the Port of Tacoma. Do you think you could get that reassigned?"

"We'll look into that right away."

There was another pause before he finally agreed to give us the first right of refusal. There were conditions, however: we must get a purchase agreement to him within thirty days, and we must agree to purchase everything—machinery and equipment, trucks and rolling stock, inventories, office furniture and equipment, maintenance equipment, and parts. I told him that we didn't want to buy any remaining finished-goods inventory because we might not be able to hold onto some of those customers after we closed. He agreed to that, but we were to purchase everything else. Before we hung up, he asked me to keep him posted on our progress in raising funds. I could tell that he had his doubts about our ability to raise well over one million dollars. He wasn't alone. I had some serious doubt as well.

After we hung up the phone, I said to Gene, "Okay, one of his primary interests is in getting rid of that building lease. They're on the hook for a lot of money should they have to pay that off. If we can get that monkey off their back, it would help with our purchase negotiations. Do you think the port would be willing to transfer that lease to us?"

"I have a good relationship with one of the guys over there," Gene said. "We won't have a problem with that, Perk."

Now that we had the green light, Gene and I embarked on a myriad of activity. The next four months would be the most stressful time of my life. We were in the midst of closing down a plant operation. Customers had been notified and were placing their final orders with us until they could find new suppliers for their packaging needs. As the operation ground down, we laid off employees a few at a time. We met with Puget Sound Bank and presented them with our business plan. That led to more number crunching because the loan officer told us we had only "half the information I need."

We had to form a corporation, so we hired Roger Johnson of Johnson, Lane, and Gallagher in Tacoma to draw up the papers. We needed a name for the new company, so we called it Box Shop, Incorporated. We opened a company checking account with a deposit of $500 to make it official, and I drove to the state capitol in Olympia with the papers to get the corporation recorded.

Once we had the name established, we met with the Port of Tacoma. They not only rewrote a seven-year lease to Box Shop, Incorporated but also gave us a favorable start-up rate of just seven cents per square foot for the 142,000-square-foot building that Menasha had leased in the past. The port directors expressed their gratitude for our courage in establishing a new business that would offer much-needed employment opportunities in Tacoma.

We had two more meetings with the banker to finalize the three-year business plan. It would require a minimum of one and one-half million dollars to get this new business up and running. The loan officer at the bank could readily see that this was a huge undertaking for a pair of novices like us. He provided the names of a couple of potential financial partners or investors. He said he would contact them on our behalf. He also suggested that we might want to inquire about a federally supported loan from the Small Business Administration. He would contact the mayor.

Mike Parker, the mayor of Tacoma, phoned me and offered to send Bart Soley, his administrative guy from the city's Economic

Development Department, down to help us put together an SBA loan. I gladly accepted his offer. He laid out the structure for preparing an economic impact statement that highlighted tax benefits to the community, jobs for 150 people in a depressed economy, and other benefits from the new enterprise.

We were also running back and forth to Roger Johnson's office, putting finishing touches on the purchase offer. There were several phone calls to Dick Johnson or his corporate accountants, negotiating prices on equipment and raw materials, and then once again revising the purchase agreement. Roger reminded us that his fee was seventy-five dollars an hour, which Gene and I would have to pay regardless of whether the purchase offer was accepted by Menasha.

Our business plan called for a nonunion operation, so we met with a Seattle labor attorney. He advised us to take certain steps in order to avoid an assumption of Menasha's labor contract with the Furniture Workers. We found his advice to be of extreme importance in that regard.

Throughout all of this activity, the plant closure was proceeding smoothly. It was an emotional time for all of us, and we were able to find jobs for only a few employees, which made matters worse. Unemployment was at an all-time high in Tacoma, and it wasn't much better in Seattle. Our customers had found new suppliers, and activity at the plant was coming to an end. In one of our conference calls with Dick Johnson, he told Gene and me that we would now be officially terminated and would have to clear out our desks and vacate the premises. In the early part of May 1980, we rented an apartment on the south side of Tacoma and made that the headquarters for Box Shop, Incorporated.

Our business-proposal document grew in volume to about five times its original size. This venture would require about $1.5 million in long-term debt, plus cash of $300,000 for working capital. I said to Gene, "We're in over our head, but we can't quit now." Menasha had accepted our seventeen-page purchase offer and wanted the deal closed within sixty days.

We had to find a strong financial partner with deep pockets, or apply for an SBA loan as our second choice. With the prime rate at 18 percent, the company would be highly leveraged, but even at a worst-case scenario, I felt that the debt could be serviced. Through our network of bankers and lawyers, we came up with some potential financial partners. Lugging our business plan, we first met with representatives of a Canadian natural gas company. They were interested in investing in the US economy but knew nothing of the paper or packaging industries. We wanted partners who would be more involved in our operation and bring more to the table than money.

We were supposed to close the deal with Menasha by July 1. Time had passed quickly, and we were now into June. We were going to need more time. I phoned the mayor's office and left a message.

Mayor Parker phoned me from his car phone. He asked me how we were doing, and I told him that we needed more time and that Menasha was being unreasonable. He said, "I'll put in a call. Who should I talk to?" I gave him Dick Johnson's number.

A few minutes later, Dick Johnson, the chairman of Menasha, phoned me. "I just hung up from talking with the mayor. How much more time do you need, Gary?" I told him we needed another thirty days.

"Have you got any firm prospects for financing the business?" When I told him we were getting into final stages, he said, "Okay, we'll give you until August 1, but we have to have cash. It's got to be cash on closing. No other way." We also met with the Nist family, owners of Seattle-Tacoma Box, together with John Kiel who owned Pacific

Container. Kiel was in the corrugated box business, and both Gene and I liked John. The Nist family, however, was second and third generation at Sea-Tac Box, and I didn't feel I could work with them. For them, this would be an acquisition and would become part of their operation. They came on too heavy-handed to suit me. I had trepidations and felt I couldn't work with them as business partners. I told Gene that I wanted to break off any further talks with the Nists. "Let's get back with the beer distributor."

We had met with the owner of Premier Distributing in Seattle before talking to John Kiel and the Nists. He had a successful Budweiser distribution business and was well-respected in the Seattle area. We needed to improve market share in Seattle, and he, with his business contacts, could be of some help to our sales effort in that regard. He was an energetic guy, a hard charger with deep pockets. He was willing to split the ownership with Gene and me equally, on a three-way basis.

When we got back to him, however, his feelings had changed. He told me that he had phoned George Weyerhaeuser and that George had told him that the box business was terribly competitive, and a new business would have a high probability of failure. I responded, "Of course George is going to say that. They don't want to compete with an independent up here. He's trying to scare you off. We provided you with some other references that would be more reliable, including a couple of local bankers."

Regardless, the beer distributor got soft in the belly, lost his courage, and backed away from us. After all, the nation was in a recession. This was an unfortunate turn of events because our personalities matched up quite well, especially he and Gene, and I think we would have had a good business relationship downstream.

We had run out of options on the financing. Gene thought we might still contact John Kiel, but we knew he wouldn't come into the deal without the Nist family. I phoned Dick Johnson at Menasha and told him that our financial partner had backed out on us.

"You guys have got us in a bind now, Gary. Don't leave me hanging. Is there no one else out there that might be interested?"

"Well, I think the Nist family of Seattle-Tacoma Box may still be interested. We just couldn't put a deal together with them."

"Do you mind if I contact them?" I gave him their name and number.

A half hour later, the phone rang, and it was Dick Johnson again. He said, "I talked to Ferd Nist, and they are willing to arrange financing but they will only do it if you and Gene are willing to take charge of the new venture. They won't enter into this without you guys." He went on to say, "At this point, you have me out on a limb, Gary. Don't leave me hanging. After all, I gave you guys first right of refusal when I could have sold off all of those assets by now."

After hanging up, I said to Gene, "Well, what do you think?"

"Perk, we've come too far with this tiger to let go of its tail. Let's give it a go."

Sea-Tac Box would be bringing in John Kiel on the financial deal. We both liked John and could potentially use him as a moderator if things became edgy with the Nists. John also had a good knowledge of the packaging business. He owned Pacific Container, a small "sheet plant" that purchased corrugated sheets from Menasha and others, then converted the ready-made sheets to small lots of boxes. The larger plants like Menasha ran high-volume, low-margin box orders while the sheet plants ran small-volume, higher-margin items for small businesses. Another positive factor was that the Nist family had the financing. Their grandfather was one of the first customers of Seattle First National Bank. The financing would be sound if we wanted it.

Finally, I said to Gene, "Okay, you're right, but I'll only give it two years. In that time, we'll know if this business will make it or not. I don't think I can work with the Nists over the long haul. If we make it through the start-up period, and the operation gains some reasonable stability after two years, I'll then decide whether to stay or leave."

When Gene and I walked into the conference room to sign the papers at closing, we were shocked to see Attorney Roger Johnson sitting there. Gene and I had hired him to represent us when we drafted the purchase agreement with Menasha, and now he had joined up with the Nist family. He had switched from our side of the table to their side. We were obviously naïve when it came to corporate financial dealings and hadn't even hired an attorney of our own for this meeting. The table was stacked against us right off the bat, which confirmed to me that this business relationship would be less than favorable in the future.

The Menasha attorney, the Nists and John Kiel with their attorney, and Gene and I all signed a big stack of papers. Included were employment contracts for me as president and general manager and Gene as vice president and production manager. Gene and I were each obligated to inject equity capital of $12,000 two years down the road. I recognized that as superb timing, based on my agreement with Gene to give this endeavor just two years. Menasha Corporation got its cash and was extricated from a five-year lease on the building. The Nist family got their new "toy" to play with, and Gene and I were each one-sixth owners of a fledgling corporation. I guess that made us the tail wagging the dog because we had to get this monster airborne in the midst of an unfavorable business climate.

We worked seven days a week, and many of those days were long. Fortunately, I had set up a critical path chart that became an invaluable tool. We spent hours identifying all the detail tasks required to start up this new manufacturing operation and then laid them out sequentially within a time frame. Some tasks could be accomplished simultaneously; others required one task to be completed before another could begin. We pasted the CPM chart (it was almost five feet long) to my office wall and marked off each task as it was completed. It helped us avoid confusion and kept us focused as we prepared for an early August start-up. It was an ambitious beginning.

One of our first tasks was to change the corporate name to Commencement Bay Corrugated, Inc. This was suggested by Mike Nist at our first board meeting, and it received unanimous approval. Once the name was established, we could then get the phones ordered and design a corporate logo to use on our stationery, business cards, and decals on the trucks and trailers. We chose blue and green colors for our logo to match those of the Seattle Seahawks. We immediately hired Judy Olson and Brenda Malloy, former Menasha employees, as office manager and customer service manager, respectively. They went right to work on the tasks of preparing customer contact files, accounting records, and the countless number of office forms that would be required. There were no computers. The paperwork would be accomplished manually, just as it had been for the Menasha operation.

We placed ads for employment, approved by our labor attorney, in the Tacoma *News Tribune.* The factory parking lot was full of applicants on the very first day, many filling out applications on the hoods of their cars. Gene selected the first six hourly employees for the production department, a shipping foreman, and a maintenance supervisor. The six-man factory crew came to work that first Monday at seven in the morning, fired up the boilers, loaded the two-ton rolls of containerboard onto the corrugator, and were making corrugated board by eleven o'clock. I had promised Allpak Container that we would deliver their first order that day, and, to their amazement, our truck pulled up to their dock by three o'clock. At Commencement Bay Corrugated, service to our customers was to be our top priority. We were off to a good start.

Gene hired more factory employees as they were needed, and I worked the phones, bringing in much-needed sales to keep us going those first few weeks. We delegated hiring responsibility to Judy and Brenda for their office staff and to the shipping and maintenance supervisors for their crews. I simply gave final approval to their selections. There had been a lot of people out of work in the Tacoma area, so we could select the cream of the crop for our new team. Most were former Menasha employees, and many were assigned to jobs with more responsibility than they had had with Menasha. We were a nonunion operation, so seniority with the previous employer was meaningless, and some of those long-time former employees weren't hired at CBC. We picked those who we felt were the best fit for this new operation.

CBC Employees, 1982

We had purchased raw material along with the plant and equipment, but that material didn't last long. We had to purchase additional containerboard on a "cash" basis since our credit hadn't yet been established. We had no truck drivers at this point, so Gene, who was also making the deliveries to our customers, would take one of the semitrucks over to the St. Regis mill in Tacoma to pick up several rolls of containerboard with an $8,000 check in his hip pocket.

We needed additional paper suppliers, but we faced an increased demand throughout the industry for containerboard despite the US recession. Much of the product was going overseas, primarily to Europe and Asia. When I contacted Louisiana Pacific, they told me that they had put their customers on a restricted allocation but would be willing to furnish us with a minimal amount. They had heard "rumors about a new independent plant in the Northwest" and wished us luck.

I purposefully waited a day or two before contacting Weyerhaeuser about containerboard. They initially turned us down. "We simply can't work you into our program right now. We have all of our customers on tight allocations, and they are all pushing us for more paper."

I was ready for that response. "We're getting some paper from St. Regis and L.P. but we need another hundred tons a month, about the same as you were selling to Menasha. You know we're the only independent operation up here in the Northwest, and if you were to add an independent like us to your customer list, it would look awfully good to the US Justice Department. They don't like to see all you big guys hogging the paper."

He said, "I'll see what I can do. I'll get back to you, Gary."

When he called back the next day, we got our one-hundred-ton allocation and, as an added bonus, an open line of credit. That filled our needs for containerboard, and we were off and running.

When I had finalized the three-year business plan, we had anticipated an operating loss for the first six months of operation. Our financial partners had deposited $300 million in our checking account at Seattle First National Bank for operating capital. They had also arranged for a $300,000 operating line of credit plus another $1 million in long-term debt that financed the purchase of plant equipment. John Kiel and the Nist family had to guarantee those loans, so they deserve a lot of credit for having the courage to back this operation when the national economy was in a severe recession. We were paying interest to the bank of about 2 percent over prime, which had climbed to 19 percent at that time.

It was crucial, therefore, to obtain credit from vendors. We were able to do that with help from the bankers and from Mayor Parker. Most importantly, the Nist family and their Seattle-Tacoma Box operation had a longtime relationship with Seattle First, and the family was held in high regard. The solid financial backing and the willingness of our vendors to offer credit provided the flexibility we needed while growing the new business. We needed to reach $10 million in annual sales as soon as possible, and that required a lot of containerboard. I would often "float" checks to vendors by writing checks at the end of a week, then cover them with a loan transfer on the following Monday. At times, that would save us $1,000 in interest over a weekend period.

Our biggest challenge was in sales and marketing. We needed experienced sales representatives to bring in chunks of business. I set up contracts with two outside salesmen, former Menasha employees, who agreed to work on a full commission as outside contractors. They brought in a lot of volume, but we needed much more. I put feelers out to others but couldn't find people who were willing to give up the security of their present jobs to "take a flyer" with a new company. Most thought this new business would fail and they would be left out in the cold. We had repeated discussions about this in our board meetings, but it seemed that I was the only one concerned about our ineffectiveness in hiring experienced salesmen. The Nists felt that they could step in and sell corrugated. They had no experience in that product line but felt they could learn enough to be successful. I knew they were underestimating the competitive nature of the corrugated box business and told them so. They suggested that I conduct some product-knowledge sessions once a week at their plant, which five or six of their people could attend. That lasted for about four of five sessions as the participants dwindled down each week. It turned out to be pretty much a waste of my time.

After the first month of operation, we held an open house at the plant. Sharon came down to Tacoma and helped Judy, Brenda, and others set up the catered food and refreshments. She was there with us to meet some of our customers, bankers, city employees, and other well-wishers who stopped in. She was supportive to some degree and hopeful that this would be a successful venture, but she was perhaps expecting the worst. She appeared to be on board but not totally committed, keeping one toe in the water, so to speak. This was evident in each of my career moves and then later on during my time in the alcohol treatment program. There was verbal support from her but nothing beyond that.

Sharon's family environment undoubtedly caused her to behave in that manner. Adult children of alcoholics will often display some of the same characteristics of the alcoholics themselves. An inferiority complex is one of the most common maladies—a lack of confidence in oneself. Perhaps we both shared that characteristic, but there was a difference in how we coped with the challenges of life. She took a tentative toe-in-the-water approach, whereas I, by plunging ahead, was able to determine the depth of the water. With her tentative approach and lack of commitment, she never really knew the depth of the challenge and feared that it might be over her head. She was definitely a "fair-weather sailor," whereas I, on the other hand, seemed to live on the edge, at least in her eyes.

I was intently focused upon the new plant operation. Through my business contacts in the Puget Sound area, we were able to generate enough sales to carry us through August and into September. John Kiel placed his corrugated sheet orders with us, and that also helped us maintain a modest level of production at Commencement Bay. We hired additional employees for the factory and a couple more people for the office. Our business plan required a much higher level of sales as we entered the final quarter of 1980, and for that we needed to develop a much higher market share. Our primary targets were industrial packaging in Seattle and Portland, produce boxes in eastern Washington, and some of the seafood packaging business on the Oregon coast. We had hoped to recapture some of the Menasha accounts and open new accounts that would fit into our plant product mix. To accomplish such market penetration, we would have to hire experienced sales representatives.

That turned out to be a most difficult task. The experienced box salesmen were reluctant to leave the protective womb of their present employers to take a chance with a new business, especially during this recessionary period. I encouraged them to take advantage of this opportunity to join a new venture and get in at ground level. Our new plant had ample capacity that would allow them to grow their sales volume over the next few years, and their personal income would increase accordingly. Despite my enthusiasm in describing the benefits of joining the sales team of an independent operation, they were unable to muster the personal courage to make a career move. One guy wanted a personal guarantee, and of course I couldn't offer that.

The Nist family wasn't concerned about building a sales force. They felt that they could provide the bulk of the sales through their contacts in the seafood industry. Their Seattle-Tacoma Box operation had been providing wooden boxes for salmon roe and other products for some sixty years. I told them that selling corrugated boxes was much more competitive, and their people lacked the necessary product knowledge. Besides, their business contacts might not be able to help them much because they would be calling on different contacts to sell corrugated. I was very concerned about our inability to attract experienced corrugated box salesmen who could bring us new business. In the board meetings, they dismissed my concern and falsely assumed that they could gain the required product knowledge in "a few weeks' time."

I had contracted Rufus Littlefield and Ray May, two former Menasha sales reps, on a straight commission basis. They furnished their own cars, paid their own sales expenses, and acted as independent contractors. We weren't obligated, therefore, to pay their salary or payroll taxes. They brought in a large volume of business, and we were now reaching full capacity for the one eight-hour shift in the plant. Rufus had customers in the Seattle/Alaska seafood industry, and Ray sold produce boxes to the growers in the Kent Valley plus some industrial accounts in Tacoma. We continued to run a high percentage of corrugated sheet business for John Kiel and a couple of his competitors in Seattle. I also hired Pete Nolan, whom I had known while working at Weyerhaeuser. He was in MIS in Chicago when I was there and specialized in the Folding Carton Division, which manufactured the pasteboard boxes for cake mixes, cereals, and the like. He had no direct experience in corrugated, but with his outgoing personality I felt that with time, he could develop some new business for us. I furnished him with a company car and expense account, but since he could bring us no business immediately, I paid him a straight salary.

We desperately needed a salesman in Portland and eastern Washington, but I was unable to attract one in either of these areas. Many still felt that Commencement Bay was doomed to fail.

We were really shorthanded in the sales department and relied heavily on Rufus and Ray to bring in the bulk of the box orders. They brought immediate results and were each earning some good commissions. The Seattle-Tacoma Box people attempted to prove their sales ability by stampeding into the Seattle seafood market with a heavy- handed approach: "We're from Sea-Tac Box, and you need to be buying your corrugated boxes from us." They quickly learned that you have to build relationships in this business, and the person buying the corrugated isn't the same guy who bought wooden roe boxes from them in the past. They had no sales plan, didn't take the time to set up a strategy, and began walking all over Rufus's accounts in Seattle. The purchasing agents would phone Rufus and ask, "What in the hell is going on? Who are these guys from Sea-Tac Box?" Rufus would be in my office the next morning, mad as hell, and rightfully so.

I tried repeatedly to get a list of sales prospects from the Nists. I wanted to review their list so we could avoid conflicts of this type. I didn't want two people calling on the same account. There were plenty of prospects to go around without stepping on each other's toes. Rufus had accounts that he was selling, and the Nists reluctantly agreed to stay away from those, but he also had some prospects that he had been working for a period of time, and those became areas of conflict. I told the Nists that they would have to stay away from those as well because Rufus was working on them and had developed a sales strategy to open them as new business. Sometimes it takes a year of more on these large account prospects.

The internal marketing conflict continued throughout the first year of business. Rufus or Ray would be in my office on Monday, and I would call one of the Nists in there the next day to get things straightened out. They didn't feel a need to provide me with a list of prospects. They preferred a shotgun approach, which made for constant conflict within our organization. I knew that I was going to have difficulty working with the Nist family and was really frustrated in not being able to hire a sales force and thereby cut the Nist group out of the marketing effort. I was forced to make the best of a bad situation. As president and general manager, I had the authority to direct the sales effort and determine the prospects assigned to each representative, but since the Nist family was holding the purse strings at Commencement Bay, they tended to go their own way. It was one conflict after another. Being president isn't all it's cracked up to be when you are holding a mere one-sixth ownership. We needed the sales. I had to make the best of the situation and try to keep everybody relatively happy.

I believe the Nists resented me for breaking off talks with them earlier when Gene and I were attempting to put this business together, and I resented their heavy-handed approach as we got underway. We kept our feelings buried for the good of the business, and on the surface we did our best to maintain a friendly attitude. They respected my business knowledge and remained somewhat restrained from interfering with the day-to-day operations as we slowly built the business. We began to show a profit during the first quarter of 1981, but I was still concerned about building future sales. I didn't want us to reach a plateau. We had to get into second gear and bring in additional box business.

Then Ferd Nist casually mentioned to me one day that he had found an answer for sales. He said they had hired a guy from Western Kraft with a lot of experience. When I didn't recognize the name, he said, "He's got similar experience to yours and could really help us down the road." They hadn't discussed the proposed hiring with me because they had put him on the Seattle-Tacoma Box payroll. That didn't sit well with me, and he explained that the new guy would also be "doing some things" for Sea-Tac Box, so they would pay his salary. It would save overhead at Commencement Bay, he reasoned. They obviously had a motive behind this hiring, and it was another example of their throwing their weight around. Then it turned out that this "experienced salesman" had no business to bring to us, and his claim to fame was in selling corrugated partitions for beverage boxes, an item that had been rendered obsolete five years prior. This hiring offered no benefit whatsoever to Commencement Bay, but I suppose the Nists felt that he could replace me if the need ever arose. Perhaps they had heard a rumor that I was leaving after two years. If so, it would have to have been Gene who told them. At any rate, this new guy should never have been hired. He was a lightweight in the corrugated box business.

As we entered the second year of business, the plant was on a relatively stable footing, and I proposed to the board that we set up a 10 percent profit-sharing plan for the employees. Our plant workforce had stayed with us throughout the start-up period, and we had only lost one employee who had hired on at the Reynolds aluminum plant for more money, so, obviously, our employees found this to be a good place to work. The Nist family offered enthusiastic support for the profit-sharing plan, and I was grateful for that. It was the right thing to do. The start-up had been risky for these employees, yet the plant had set a high standard for productivity, and that was a key factor in keeping us competitive and allowing us to turn a modest profit within the first six months.

The labor union that had represented the Menasha employees in the past had tried to organize our people. Shortly after we began operation, they showed up one afternoon in our parking lot with cases of beer. They had made a second attempt about six months later, and our employees rejected the union both times in NLRB-sanctioned elections. We remained the only nonunion operation on the Tacoma waterfront.

It was in early 1982 that the Port of Tacoma officials contacted Gene and asked him to set up a meeting with the "principals" at Commencement Bay. They informed us that Sea-Land, a container cargo exporter, wanted to move from Seattle to Tacoma and that the Port of Tacoma would need our waterfront location to accommodate them. They would be willing to cancel our lease agreement on the building and offer us cash up front and some low-interest loans to construct a new building on a new site.

This would be a big financial break for us, and the thought of a new plant was exciting. The Nist family and John Kiel told Gene and me that they would handle the financial negotiations with the port and that we should begin drafting a plant layout for a new facility. Gene jumped into the project with enthusiasm. I had my hands full with the current operation, and as our financial partners got more and more involved with the financial settlement, the proposed building sites in the area and new production equipment, I became less and less involved, primarily due to my choosing. I could see where this was going.

Seattle-Tacoma Box would own the new building and then lease it back to Commencement Bay. They would also purchase a brand-new corrugator—a huge investment—and lease that to the company as well. They visited several potential building sites before selecting some acreage near the town of McMillan for the new plant. They told me that they had selected a corrugator manufactured in Germany with a state-of-the-art, computer-assisted control panel that was ideally suited to run sheet orders. The new plant would continue to manufacture some corrugated boxes, but the emphasis would be on producing corrugated sheet orders for the small sheet plants in the Puget Sound area. I could readily see that this new plant would be owned by Seattle-Tacoma Box and would no longer be the full-line corrugated box plant that Gene and I had envisioned. CBC would in all respects become a division of Sea-Tac Box, and we would all be working for the Nists. This would make my decision much easier. I began to think of myself as a short-timer. Gene tried his best to get me excited about this new development, but I wanted no part of it. I stayed with the day-to-day operation of the plant and kept the sales force motivated as best I could.

Gene and I had little sway in the board meetings, and the conflict remained in marketing our product. John Kiel tried to act as moderator when discussions became heated. Gene was more malleable than I and tended to go along with the flow of things. On one such go-round at a board meeting, the board passed a resolution of reprimand regarding Gene's personal use of a company truck and my approval of same. There was no need for a formal resolution to be added to the minutes. We could have had an off-the-record discussion. It was an example of the majority owners exercising control. Now that the plant was making a profit and the risk had diminished considerably, these guys were reminding us of who held the purse strings. As president, I still had to answer to the board of directors. They were beginning to rein me in and take control, knowing there wasn't much I could do about it.

I've always felt that if you can't control things and you can see no way of improving a difficult working environment, then you have to make a change. If you don't, it will affect your health and well-being sooner or later. Too many people in this type of situation will hang in there until retirement, enduring a stressful, unhappy work environment. Gene was willing to do just that. I was not.

CHAPTER 18

# VENTURE INTO SMALL BUSINESS

When Sharon and I discussed this situation, she didn't want me to walk away from the business, but I felt her interests had more to do with the money and security than in my well-being. At any rate, she and I had difficulty with my decision to leave the box plant and resign as president. My contention was that I would have had to borrow $12,000 to maintain a one-sixth ownership, and I really couldn't work with the Nist family. Our financial partners were now bullying their way into the plant operation and changing the mission of the business that Gene and I had envisioned. I wasn't comfortable with what was happening, and my pride prevented me from accommodating these people. It would not be wise for me to invest any more money.

I told her that I needed to slow down, that I was approaching the stage of burnout with the stress of working long hours and having to deal with this board of directors. With me working such long hours in

Tacoma, forty miles away, we had little family time. I had been doing a lot of thinking the past few months and asked her what she would think about us buying a little hardware store. I said maybe the boys could work with me on a part-time basis and it could become a low-stress, family business. She said the boys wouldn't be interested. (It later turned out that she was right about that.)

The idea of owning a small hardware store appealed to me for several reasons. Over the years, I had demonstrated an ability to work well with people, and I felt that I had a good head for business. I had applied sound management skills during my years of employment with Weyerhaeuser and Menasha and had just recently guided a good-sized manufacturing operation through a difficult start-up period in the depths of an economic recession. These skills, combined with my product knowledge, convinced me that I could easily manage a small retail hardware store. I had always enjoyed browsing around in hardware stores, was an accomplished "do-it-yourselfer," and had a vision of the old-fashioned style of store where I could wait on customers and provide them with sound advice. It would be a more relaxed work environment and a welcome change from my most recent experiences with the large companies.

The primary reason for pursuing this course, however, was to involve my family, or perhaps more accurately, to bring me closer to my family. Sharon and I could man the store during the week, and I believed that our kids would willingly join us there after school and on Saturdays. Looking back at this in later years, I realized that I was subconsciously seeking a relief for my burden of guilt. During my career in the packaging industry, I had been an overachiever at the expense of family time. I undoubtedly felt guilty, and this was to be my unspoken attempt at making amends.

Guilt and remorse are frequent companions to an alcoholic or chemically dependent person that he or she carries around like a heavy backpack. There are other characteristics as well. We tend to manipulate people and experience periods of depression and low self-esteem, leading to overachievement. Many who are afflicted will possess an above-average level of intelligence and feel a need to be well liked by everyone. Every alcoholic, and most adult children of alcoholics, will display some of these characteristics.

I would be turning forty-three in August 1982, and by this time I knew that I had a serious drinking problem. I had considered seeking professional help on a number of occasions, but that thought soon left me. I felt that I could resolve the problem on my own. For someone like me, who had always been in control and had always stayed with the long-range life plan, it was extremely difficult to admit a need for outside help. I steamed forward, "torpedoes be damned."

It would be two more years before I came to realize that I wasn't going to win this battle with alcohol on my own. Alcoholism is a progressive disease that worsens as time goes on, and one who is afflicted must hit bottom before reaching out for help. There had been five instances in the past where I was pulled over by the cops while on my way home from a bar late at night. On four of those incidents, I was issued a DWI ticket and had to appear in court. On two court appearances, I had hired an attorney, and that cost me (and my family) several thousands of dollars in attorney fees. There were also fines to pay, and at one time I had my driver's license suspended for six months. These instances were occurring at two- to three-year intervals from the time I reached my late thirties. Each time I would be laden with guilt, be mad at myself for being so stupid, and would vow, "Never again!"

Despite the extraordinary success in my business career, I remained down on myself (the low self-esteem) and felt a personal need to climb yet another mountain, to make another move, to gain another promotion. I never felt nearly as successful as others believed me to be. I remember that a top executive at Weyerhaeuser had told me, back in 1968 or 1969, "Don't undersell yourself, Gary," but of course I continued to do just that throughout my life.

So now, in 1980, I had climbed my biggest mountain of all. The new Commencement Bay Corrugated business was climbing upward, and it was apparent by early 1982 that it would be a successful venture. I had proven my management ability once again, and my twenty years of broad business experience within the packaging industry had become an impressive resume. I liked to think that I had crammed forty years of broad business experience into twenty years of time. I had achieved success at every step along the way, and, now, this should have been the time for me to go into a cruise mode and reap the rewards of a long and successful career. As president and general manager of a solid business enterprise, I should have been able to reorganize my personal life: delegate more responsibility at work; spend more time with my family; take an extended vacation; join a golf country club.

I knew, however, that it was not to be. I had found myself in an untenable situation, at cross-purposes with our financial partners at CBC. I tried my best to explain to Sharon that, for that reason, I could not continue in this capacity with the Nist family as my partners. The business was not going to resemble what Gene and I had envisioned, and since our financial partners held the purse strings, they would bend it in their direction and treat it as part of their Seattle-Tacoma Box Company. I was too proud to let that happen, not while I was a part of it.

I told her that I was also reaching a burnout stage with all of this tension. I simply couldn't see any justification for investing the additional $12,000 in a business that I would no longer control. I would

have to resign my position as president. I had given Gene the two years
that I had promised, the business was on a stable footing, and now I
needed to gear down. I was hopeful of buying a small hardware store
where I could utilize my business skills in a low-pressure situation. I was
certain that I would enjoy operating a small family business.

We had our eye on a Coast-To-Coast hardware store in Duvall, a
small town just a few miles east of our home in Redmond. The present
owner and I had agreed on a price. I had taken my local banker out there
to look over the inventory, and he approved the financing the following
day. The owner and I had scheduled a closing date of the following
Monday for the purchase.

But then, on Sunday evening, the night before closing, the owner
phoned me to say that he had decided not to sell the business after all.
He said his daughters had talked him out of selling the business. This
was a shocking development. He had seemed eager to sell the business
up to now, and our negotiations over the price and terms had proceeded
smoothly. I didn't expect him to suddenly change his mind like this,
but after further conversation, I could tell that his family had firmly
convinced him not to sell the business.

This action, of course, was a breach of contract because we had
reached an agreement on his sale of the business, but after I thought
more about it, I decided not to take any legal action. Duvall was a small
town, and the owner had spent his lifetime there. He was a member of
the chamber of commerce and chief of the volunteer fire department.
A successful lawsuit against him would be severely detrimental to my
business in the future, because I would have had to rely heavily on local
business to be successful.

Sharon was really worried now. I had already resigned my position
with Commencement Bay Corrugated when this deal fell through. I

think she said something to the effect of, "This is a fine kettle of fish. You'd better find a job somewhere!"

Always the optimist, I went back to my banker and told him what had happened. He thought that I should pursue legal action against the Duvall owner, but I explained to him why that would be detrimental in a small town. He said he could see my point, but I think he was primarily disappointed about not getting the loan package.

A few days later, the banker phoned me about a local business opportunity in Redmond. It wasn't a typical hardware store but somewhat related, he said. When I met with him later, I learned that the owner had a hardwood lumber and plywood business where he also sold woodworking tools, books, and supplies. He sold these products to contractors and finish carpenters, schools, cabinetmakers, and woodworker hobbyists. I went down to this place of business in a small industrial park and talked to the owner. While woodworking and carpentry were hobbies for me, I didn't have an in-depth knowledge of these products, but I found the business to be quite interesting. I interviewed his three employees, one of them a woodworker designer/craftsman, and gained some background information on inventory and marketing practices. They all told me that their immediate need was for increased sales. It appeared that their business was slow, and after the owner provided me with his financial records, that was confirmed.

He had some long-term debt from when he purchased the beginning inventory and equipment a couple of years prior. His accounts receivable were current, and he had a good credit rating with his suppliers. Most of his sales were to professional furniture makers and cabinet shops and to a couple of finish carpenters. There were some sales to the local high schools and a bunch of consumer hobbyists, maybe a couple hundred regular customers. He had a mailing list of 2,500 names, but most retail woodworkers don't purchase these products often because, for them, it's merely a hobby. Because of the low level of sales and long-term debt service, he was unable to show much of a profit month to month, and according to his books, the net worth of his business was a miniscule seventeen dollars! His financial records were prepared by a local CPA, and I met with him as well.

The business, named Northwest Woodcrafters, needed to broaden and deepen the inventory in order to obtain increased sales and cash flow. The owner said he preferred to take on a financial partner but would sell the business outright if I wished. I told Sharon that I would feel more comfortable keeping the present owner, Jim Sypher, on board because I knew very little about the hardwood lumber business, and Jim had established personal relationships with his vendors and customers. It was the sales to those contractors and cabinet shops that were keeping the business afloat at the present time. The business needed a minimum of $40,000 in capital to get it geared up, and I would have to provide that as his business partner.

I hired an attorney to draw up the papers, and as we signed them, I told Jim that our first priority would be to get a long-term lease for our store. He had been renting space in an industrial building on a month-to-month basis, which I found to be risky. Since the current landlord would not provide a long-term lease, we would have to relocate the business.

We looked all around Redmond but couldn't find anything suitable with a minimum ceiling height of sixteen feet and five thousand to ten thousand square feet of warehouse space. We found a location in Bellevue in a retail shopping area that would provide good visibility for our business, although the rental fee per square foot was a lot higher than in Redmond. After signing a five-year lease, we spent evenings and weekends in our new building, demolishing walls and reconstructing a new layout with a retail section in the front and ten thousand square feet of warehouse in the back. We also built an eight-hundred-square-foot millwork shop and set aside space in the warehouse for a classroom with a half dozen woodworking benches. We would schedule woodworking classes in the evenings, and that program would be managed by our master designer/craftsman employee, David Eck, who had a fine reputation for high-quality custom furniture design and construction.

We held a grand opening at our new Bellevue store location and signed up a lot of new customers for our mailing list. Our goal was to increase the retail sales portion of the business and improve the gross margin. We still needed the high-volume business from our professional contractors and cabinet shops to get the required inventory turnover but hoped to get half of our sales from retail customers who would provide the higher profit return.

Sales increased dramatically in Bellevue, and we took our customer mailing list from 2,500 to 10,000 after we began publishing a monthly newsletter. We built our inventory up to include some forty species of hardwood lumber, including the exotic imports, several species of hardwood plywood, and industrial-grade particleboard for cabinetry. The woodworking classes proved to be popular, so we added more. David hired the instructors for these evening classes consisting of four to five sessions each, with a class limit of twelve people. We kept the cost low at thirty to thirty-five dollars, just enough to recover our out-of-pocket cost. The classes generated more sales of lumber, supplies, and tools because they kept our customers active in woodworking. After finishing a class, the student couldn't wait to get started on another project in his or her home shop and put those newly learned techniques to work!

Jim Sypher and I each had a strong sales background, so we were compatible in that regard. He worked primarily with the contractors and cabinet shops while I chose to build up the retail part of the business.

I worked closely with Dave to keep the woodworking classes full and put together the first few issues of our newsletter. My daughter, Pam, came down and helped me run off the mailing labels and apply them to the newsletter each month. Then Dave took over the responsibility of writing the newsletter, and we paid him a few hundred dollars a month to publish it on his computer. He had the technical knowledge of hardwoods and wrote about different species each month and also described the use of tools and techniques in woodworking. We inserted discount coupons, making every effort to increase retail sales.

I set up the accounting system for the business, and Jim agreed to handle the credit accounts for the contractors and cabinet shops. We hired two more employees as the business grew and were making deliveries on a regular basis to the cabinet shops. We had been banking with Seattle First National Bank from the time that Jim opened the business, and they increased our line of credit as the business grew. By the middle of 1983, we were approaching an annual sales level of a million dollars, and we were going to need to inject more capital. If we could buy truckloads of lumber and plywood directly from the mill, it would reduce our cost of sales. To support the increased volume, we would need more working capital.

Sypher informed me that he had promised Jim Anderton an opportunity to buy into the business and that maybe this would be the time to consider him as a partner. Sypher had hired Jim to sell hardwood lumber and panel stock to our contractor and cabinet shop customers before I became involved in the business. He had been working for a hardwoods distributor in Seattle and brought some of those customers to us. He was moving a lot of product for us, but I didn't know that Sypher had made him a promise of ownership when he hired him. Somehow, he failed to mention that. I was beginning to regret my earlier decision to keep Sypher as a partner. He hadn't been carrying his weight in this venture and seemed to lack ambition. He liked to drink coffee and visit with the customers. It seemed like he wanted to be the public relations guy while Anderton and I did the heavy lifting.

I liked "Chico" Anderton. He had an outgoing personality and was an outstanding salesman. Unlike Sypher, he had a lot of energy and a lot of good ideas. He was really excited about working at Northwest Woodcrafters and was always willing to jump in the truck and make a rush delivery to one of our customers. He stayed late at night to straighten up the warehouse. I felt that he would make a better partner than Sypher.

Jim Anderton borrowed $40,000 from his dad and came in as a third partner. He took responsibility for contractor sales, trucking, and warehouse operations. I had the retail sales and accounting responsibility while Sypher took care of customer credit and some of the vendor purchases. One of our employees, Ryan Stute, was an accounting student at college, and he worked primarily for Jim Anderton, making deliveries on our two-ton flatbed truck. He also made some sales calls for Jim and spent time with me on accounting tasks. He was well-motivated and grateful to get some business experience. He told me once, "You know, I've learned more here from you, Gary, than I'll ever learn in college textbooks" about business.

My two sons, Pete and Patrick, came down and helped out periodically, and it really made me feel good to have them around. I was a proud papa. This hardwoods business would be similar to a hardware store, and I was close to realizing my dream of owning a retail business. It wasn't mine totally because I shared ownership with business partners, but I was excited about this opportunity. I also welcomed the challenge of taking a weak business to new heights. Having been successful in business as a corporate manager, and in starting up a complex manufacturing operation at Commencement

Bay, I felt that my business plan for this much smaller business would certainly be successful. I was eager to crank it up and take it to a more profitable level.

I envisioned our three kids there with me, helping out on Saturdays. I wanted to share this experience with the family. Sharon said, "Don't expect our kids to be down there. They have their own lives to live." She was right, of course. We had raised them to be independent and responsible. Still, I was disappointed when they didn't come around very often.

I purchased that share of Northwest Woodcrafters in August 1982, and two years later we were approaching our sales goal of over a million dollars in annual sales, but the sales mix was disappointing. We were not yet meeting the retail sales goal. The vast majority of our sales dollars came from the high-volume, low-margin contractor market. The smaller segment of retail sales meant a shortfall in our overall net profit, or bottom line. Our retail sales promotions, the monthly newsletter, and the woodworking classes all proved to be successful, but we had overestimated the rate of retail sales growth. Our newsletter mailing had grown to more than ten thousand customers, and our woodworking classes had grown from four to twenty-three by 1984. Our customers called Woodcrafters the "College of Woodworking." The retail sales had grown to about 35 percent of the total, but that was far short of our expectations. We remained far too reliant upon contractor sales for the needed cash flow and higher turnover of the inventory. It would take more time to reach our retail sales goal and improve our profit return for this business, but we were on the right track and feeling good about the future for Northwest Woodcrafters. We weren't making a lot of money, but we were above the grass.

I really loved the challenge of this business and was happy in my work. But then, I had always made it a point to be happy in my work, often working long hours but living the "American Dream."

I would have some private moments when I would reflect on my past: coming from a life of poverty to work my way through college; hooking up with large companies and climbing the "corporate ladder"; playing a key role in starting up a big manufacturing plant; buying a small business and making it grow. Although it wasn't my own business since I had kept on a partner, I was in control just the same. Sypher was along for the ride. There could have been a different chain of events. Had I not given up my career opportunity in 1980 and accepted the position with Menasha Corporation as general manager at the showplace plant in Wisconsin, there was a good chance I would have been in line for a position of vice president for that company. Len Tweedie retired a few years after I turned down that relocation, and it's unlikely that Norm Koski would have taken it. He wouldn't have left his native California for the frozen tundra of Wisconsin. I had a great track record with Weyerhaeuser and Menasha; I could have solved the business problems at that Wisconsin plant and been seriously considered for a vice presidency. It would have meant moving the family one more time, however, and I wasn't willing to do that. I had promised the kids we would stay put until they finished school, and, besides, my marriage wouldn't have survived another move.

Then, at Commencement Bay Corrugated, I could have stayed on there after the successful start-up. The business was healthy and was destined to become successful, but I found no compatibility with the people holding the purse strings. My financial partners and I were at cross-purposes. That would have been a stressful and disappointing relationship for me. For many people, the American Dream isn't solely about financial gain, or owning the biggest house, or acquiring all those unnecessary consumer goods. What turns me on is that feeling of accomplishment, productivity, and recognition. It's all about being happy in your work. America is the land of opportunity, but it's not necessary that you compromise your principles. Stay above the grass.

In 1984, I had no regrets. I was a happy man. I liked this hardwoods business and enjoyed making the coffee in the morning and sharing it with our customers, offering woodworking advice, tracking the sales, and maintaining the financial records. There was always plenty of work to be done at the store, and I was happy in my work. I enjoyed being a merchant. I was bringing home a good salary, comparable to what I had been earning in Tacoma, so in that regard I was taking good care of my family.

I had never shed those drinking habits, however, and I usually got into trouble during one of my happy moments. And since I was happy most of the time, I drank a lot. I think it was in late May 1984, after a drinking session with buddies, that I found myself late at night sitting in my Suburban at the marina parking lot in Ballard, a northern suburb of Seattle. The last two cans of a six-pack of beer lay on the seat next to me, and I had no memory of driving there. I next remembered driving in downtown Seattle with red lights flashing in my rearview mirror. The cops pulled me over and took me to the station for a Breathalyzer test. That was the sixth and final time that I was arrested for drunken driving.

The next day, I found a lawyer, Cohen, who specialized in defending drunks, and asked him if he could refer me to the best treatment center in the area. He asked, "Do you think you have a drinking problem?" I told him, "I know I have a drinking problem. I need to do something about it." That was the first time I had made a public admission. There were several occasions in the past when I had privately considered treatment, not just for my sake but for my family as well. Over the years, I had accomplished a great deal in my work, had an exemplary career and a wonderful family. All of this would be wasted if I continued on a downward spiral. I had been fighting this demon unsuccessfully for all these years, and now I was determined to get some help.

Cohen recommended a local treatment center that was affiliated with the Betty Ford enterprise in California. I passed the entrance exam at First Step in Bellevue, Washington, without any difficulty, and the counselor told me that I had qualified for the two-year outpatient program. It would cost more than $2,000, but, looking back, it was the best decision I could have made. It would be a major turning point in my life. I owe a lot to the Man Upstairs because I never would have gone there on my own.

I later learned that only one in thirty-six alcoholics ever get treatment in their lifetime, and only one in three make it through a two-year program such as this without suffering a relapse. Those are not good odds.

I had my last drink on Saturday, July 8, 1984, a week before entering the program. It was a Manhattan cocktail that I drank before dinner when Sharon and I went out with our neighbors, the Johnsons.

There were about a dozen patients in my group at First Step, and the counselors told us that there are two instances where relapse is most likely to occur: the fifth week and again during the fifth month of sobriety. They explained that alcohol and other drugs affect every cell in the human body, including those in the brain. During an extended period of sobriety, many of the cells heal themselves while others do not. By the fifth week of sobriety, brain cells in the brain that affect human emotions are the first to heal. The "electric circuitry" that had been numbed by the alcohol begins to fire, and suddenly you feel emotions that you hadn't felt in years. As emotional sensitivity spikes, it causes feelings of instability in the human psyche, suddenly tearing up over a sad movie, for example. One can experience an emotional roller coaster after that five-week period that can set the stage for a relapse: going "off the wagon," so to speak.

Just as the counselors predicted, I came really close to a relapse in September, and it was my daughter, Pam, who unknowingly came to my rescue. It was about ten in the evening, and I was home alone. I had a sudden and strong urge for a drink and reached into the cupboard for a bottle of whiskey. I had it in my hand when something made me stop and put the bottle back on the shelf, unopened. I immediately picked up the phone and called Pam, "Let's leave for Pendleton tonight."

"You want to leave now? I thought we weren't going to leave until tomorrow."

We had tickets for the Pendleton Round-Up. She and I liked rodeo and had been going to Pendleton together in September the past two years. We hadn't planned to leave until the next day, but I needed to get away from the house, away from that whiskey in the cupboard. I was in need of company and some support, and my daughter came through. She packed her stuff, I picked her up in my Suburban, and we left around eleven that evening for a six-hour drive to Pendleton, in eastern Oregon. This was in September, that critical fifth week of sobriety, and thanks to Pam and God above, I avoided the relapse.

As part of the two-year program at First Step, there is a family night held once each week. Despite my urging, none of my family members attended those sessions. There were very few families who showed up on family night because they didn't realize the importance of being there. "The drunks and junkies need treatment. Not us," was the prevailing attitude. My primary counselor, James Fouts, made it clear that the family needs treatment as well as the patient. Drug dependency by a family member affects the entire family. As addicts go through treatment, there are notable changes in their personalities that affect their relationship with other family members. I told James that Sharon failed to see any reason for her to be attending these weekly family sessions, and my kids followed her lead. They wouldn't be attending the family night program, either. He said, "Don't worry about it. All you can do is ask them. Don't push it. It's most important that you're getting treatment. That's your number-one priority."

My support came from the counselors at First Step (who themselves were chemically dependent with several years in recovery) and fellow drunks at the AA meetings that we were required to attend on a regular basis. Those of us who graduated from the two-year program were told that we now knew more about alcoholism than 95 percent of the American public, including the medical profession. They said doctors don't get involved in treating drunks and junkies. Many don't recognize it as a disease, and there's no money in it. Chemical dependency on drugs and/or alcohol, however, is an incurable disease like diabetes; unlike diabetes, it's progressive. The older one gets, the worse the disease. Alcoholism is a baffling disease that grows worse with time whether you're actively drinking or completely sober. One of the men in treatment with me at First Step told me that he had quit drinking for fifteen years when he relapsed during a European vacation. When he arrived home, he not only continued to drink but also found that his drinking was fifteen years more advanced than when he had quit! He had gone back into the program at the time I was there, beginning a new period of sobriety.

They told me at First Step that my life would change dramatically, and it certainly did. First, my marriage finally crumbled altogether, then my business went down the tubes—or maybe it was the other way around. The marriage had weakened, but the business failed more suddenly, so it's difficult to tell which came first. I was able to cope with these traumatic changes because I was well into recovery. The burden of guilt and remorse had been lifted after gaining a period of sobriety through treatment, and that burden had been replaced with a genuine feeling of peace. The Serenity Prayer had become my rule of life. I had finally gained an understanding of this incredible disease and its effect on the addict, and I now realized how the drinking had affected those close to me.

When our business, Northwest Woodcrafters, failed, I was shocked. I didn't expect that there was any chance of failing. I had always been successful in business and had had an excellent track record throughout the past twenty-one years.

This was a wake-up call. I had read somewhere that every entrepreneur needs to experience a business failure to remain grounded. Like riding a motorcycle, overconfidence can lead to disaster. I was overconfident when I bought a major share of the Woodcrafters operation.

After relocating the business to Bellevue, sales doubled within the first two years. We had drawn up a three-year business plan, and we were well on our way, confident of success. Jim Anderton had come aboard to sell hardwood lumber and plywood to the commercial market: cabinetmakers, interior finish carpenters, and furniture makers in the greater Seattle area. He came to us with a long list of sales contacts and opened many new accounts for us. He did a fantastic job of bringing in the much-needed new sales accounts.

Retail sales, on the other hand, were much more of a challenge than we had anticipated. We employed several marketing strategies: newspaper advertising, a monthly newsletter, and woodworking on site. The mailing list for the newsletter grew from 2,500 to over 10,000, yet the retail sales volume was lagging far behind our plan. That resulted in a lower gross margin on sales despite the increased volume. We had to increase our credit line at Seattle First National Bank to fund the increase in inventory and receivables required to support the sales growth.

As we began our second year of operation in Bellevue, I told my partner, Jim Sypher, that we needed more equity in the business. Most small businesses fail due to underfunding. He then told me for the first time that he had promised Jim "Chico" Anderton at the time of hire that he would have an opportunity to "buy in" as a part owner. Sypher had not disclosed this to me when we negotiated my purchase of 40 percent of the business. Nevertheless, I liked Chico, and he was an energetic guy with a solid background in hardwood sales. If he wished to invest as a partner in Woodcrafters, it was fine with me. We needed an infusion of equity capital, and, after learning that my partner Sypher was lazy, I appreciated that Chico would bring the energy needed to build a small business such as ours. Our attorney drew up the papers, and Chico invested $40,000.

We were now able to pay down some of our bank debt and had enough working capital to buy some of our lumber in truckload quantities directly from hardwood mills in the Midwest and Eastern United States. These purchases resulted in higher margins on commercial sales.

My main concern now was the growth in accounts receivable driven by a higher volume of commercial sales. I wasn't confident of Sypher's ability to manage the receivables. We now had three owner/partners in the business, and that proved to be a problem due to a lack of communication. Chico was responsible for commercial sales and management of our ten-thousand-square-foot warehouse. Sypher took charge of the retail sales floor, purchasing, and customer credit. I handled finance and accounting, sales promotions, and the woodworking classes.

Our accounts receivable began to age. We weren't getting paid within the thirty-day period. Few customers were taking the ten-day cash discount, and many were stretching out their payments to sixty to ninety days after shipment. Sypher was losing control and letting customers exceed their credit limit as well. When the three of us sat down to discuss the situation, he admitted that he had been giving some of our customers a break when they didn't have funds to pay their bills on time, but he felt that they were good for it.

Partnerships are known for having disagreements and personality differences, but with three owners, the problems are compounded by a lack of communication. One tends to assume that the other two are taking care of their responsibilities, so you don't communicate enough.

In 1983, the housing market in the greater Seattle area had stagnated due to overbuilding. There were too many luxury homes on the market. As a hardwoods supplier to finish carpenters, we were indirectly impacted. Our customers, cabinetmakers and finish carpenters, were the last suppliers to the project. When the money ran out, they didn't get paid and, as a result, were late on their payments to us. Collecting from some of the smaller businesses was futile. Many simply locked their doors and walked away. Others had no assets to speak of, and we had granted them way too much credit.

Seattle First National Bank cut off credit to many residential builders and considered our business as a supplier to be risky as well. They had changed loan officers twice during our time with them, and that weakened our relationship with the bank. We were not able to prevent them from continually reducing our line of credit.

Our capital had been squeezed from two sides. After losing $40,000 in uncollected receivables and the reduction of our bank line of credit on the other side, we were forced to sell product on a cash basis. We lost most of our commercial accounts when they switched to other suppliers who could offer them credit.

Chico and I had finally managed to buy out Sypher after a year of negotiating, but it was too late by then. The business was a mere skeleton, and employees were laid off one by one. Chico resigned to save us the expense of his salary, and I agreed to stay on with just two employees, with the slim hope of salvaging at least a portion of the business.

We didn't have nearly enough cash coming in to meet our obligations, so I had to take up this issue with our creditors. I called a meeting at the store and explained the situation to most of our suppliers of lumber, plywood, and hardware. I told them the truth of the matter; we had absorbed some $40,000 in uncollectible receivables on one hand and then were forced to pay off the entire bank debt at Seattle First National Bank. We were not planning to file for bankruptcy protection but would work out a payment plan with each of our creditors, with the goal of paying them off over time. In the meantime, we would continue doing business on a cash basis.

It was obvious to me that the creditors who attended that meeting were favorably impressed that we had laid everything out for them and revealed our financial situation. It was also apparent that some of them had serious doubts of ever seeing full payment from us.

Over the next four months, the remaining two employees and I put in some long hours to keep the store open and bring in whatever sales we could. The sales income was a fraction of what it once was and kept trending downward in volume despite our hard work. I could see no way to turn this around. I was physically exhausted and, after four months, made the ultimate decision to liquidate the business. We then paid our creditors as much as we could after filing for Chapter 7 bankruptcy.

We learned much from this experience at Woodcrafters, but my major lesson was to never again work with a large bank when you're running a small business. The large banks like Seattle First (later merged with Bank of America) are not capable of serving as a financial partner with a small business. We had three different loan officers over a five-year period, young guys who were focused on the larger bank clients and had to be reminded who we were each time we met with them. I never again did business with a big bank where there is no opportunity to develop a personal relationship.

In a letter to my mother dated May 15, 1987, I wrote:

*Dear Mom,*

*Well, I hope to get this package in the mail within the next few days, along with some snapshots we had made from last Christmas that you requested. We've enclosed some of each of us, including Max [the family's boxer], who thinks he's a Perkins too.*

*We are all in excellent health out here, and Pam and the boys are all living away from home, so Ma Perkins and I have had to adjust to that. This has had a major effect on Grandma Florence too. She would like to see them here for dinner every weekend and tells them to bring their laundry.*

*We have heard from Ruth and Judy, and I got a letter from Kelly recently, so it's always nice to hear from all of you. It's been three years since I've been back to Benton, so I'm going to try to get there for Labor Day.*

*Since it's been so long, I am enclosing an update on the family so you can keep track of their movements. Sharon has been flying all over the globe, and Florence and I chart her itinerary from here at the home front. My biggest trip is to the nearest fishing hole or golf course and an occasional overnight campout whenever I get a chance. Haven't done much of that lately, though.*

*We don't like to go off and leave Florence alone in case
she has one of her dizzy spells like the time she fell in the
hall and broke her hip.*

*I am enclosing some cutting boards I made of cherry
and maple for you, Ruth, and Judy, so you have quite a
package here!*

*Please write when you get a chance, and I'll enclose
the kids' addresses. They would like to hear from you too.
Especially Pam; she's stuck in Alaska.*

*Judy is planning to come out this summer, so we hope
to hear from her soon. Anytime is fine except for the last
week in July—I'll be at the Cheyenne Rodeo.*

*Love, Gary*

*P.S. Don't forget your homework assignment! [providing
family history information]*

I attached the following update on the family:

*Pam is up in Alaska this summer again. She had taken a
job last year in the Seattle office of Sea Alaska Packers, the
company she had worked for in the summers during her
college years. They hired her into the Credit Department
with an indication that she would later be trained for
marketing and sales, her primary interest. She did a good
job of straightening out their accounts receivable and
pushing for needed credit policies to be established. This
required some confrontation with the male managers and
sales executives, so there was quite a lot of conflict. She*

*stuck to her guns, though, and earned a lot of respect from the management.*

*Last winter, this company was merged into two or three other Seattle-area seafood packers, so there was quite a lot of confusion. Obviously, the managers and executives of these companies were all jockeying for position, and it was—and still is—a political mess.*

*It was wearing on Pam emotionally, and she got fed up with the whole situation. She volunteered to go up to Sand Point, Alaska, for the summer runs and help get some problems straightened out up there. They would be a "snap" compared to the mess at the Seattle office. She also has experience with the paperwork and documentation for international shipments of seafood, and she suggested to management that she set up those procedures at Sand Point and show the girls up there how to prepare the papers.*

*She has been up there since the first of May and phones us once or twice a week. She is working in the office but occasionally helps out on the packing lines when the fish come in heavy. They only have a few hours to get them all processed before they start to spoil. Some days are quite long, and she sounds tired on the phone.*

*Sand Point is out on the peninsula in the middle of nowhere, with a minimum of facilities. They bring college students up there from all over the U.S., and they stay in a type of dormitory building, but I think Pam shares an apartment with some other girls in the office.*

*Pam and I were going to go to the Cheyenne Rodeo in late July, but now, of course, she won't be going. We've gone to the Pendleton Round-Up every year and were looking forward to Cheyenne as well. We already bought the tickets, so maybe I can talk Sharon into going.*

*I like to drive and sleep on a bunk in the back of the Suburban, but Sharon doesn't like to "rough it." She has been staying in some of the nicest international hotels all over Europe and the Orient. She has been to Mazatlan and Puerto Vallarta, Mexico; Spain; Yugoslavia; Austria; Hong Kong; Seoul, Korea; and just returned from Germany last week. I went with her to San Diego last year and then later to Monterey and Carmel, California, where Clint Eastwood is mayor. We didn't see him but went to his bar and restaurant in Carmel. Monterey is a former fishing village on the coast and is the setting for John Steinbeck's* Cannery Row. *It is pretty as a picture there, and we could have stayed longer if it weren't so expensive. It cost me $18.00 to play a round of golf. That's why I prefer to "rough it"!*

*I haven't joined Sharon on any of the international junkets. (I could have gone to Germany with her for $159.00 for airfare.) The travel agents usually tour about three or four hotels a day, pack and unpack, meet the tour bus at 7:00 a.m. to get to the next stop, go through museums and castles, and so on. I prefer to go someplace and stay there, or maybe take a few side trips of my choosing. In other words, I like to plan the next ten minutes. The castles of Europe don't interest me, but I would like to go to Cornwall and Ireland sometime and visit places of our family heritage. I've been doing a lot of studying in that area, and Florence and I have taken a genealogy course.*

*Sharon really enjoys the travel business, and it's too bad she doesn't have her own business. They are usually not a good investment, though, because they seldom make much profit, and the owners typically use them as a hobby so they can get cut-rate deals on travel. Most people in Redmond think Sharon is the owner. She started it up and books most of the business, while the owners are more or less "silent investors." They put the money into the business so their wife will have something to do—in this case act as an outside sales rep who sells a few tickets to her friends and takes her husband with her on a few trips each year. It's tough on Sharon; she does all the work, and the owners really don't care if the business makes a profit, only that they don't lose their investment. She is carrying the burden on keeping the sales level up, and at the same time is responsible as manager to handle all of the administrative chores. She is toying with the idea of getting out of management and just concentrating on sales. She has enough of a following that she could earn a decent commission and not have to spend such long hours at the office. Now that our kids are gone, we should have more time to spend with each other.*

*Our finances are pretty well shot now that Woodcrafters went bankrupt last year, so maybe both of us should stay in the sales end and keep life simple, for a while at least. I took a second mortgage on the house and borrowed some more money to try to get Woodcrafters "over the hump." If we had made it (and we had a good chance to do it), we could have sold that business for a big chunk or could have turned it over to the kids. Some things worked against us, though, and we went down the tube. I have a lot of personal debt to pay off. As Grandpa Cook would say, "After the dance, it's time to pay the piper." I don't regret what I did, but it is unusual for Perkinses to take big risks like that, I guess; we're a pretty conservative bunch.*

*I'm doing okay now as a lumber salesman, though, handling a line of finish lumber, door, and millwork on a commission basis. I told Pete that when he graduates and becomes a contractor, maybe I could sell him a couple of boards. Pat and I had dinner down in Tacoma a couple of weeks ago (after I filled up his refrigerator), and he suggested that I get a truck and a warehouse someplace and set up my own business in millwork supply. There is a man in Mercer Island who said he would put up the money to back me in a business, but I don't know if I want to go through that again. It's a lot of work and long hours. I've done that twice and helped Sharon start up the travel agency, so I know what it takes. It's interesting that she and I are at the same point in our lives, where we've raised the kids and are each at the same crossroads in our careers. We each have a following in our respective line of "product," so maybe, as I said above, we should just continue selling for others and keep life simple for a change.*

*Florence is doing just fine in spite of her plastic joints and continual pain. We got her a new swivel chair for Christmas that is small, and the seat is a little higher, so she doesn't have to bend so far to sit in it. She watches all of the nighttime "soaps" and knows all of the actors and all about their backgrounds. Her mind is really sharp, and she keeps up on all the latest news and politics despite the fact that she seldom leaves the house. I think she knows more about Reagan than Nancy does! She thinks he's senile and ought to be impeached. She reminds me of Grandpa Cook when he would talk back to Gabriel Heatter on the radio and cuss out the Democrats.*

*She has volumes of information on her family history, and we want to get it organized and recorded before she leaves for Wisconsin June 21. I came home one night in January and told her I had signed up the two of us for a class in genealogy at the community college. She said she wouldn't be able to go to the classes and didn't want to risk injury before going to Wisconsin. I said she wouldn't have to go—that I would pay attention and take notes, then we would review them each week and do our homework together. We haven't gotten too far yet with the organization of material, but I learned how to look up the census and military records in the National Archives. There is a branch in Seattle, so I spent a day in there with my classmates: seven women! Sharon gave me a hard time about being in class with all those girls (average age sixty-five). Needless to say, I was the teacher's favorite. She is about seventy.*

*Anyway, I pored through all the census listings for New Diggings and Benton from 1840 to 1860 but just made a dent in the project because of all the relatives I found. I'll have to go back over to get the Jo Daviess County [Illinois] records and also the Seymour records for Florence's family. 'I found the Cooks and Raisbecks, a bunch of Bennetts and Hockings, but I need to get more dates and places for some of these families so I can go further back. I'll need you to look up whatever records you have and birthdates* and birthplaces, Mom, and fill out a couple of the enclosed sheets as much as possible.

The Seattle library has microfilm of all the newspapers in the country, too, including the Benton Advocate and the [Shullsburg] Pick and Gad, so I might get information from the obituaries if I have an approximate date of death.

Florence has her family records back five generations, and we need to get some information from the Baltimore area. [Uncle] Willie has the Perkins records back five generations also, but I'm having trouble backtracking to England. The Church of England told me to try the Mormon Church in the U.S. They have records right here in Seattle.

Florence keeps busy here at the house, too, with the washing and the dishes. She has to feel she is contributing and keeps constant tabs on our "kids." She always asks them when they are coming to visit and if they can stay for dinner. They've always been good to her and will patiently listen to her advice and counsel. I planted flowers while Sharon was in Germany, and Florence stood out on the back deck with Max to supervise the project. She is frustrated by not being able to plant. She has always been a good gardener. Of course, I had to tell her about Uncle Foss's secret for planting potatoes: he claimed he put an onion in every hill so it would make the potatoes' eyes water.

Florence is still trying to sell her house in Shullsburg and hopes to do it when she is back there this summer. She will clean the house out and wants one of us to go to Wisconsin and drive a rental truck back here with the furniture, etc., that she wants to keep or give to the kids. I *think maybe Sharon or one of the boys will have to fly back with her in June, although she insists she will be perfectly okay by herself. I would like to go to Benton for Labor Day if things work out then.*

*Pete is a junior at the University of Washington and is studying building construction. He was just recently accepted into the School of Architecture, Building Construction Department. They only accepted about thirty-five applicants this year (50 percent), so that is quite an honor for him. It is a nationally recognized branch of the university.*

*He has been studying hard all year and seems to like the construction business. He worked a couple of summers as a framer and also for a remodeling contractor, so he has a lot of practical experience as well.*

*He and one of his friends, Kelly, are building a 1200-square-foot deck for Kelly's sister and her husband at their new home near Redmond. He called me on Wednesday and wanted delivery the next day on 1400 board feet of fir joist material and 1200 square feet of decking. I said, "Hell, you're just like these other 'contractors,' placing orders with no lead time." I gave him a good price, though, and didn't rip him off too badly.*

*I went up to their job site today to see how they were doing. They were taking twenty minutes to set each pier block and were using an engineer's sextant to get them all perfectly level. They hadn't even started laying the joists yet. I told them they were slower than [my cousin] Duffy Mulligan. It's a good thing the brother-in-law wasn't paying them by the hour!*

*Pete, Kelly, and another guy from Lewiston, Idaho, share an old apartment in North Seattle, just a mile or so from the U. It's an old store that was converted into an apartment, so it sits right on the street, and the large windows have been closed off to make it a little more private. The rooms are quite large, and the place is pretty well beat up, so Pete says they don't have to worry about damage, and they can be "comfortable." I took Sharon and Grandma Florence ("Granny") over there, and I think Granny was a little bit shocked. There was stuff lying all over the place, four big stereo speakers nailed to the walls, and speaker cords running everywhere. The kitchen table was surfaced with a piece of Masonite, which was all carved up. The table came from the university laboratory; I guess they talked a maintenance man into giving it to them. It wasn't very sturdy, but I guess it does the job.*

*Of course, we all guessed which bedroom was Pete's. It was relatively tidy, and I recognized the posters: Bo Derek and the Ferrari.*

*His brother, Pat, and roommates are another case. He had to go down to Tacoma to help Pat fix a wall at their apartment before they moved out. It seems Pat and Tom Magruder were wrestling, and Tom got pushed partway through the plasterboard wall. Pat said he hung a picture over the hole, but it was kind of low on the wall, and he thought maybe the landlord would notice it. They had gotten into trouble with the landlord on several occasions. (He lived downstairs.) They were now going to move into another apartment, and he requested assistance from Pete to help them fix the wall.*

*Sharon and I can't get over how the boys have changed as they've gotten older. They used to fight all the time when they were young, and Pete never had much time for Pat, so each had their own friends. Now when they get together, they sit and talk—just the two of them.*

*Pete never did much dating in high school. It was always baseball and running with his buddies from the ball team. The past two years, he's made up for that! Sharon and I can't remember half the names of the girls he brings to the house. Of course, we're getting older too, and they say the memory is the second thing to go after you turn forty. I can't remember what the first thing is.*

*He has been dating one girl pretty regularly lately, though. Her name is Maryann, and I think Pete likes her quite a bit. Her family lives here on the east side, but she goes to college in Bellingham, 150 miles north of here. He brings her to the house quite often, and she seems really nice, with a good sense of humor.*

*I guess Pete will be painting houses this summer with his friend Keith.*

*Pat had his best year in baseball as a senior in high school last year. He broke a finger twice, though—two different fingers on two different occasions—when he was sliding into bases. Once, the pitcher accidentally stomped on his hand while trying to tag Pat at third base. He was safe, but his finger was lacerated, with a minor fracture.*

*He was invited to play in the "feeder game" at the end of last year, but he couldn't play because he had another finger in a splint. The "feeder" is sort of an exhibition game where high-school seniors are reviewed by the college scouts for possible scholarships. He obviously did not win a scholarship, but he was invited by the coach at Pierce College to come down and try out for baseball there.*

*Pierce College is a community college (or junior college) in Tacoma. Two of his high-school buddies were given scholarships there of about $1,000.00, and Pat was happy to be going down there with them.*

*Of course, Granny wasn't too happy about Pat leaving home. He was the last one, with both Pam and Pete living in Seattle. She was hoping he would go to a school close to home. Pat, however, was excited about living away from home with his buddies in their own apartment and also about getting an opportunity to play ball. It was going to be interesting to see how he made out with managing his own money and living expenses; he had never managed money as well as his brother. With Pat, it was always deficit spending.*

*Well, he took a job waiting tables at a bar and restaurant in Tacoma, signed up for some easy classes, played baseball, and began dating some Tacoma girls. Surprisingly, he has learned to manage his money well. He has set up a budget and schedules his phone, rent, and other payments much better than some of his friends, who call home quite often because they overdraw their checkbooks. He doesn't have a car down there, so he rides the bus to work and has to bum a ride home once in a while. He doesn't come home often because he works most weekends at the restaurant and serves brunch every Sunday. I tell people when asked that Pat is majoring in baseball and girls. He's taking some serious classes now, though, and gets good grades. He will probably major in business.*

\* \* \* \* \* \*

Shutting down the business wasn't so difficult after having phased out the Menasha operation four to five years earlier. I was now saddled with a lot of personal debt when my two partners at Woodcrafters filed for bankruptcy, but I kept a cool head and knew that I could work my way out from under. After all, money can be a temporary possession in many cases and, as they say, "comes and goes."

The divorce, however, was another matter. It was far more traumatic for me than I could ever have imagined. Sharon was extremely distressed over the failure of the hardwoods business. She had become deeply concerned about the financial implications and wanted me to file for personal bankruptcy. She was understandably frightened, and I tried my best to assure her that these debts could be settled through negotiation and that I was sure we could reduce them to a fraction of their face value. It would pinch us temporarily, but we could get the remainder paid off within a few years' time. I argued that bankruptcy should be the last resort. We weren't at that point, I insisted, and I didn't want to needlessly betray a friend of ours who had loaned money to the business. The other debts were considerably more, due to our having to sign personal guarantees for the corporation, but I was certain that I could negotiate with those parties and settle for pennies on the dollar. After all, they expected to incur a total loss when our business went down; therefore, any money gained would be a real plus for them.

She reminded me that my two partners had already declared bankruptcy and "now you are left holding the bag" for the entire debt. "You should follow their lead and file for bankruptcy too," she declared.

I couldn't do that. It wasn't in my character to stiff people if I could avoid it.

My refusal to file for bankruptcy was undoubtedly the final issue that brought on the divorce. Despite my confidence in resolving those debts, she determined in her mind that financial disaster lay ahead and wanted no more discussion of the subject. She filed divorce papers against me shortly after that. I have a vivid memory of her serving me the papers. It was in the evening, after dinner. She and her mother had been watching television in the living room, and I was lying on our bed, reading a book. She came into the bedroom and handed me the divorce papers, saying, "I have filed the papers. I told you I would. You don't have to move out right away. You can stay here as long as you need to."

My heart sank. I don't remember what I said, maybe something like, "This isn't necessary, Sharon; you didn't have to do this." My mind was blank, in a stage of shock, I suppose, but there was no anger, thank God. I didn't sleep much that night.

It was difficult to focus for the next couple of weeks as I removed some of my personal belongings and moved into a small apartment. The worst part was having to bear this trauma alone. I had never felt so lonely in all my life. The recent counseling at the treatment center kept me centered to some degree, but now that I was more in touch with my feelings, my emotions ran wild, up and down like a roller coaster. I had deep regret for having failed in marriage and being at least partly responsible for bringing us to this emotional trauma. I could have said or done some things differently, but I knew that I could not have compromised on the bankruptcy issue. Looking back now, this was likely another example of my Cornish independence. I couldn't lower my principles. I had to remain above the grass.

I found a small apartment in Monroe, Washington, a few miles north and east of Redmond. I didn't have many furnishings: a bed and a couple of chairs, a sofa and some plastic dairy cases to use as lamp tables. I had built an oak poker table that now served as a kitchen table, and Sharon allowed me to take the stereo receiver and speakers. I had no television, nor did I need one. Most of my books were left behind, but I took a few for nighttime reading. I joked to friends that the only dish she allowed me to have was a yellow plastic bowl that we had gotten as a "premium" with a sack of dog food. I made several trips to The Yellow Front discount store to buy a few more dishes and house ware items.

I began to focus on my immediate task of helping Neal Schwartz, one of my former customers at Woodcrafters, start up a new hardwoods business or, to be more accurate, a new business for him. He had first approached me when we were liquidating Woodcrafters. He said that he liked the way I ran a business and that if I were willing to help him get a similar business started, we could form a partnership. Neal had been a salaried technician for the 3M Company for many years, and operating a small business was to be a new experience for him. He would put up the money but wanted to remain employed at 3M and would count on me to be the manager. I was to locate a building to lease, line up vendors, stock the inventory, sell some commercial customers, and get the business rolling. He would be available to help on Saturdays and weeknights. He said, "You will be the manager, and I will work for you." I agreed to take on this task, but told him, "Let's get it going, and if we still have a viable business after two years, we can discuss forming a partnership. For now, you can pay me a small salary that won't overburden a new business, plus a commission on commercial sales that can be deferred and paid to me later on." He agreed to this, and I had the papers drawn up by a Redmond attorney.

This business was just getting off the ground when I was served the divorce papers. The new business became my main focus while going through the divorce. I worked seven days a week at the hardwoods store: bidding jobs, handling retail sales on the floor, running shop machinery, unloading truck deliveries, stacking lumber and plywood, and keeping the books. The hard physical work and mental challenges kept me focused and relaxed at the same time. Neal worked just as hard when he was available. We worked every Saturday and Sunday. After opening the business in January 1987, I took my first Sunday off in November of that year. My concentration on this new business venture was certainly a key factor in my ability to deal with the ending of my twenty-six-year marriage, but as I thought about it later on, there was a much stronger influence gained through the alcohol treatment program and the guidance of a Higher Power. Together, that supported me through the crisis and brought me an inner peace that I have been blessed with ever since.

The professional counseling obtained during my alcohol treatment program has paid huge dividends in my life. I am no longer driven with anxiety and stress. In my former life, I would get unduly concerned about an issue or feel the need to take action or to solve a problem. Now it is not an obsession, but a measured approach to the situation. As I dealt with the emotional trauma of the separation and divorce at age forty-eight, I was able to sustain that inner peace. I was now significantly more in touch with my feelings, and while emotions were present, they were less extreme. I had a much better understanding of my past behavior and the reasons behind those undesirable actions. At the same time, the counseling taught me to not be apologetic, not to be sorry, but instead feel regret for any past actions that might have hurt family members and friends. My chief counselor, James Fouts, told us, "It's good to regret past actions because it's part of the healing process, but never say you're sorry. Feeling sorry will bring back that burden of guilt that you are trying to eliminate from your past." Guilt feelings are the biggest danger, an obstacle to one's recovery, because guilt often leads to hurt, then anger, and finally a strong sense of resentment. Resentment is a common cause of an alcoholic's relapse, we were told. "You have to get rid of the baggage you've been carrying around all those years."

During the first few weeks of treatment, the counselors forced us to individually recall as many bad behavioral experiences as we could where we had hurt other people and caused embarrassment to ourselves. They pounded at us over and over to get those past experiences out into the light and examine them one by one. This was a painful experience and reminded me of the psychological mind games of boot camp in the US Navy. As I dredged up the bad behavioral episodes of the past, one would lead to another and then another, like a magician pulling a chain of silk handkerchiefs from his sleeve. Once I began the process in the counseling sessions, it continued for weeks afterward—while I was sitting at home, or driving down the highway, or even when I was at work. I kept vomiting the stuff up that had been buried deep within the recesses of my mind over the many years of drinking.

Later on, as I continued on the path of the Twelve Steps to recovery, I had to make a most difficult attempt to make amends to those persons who I had hurt in the past. I'm sure that some of those attempts were clumsy, but I had good intentions and felt a great deal of relief as some of those burdens of guilt were lifted from my mind. The entire process was painful but effective in my healing process.

After about six weeks into the program, it was apparent that my personality had changed. For the first time in many years, I had a better understanding of myself and felt better. I could discuss my feelings openly with others. As Fouts predicted, by the fifth week some of my cells in the emotional portion of the brain began to heal after the effects of alcohol, and my emotions rose to the surface. I would find myself welling up over a sad or heartwarming movie, often with tears running down my cheeks. I couldn't remember that happening to me since childhood.

My behavioral change after treatment didn't save our marriage. On the contrary, it widened the breach between Sharon and me. Having cast off my burden of guilt, I wasn't the same guy. I was no longer on the defensive, didn't visit the "doghouse," and was no longer as manipulative or as prone to agitated reactions. I was truly at peace. Fouts had forewarned me, as I reached the end of the first year of treatment, that these changes could have an adverse effect on my marriage because I would become a different personality. He said, "This is often an unfortunate outcome of successful treatment. It would be extremely helpful if your wife and children would attend the family segments that are part of our program." He said that I should bring this up as a suggestion to them and cautioned me not to force the issue, because they would probably feel that this treatment problem was mine and not theirs. They don't realize that the family members require treatment as well as the alcoholic or drug-dependent family member. Again he cautioned me not to force the issue: "From here on, you have to look out for yourself first. Your main purpose is to maintain your sobriety." I took the Serenity Prayer to heart: accept the things I cannot change, have the courage to change the things I can, and have the wisdom to know the difference. I had turned an important corner, and whatever happened from here, I had to move on with my life.

The single life after a twenty-six-year marriage was a lonely and difficult time of adjustment. Since my social life was limited to the AA meetings and a restaurant meal on occasion, I buried myself in work. I spent twelve-hour days at Hardwoods Supply, and the new venture needed all of my attention. Neal came in to help in the evenings and on the weekends as sales steadily rose. It took us about six months to reach a break-even point, and I could then hire a bookkeeper and a warehouse worker. I prepared most of my meals at home. My sister Judy mailed me a recipe book published by the Leadmine Ladies' Aid Society, and Aunt Bertha sent me a recipe for her baked beans and yeast buns. Bertha learned her cooking skills from Grandma Perkins and didn't have any recipes, so she said, "As I prepared a pot of beans, I measured and wrote down the ingredients as I went along." It was the same for the bread. I ate my meals at the poker table and washed dishes by hand. I had the stereo to keep me company, and I enjoyed reading, mostly spy or detective novels. With the twelve-hour workdays, I often fell asleep with the book on my chest.

The divorce proceedings in 1987 had caused a rather distant and cautious relationship with my three adult children. I would meet them for lunch on occasion, and the boys would come by Hardwoods Supply, sometimes to work a few hours. I was very conscious of not discussing the divorce or bringing up the recent past with any of them. I knew it was a difficult period for them as it was for me. I remember Pat early on said, "Dad, I'll have lunch with you, but I don't want to discuss anything between you and Mom." He was setting the ground rules before we went to lunch. I appreciated his expressing his feelings, but it was unnecessary on my account; I wouldn't have brought up the subject. I just wanted to spend time with him.

We were all uncomfortable during those early meetings, and I sometimes felt that I was being patronized, but I'm sure it was an awkward approach by my kids to reach out to me. I was extremely grateful for any time they were able to grant me. After a twenty-six-year period as a family, I felt awkward as well. It was a tough deal for all of us. In spite of the two years of deep introspection through counseling and the Twelve Step healing process, I couldn't prevent flashes of guilt, like old bruises, barely beneath the surface. I was now much more sensitive as well. After digging deep within my "baggage" to recall those terrible experiences of the past, I found that those devils would resurface at times, and then one memory would lead to another and another, just as before. They were no longer buried but popping up to the surface, boiling over. Hopefully they would eventually vaporize and be gone forever.

My counseling taught me to recognize these experiences (some called it the "bleeding process") and to avoid any feelings of guilt because that can lead to relapse, and I was determined to maintain total abstinence from alcohol. I continued to go to the AA meetings. The support of those fellow addicts and my belief in God kept me on track. My close friend, Ron Reid, had entered recovery a few years earlier. He agreed to serve as my sponsor and mentor. I still keep in touch with him.

Regrettably, I had to avoid many old friendships because they had centered on drinking, and I had to change my social habits. But then, I had no social life to speak of after the divorce aside from a meal out at a restaurant once in a while. It was two years before I dated. She was a waitress at a restaurant in Monroe. Later on, I met a woman at Hardwoods Supply who came to our annual tool swap held in the parking lot. She had no interest in woodworking but said she just stopped by with her girlfriend out of curiosity. I served them a bowl of my famous Terlingua, Texas, chili that I always cooked up for the outdoor swaps. She said the chili was hot, and maybe she thought the same about me, because we dated a few times after that.

# CHAPTER 19

# STARTING OVER AT AGE FIFTY

I met Rose on the twenty-third of June 1989. I had eaten dinner at a restaurant in Monroe and then decided to check out a country and western band that was playing at the Hayloft Saloon. Having taken an available seat at the bar and ordering a Pepsi, I turned around on the barstool to face the band as they played. The place was packed. After a while, I noticed a group of four women at a table who were frequently being invited to dance by different guys, and they seemed to be having a really good time. I took special note of one woman with spiked hair who was wearing white jeans. After a couple more numbers, I decided to go over to their table and ask her to dance. Before I could get up, some guy beat me to it, and she danced with him.

A few numbers later, I had finished my second Pepsi and was about to leave. As I passed the table of women, the brunette in the white jeans was standing right there, in front of me, so I asked her to dance. It was a Texas swing type of number with a nice easy tempo. After the dance, I followed her to the table, where we made small talk while waiting for the band to strike up the next number. We danced the rest of the night until the band closed down for the evening. We exchanged phone numbers, and I promised to phone her the next day.

We dated on a regular basis after that. She was in the final stages of a divorce settlement and had two teenagers at her home in Monroe. She was in the process of gaining formal custody of David and Jolynn. It had been a bitter divorce. Rose's husband had deserted his family to be with a woman in California whom he had met during a business trip. There had been succeeding trips to California, followed by his decision to abandon his family with no apparent warning. It had been a traumatic shock for the kids as well as for Rose. After all, they had been married for eighteen years.

As our relationship grew closer, I learned that there had also been abuse in the family: verbal abuse where he often disrespected Rose in front of the children. He was a controlling individual who felt a psychological need to put others down, especially his wife. As a result, Rose had very low self-esteem and now found herself abandoned by her husband, the breadwinner. She was scared to death of the future. She had not held a job since she was in her twenties, working as a waitress. With no training and no recent work experience, her job opportunities would be limited.

Speaking from experience, a family breakup is one of the most traumatic times of one's life, and for Rose and the two kids, that was extremely so. I soon found the family to be highly stressed and dysfunctional as each member was forced into a new role when the husband/father left them on their own. Because Rose had often been disrespected by her husband in front of the kids, she now had difficulty with maintaining parental authority. When I came to the house to see

Rose, I often witnessed arguments, shouting and screaming, and objects thrown across the room. My first inclination was to get the hell away from that situation! After all, I was still in the process of healing in my own regard and had to concentrate on my sobriety. I didn't need this additional turmoil in my life right now. I was thinking that I shouldn't get into a relationship with a woman in her situation. She and her two teenagers displayed emotional outbursts, insulting and personally destructive remarks to one another, and, at times, violence—ripping the phone off the wall, for example.

Rose said in later years, "I don't know why you didn't just take off running, as far away as you could get!"

There was a great deal of emotional pain in this family, and I could feel them hurting. Having just gone through a two-year counseling program, I recognized the signs and felt I could help in some way. There was something or Somebody who told me that I could not simply walk away. These people were hurting, and the hurt, left untreated, leads to anger. Maybe I could help ease some of their pain.

I had grown fond of Rose these past few months and, as any psychologist will tell you, love is an emotion, and emotions seldom make sense. Love and logic are often not compatible. I was physically attracted to Rose, who reminded me of Angie Dickinson through her mouth and eyes. She had a great sense of humor and was fun to be with whenever she could set her recent troubles aside. She was uncomplicated and enjoyed the simple things in life, just as I did. She was open and honest with a good sense of values, which I respected.

Had I not recently gone through the extensive counseling program, I might have walked away from this dysfunctional family. However, I felt that I understood the tremendous hurt that they had suffered. Rose's low self-esteem from the years of abuse would be more difficult to overcome and might never be totally reversed, but maybe we could improve the situation somehow. It certainly was worth a try, because after those two years, I found that I loved her very much. Besides, I looked forward to the challenge. As they say at the Pendleton Round-Up, "Let 'r Buck!"

Most of us learn from life's experiences. I've always been a good student of life and have applied what I have learned. I don't leave it "in the classroom." My ability to learn was borne out during boot camp in the US Navy where I scored sixty-nine of a possible seventy-two on the GCT test, which measures an ability to learn. I've been fortunate. My ability to build on past experiences in business allowed me to confidently venture into new endeavors with a good degree of success: the youngest office manager in Weyerhaeuser's Shipping Container Division; project leader for computer system development, guiding those projects through uncharted waters in the 1960s; a leading salesman of packaging in the third most competitive industry in the Chicago market; and the planning and successful start-up of a new manufacturing operation in the midst of the deep recession of 1980. I take pride in those accomplishments as a leader and manager.

There were second thoughts about my dubious decision to walk away from a successful career in the packaging industry in 1982 at age forty-three, but I remain convinced that it was the right decision. My career path was pulling me away from a commitment to family responsibilities at that time. I had always tried to put family first. When my employer wanted me to relocate my family once again to the Midwest, with a promotion to manage a much larger plant with high visibility, despite a golden business opportunity, I felt an obligation to fulfill my promise to remain in Redmond, Washington, until our kids finished high school. I would be passing on one hell of an opportunity that could have paved the way to a vice presidency. I struggled with the decision for a brief time but stayed true to my convictions and resigned from Menasha Corporation. It was the right thing to do. Our three kids were able to finish their high-school education in Redmond, graduated with their close friends, and went on to become successful in their life's plans. I am really proud of each of them.

My life wasn't without failure. The Woodcrafters business had failed in 1984 and had to be liquidated. Then my marriage failed a couple of years later. These setbacks are a basis for learning but can be beneficial only after you get past the deep trauma and emotional turmoil of personal failure. Outside counsel can be very helpful, and for some, it is necessary during those periods.

The one underlying thread throughout most of my adult life, one that impacted my life greatly, was the demon of alcoholism. Because there is no cure for this disease, the characteristics and side effects will always be with me. As a result of my two years of counseling, I can recognize them and limit their impact to some degree, but I know that I cannot change them. I've often had periods of low self-esteem, for example, going way back to my high-school years. My classmates elected me senior class president because they apparently saw me as a leader, although I saw myself as an underachiever. At the time, I thought my feelings were due to childhood poverty, but learned in recent years that low esteem is a common characteristic of alcoholics. It's likely that I will always be an overachiever, a workaholic, due to the low self-esteem that often accompanies this baffling disease.

Someone up there guides us through those life experiences brought on by our unending string of life choices, good and bad. But then, some of the bad choices can have good results if you keep the faith. A Higher Power is involved in our day-to-day living, despite our individual beliefs. I experienced a chain of events between 1984 and 1989 that completely changed my life. First, there was my unforeseen decision to get into an alcohol treatment program. That was followed by two traumatic experiences: a business failure and the final collapse of my twenty-six-year marriage. During that period, I was able to take a personal inventory of my life and determine a course for the future. Toward the end of that five-year period, Rose and her two kids came into my life.

I had made the decision to change my social life in order to maintain my sobriety. I had to avoid old hangouts and former drinking buddies and create a whole new environment. I needed to start a new life, and I wanted Rose to be a big part of it. We talked and talked during that time. Both of us were going through our respective healing processes, and we were in harmony. She became a bright light in my life at a time when I was absorbed in deep thought and emotional strife. I was pretty much antisocial until I met Rose.

Her son, David, and daughter, Jolynn, were going through transition as well. They were still in denial and refusing to deal with the pain brought on by the hurtful divorce. I succeeded in getting them to go to a counselor in Monroe only once or twice. They didn't want to be there, and the counselor was ineffective, so I didn't push it any further.

David was graduating from high school in Monroe, Washington, but Jo was having serious problems at school with low grades. She wasn't concentrating on her studies and was hanging out with a bunch of undesirables. Rose and I together decided that with Jo's problems at school, and her association with the wrong crowd, it would be best to change our environment. All of us had come through traumatic experiences due to the divorces and broken families, so it would be of further benefit from that standpoint as well to leave the area and begin a new life experience. We needed to make a major move geographically.

Rose and I had some preliminary discussions about relocating, but before I asked her to marry me, I asked David and Jolynn for their permission, or at least I wanted to get them to tell me how they felt about me marrying their mom. I was encouraged by their response.

They both felt that I would become a good influence for her and that she needed some "positives" in her life. She had been burdened with a lot of baggage from her past marriage and had suffered through a verbally abusive relationship.

We agreed that it would be best to leave the Pacific Northwest and begin a new life. We both liked western Montana as a first choice, but after making some phone calls back there, we learned that economic conditions were depressed, and it would be difficult for me to find satisfactory employment in the wood products industry. We then discussed the merits of settling in her home state of Vermont or in my home area of Wisconsin. She favored Wisconsin primarily because I had family there, and she had never been associated with a large family. I had described my happy family life in Benton with gatherings for holidays and Sunday dinners with relatives, and that type of experience appealed to her. Conversely, her early life in Vermont had not been a happy time for her, and she said she wasn't close to any of her relatives back there. It had been over thirty years since she left Vermont, and she had left at the young age of seventeen to "get away from unhappy memories."

We acknowledged that there would be a serious downside to moving some 2,100 miles from the Seattle area. I would be leaving my family behind and would miss seeing my three adult children and, potentially, grandchildren on a regular basis. But then, some of my family might relocate someday as well, due to a job transfer or for other reasons. Regardless, we rationalized that we would only be a plane ride away no matter where we lived.

The positive side of the move was a chance to start over for the three of us. Since David would be going on to college, Rose, Jolynn, and I could establish a new home in a new environment, gain new friends and neighbors, and Jo would have a new school environment where her teachers wouldn't be constantly comparing her performance to that of David, the older brother, as they had done in the Monroe schools.

This would be a serious challenge for Jo initially. Uprooting a teenager of junior-high or high-school age was generally not a good idea. After all, I had refused to do that to my kids and gave up my career in the packaging industry back in 1980 to prevent just such a traumatic experience for my family. Rose felt, however, that in Jolynn's case, the move could prove beneficial to her in the long run because she appeared to be on a downhill slide in Monroe, and something had to be done. By moving to a new region of the country, Rose knew that Jo would be forced to break away from some undesirable associates and a disappointing school environment.

We didn't kid ourselves. This relocation would cause some initial pain and stress for all of us, and we would have to maintain a positive attitude, especially for Jo's sake. For me, now past the age of fifty, it would be a tremendous challenge as well. I considered this as I began packing the rented truck with household goods and wondering if I wasn't too old to be starting over in a new career with a new set of family responsibilities. The twenty-four-foot truck was packed literally to the tailgate. I left my wheelbarrow for the neighbor and gave Pat my salmon rod and bowling ball. He thought I could surely find room for those in the truck, but I told him, "There are no salmon in the Mississippi River, and I won't have any time for bowling!" We headed east on Interstate 90 with all three of us in the cab of a Budget rental truck, Jolynn's two pet rats in an aquarium on the floorboards, and Jolynn bawling her eyes out! Thankfully, our trip improved after we crossed the Cascade Mountains.

* * * * * *

On Wisconsin!

Rose and I were married just shortly before the move, on April 19, 1991. She was a pretty bride in her pink dress as she held a bouquet of red roses. Jolynn, at age fifteen, was the maid of honor. My close friend and AA sponsor, Ron Reid, was best man. The wedding was held at Pete's home with a small gathering of family and close friends.

The day after the wedding, I drove back to Wisconsin to start the new job while Rose got things in order for our move, which was scheduled for the end of the month. I had accepted a job as a building material sales representative for a business just north of LaCrosse, Wisconsin. That was not my original plan for a career change, however. I had flown back there a month earlier for a scheduled final interview with a Weyerhaeuser Company subsidiary, Northwest Hardwoods, Inc. I had met with their regional vice president in Tacoma, and he had described a need for a hardwood lumber sales representative in Wisconsin. He had set up a meeting for me with the sales manager in LaCrosse. The day before the scheduled interview with the Wisconsin regional sales manager, I learned that he had suffered a heart attack while on a trip to Japan and wouldn't be available to interview me for some time. That put me into a bit of a crisis because I was in immediate need of a job.

When I arrived in Madison, I borrowed my sister Judy's car and began job-hunting near my hometown of Benton in the Dubuque area and then explored possibilities farther north along the Mississippi toward the LaCrosse area. That's how I eventually landed the job as a salesman for Beaver Builders' Supply on Beaver Creek in the city of Galesville, Wisconsin. I had interviewed several prospects as I traveled north from Dubuque.

It had been an interesting interview with Greg Stellrecht of Beaver Builders. I had simply walked in there cold, unannounced, and he asked me if I was responding to the ad. I said, "What ad?" It turned out that he had placed a newspaper ad for a sales representative one week earlier. I told him that I didn't know about the ad. He said, "What are you doing, just tripping up and down the river, looking for work?" There was a home show going on at the time in LaCrosse, and I told him that I had picked up some literature about his company at the show, and since I had experience in supplying hardwood and millwork to contractors, I could probably be of service at Beaver Builders' Supply. The interview progressed well, and he asked me to stay over and continue discussions on Saturday. I spent a couple of hours with him the next morning, then drove back to Madison, dropped off my sister's car, and caught a plane back to Seattle.

Greg contacted me the next week, and we negotiated a salary figure over the phone. He wanted me to start right away, but I told him I was to be married later that week, on the nineteenth of April, and could be back there to begin work on the following Monday.

The wedding was on Friday, and on Saturday I kissed my new bride good-bye and pointed my Suburban east for the 2,100-mile trip to Wisconsin. I drove straight through with a brief rest at a roadside park in Gillette, Wyoming. I crossed the Mississippi early Monday morning and drove into Galesville to start my new career.

My first assignment was inside sales, working with contractors on cost estimates and special nonstock material orders. This position provided me with a basic knowledge of the company's line of products. From my past experience with remodeling my homes, I was familiar with most building materials, so I quickly got up to speed. While in Washington, prior to the wedding, I had spent some time with Pete, who had been working several years for contractors, and he showed me how to perform a material list "take-off" from a set of builder's blueprints. He also gave me a quick course on some important building material nomenclature. Beaver Builders supplied a complete line of materials for residential construction from the foundation up, including doors, windows, siding, and roofing. They had their own roof truss plant to build custom roof systems as well. Thanks to my son Pete, I was able to hit the ground running.

After a week on the job, Greg agreed to give me a few days off so that I could fly back to Seattle, load up the rental truck, and bring Rose and Jo back to Wisconsin, along with her two pet rats that I named Homer and Jethro. David was staying with friends in the Seattle area. After loading the truck and getting on the road with Rose's Mercury Tracer in tow, the trip was uneventful once we crossed the Cascades, and just a bit boring as we drove through South Dakota. The women passed the time by counting road kill and keeping score by species. Jo identified some of the flattened masses as UFOs, "unidentified flattened objects." We finally crossed the river and into Galesville where we located a storage space for the load of household goods. After unloading, I managed to get the rig stuck in loose gravel that had not been compacted. We were just a block away from Beaver Builders' yard, so one of the employees brought over a truck, hooked up a chain, and managed to pull the front bumper loose from the Budget rental truck before getting us out of there. Fortunately, the agency didn't notice the damage when I turned the truck in at Minneapolis.

I had been staying in temporary quarters, a small brick building with just two rooms, across the river in Homer, Minnesota. This rental unit was on the Mississippi shoreline, complete with a fishing dock. The three of us stayed there while we hunted for a house to rent. There was one large room that served as a kitchen, dining, and sitting room, then a small bedroom with a double bunk bed. Rose and I cuddled up in the lower bunk. We were still on our honeymoon, so to get some privacy we would sneak out to the Suburban late at night after Jo fell asleep. The rental place was cramped but served as a "summer cottage" where we could fish from the dock. The tugboats pushing barges up and down the river blew their horn as they passed within a hundred yards of us.

We couldn't find a single-family home to rent in Galesville, but there were several older homes for sale, some of which had been listed for over a year. It was a buyer's market. The local Bank of Galesville agreed to finance the purchase of an older home that Rose fell in love with, but we would have to raise money for the down payment. That posed a problem because we were both heavily in debt when we left Washington.

On paper, I owed more than $100,000 in personal guarantees on the failed Woodcrafters business, and she owed money on the mobile home in Monroe that her ex-husband had dumped on her in the divorce. This bank, however, was locally owned. Since Galesville was a small town and business there was done on a personal basis, the loan officer agreed to make a conventional loan if we could come up with the down payment. I soon realized that word traveled fast in Galesville, and many of the townspeople knew about my hiring on at Beaver before we arrived. They knew me as the new guy at Beaver. Greg had a good reputation there, and I'm sure that also contributed to our loan approval at the bank. We lacked the cash for the down payment, and after selling my Suburban, we were still about $800 short. I managed to borrow the remaining cash from my uncle Bill Perkins in Blue River, and we moved into the house in Galesville. I insisted on writing Uncle Bill a personal note with 8 percent interest.

The move to Wisconsin turned out to be good for us in the larger scheme of things, but I couldn't help but realize at that time just how much my life had changed over the past few years. This was a far cry from being in line for a vice presidency at a large corporation like Menasha, or from being president and general manager of Commencement Bay

Corrugated. Here I was, struggling to come up with a few hundred dollars to get my new family in off the street!

However, that move to Wisconsin turned out to be the best thing that could have happened for me and my second family. Once again, Somebody up there was looking out for us. We adjusted to the new lifestyle and even joined a local church. Rose and I are both divorced Catholics and could no longer receive the sacraments, so we decided to join the First Presbyterian Church in Galesville and went to church almost every Sunday. It was close by, next to a park, and a pleasant three-block walk from our home. We had many blessings for which to be thankful. During the ten years in Galesville, we managed to not only get out of debt (I was able to negotiate settlements of pennies on the dollar) but we were also able to update our home by building a new garage and woodworking shop. I was earning a decent salary at Beaver Builders' Supply, and Rose was hired at a local factory with good pay and benefits. After settling the debts, we were able to invest money in mutual funds. At one point, we had money in five mutual funds through 401(k) and IRA programs. We were once more above the grass.

Jolynn's first year at Galesville High School was very difficult. She was an outsider coming into a small-town school, where she was met with skepticism and outright rejection by some of the local students. Needless to say, newcomers were not readily accepted. But during her second year at Galesville, she won a spot on the gymnastics team and gained the respect of a better class of friends, and her grades steadily improved. She has always been bright with a quick mind, and when she applied herself in a more positive manner, she finished high school as an A student.

There were some sad times in Wisconsin too. In September 1993, I lost my sister, Ruth, at the young age of fifty-two to complications of primary biliary cirrhosis. We learned that it's a genetic strain in our family. Our father had died in 1965, and it was later learned that he likely had that same disease. After Ruth died, Judy and I both had blood tests, and it was revealed that Judy had the same affliction, but it was in the beginning stages. She has to take medication for the rest of her life to control the progression, and I have repeatedly reminded my three children to monitor their liver enzyme count as I have done on a regular basis.

Earlier, in March of that same year, my mother died at age eighty-five. Her heart finally gave out after years of trouble. She had rheumatic fever when I was young, back in 1953, and she also had Bright's disease as a child, so her heart remained damaged throughout her adult life.

My mother and both of my sisters were fond of Rose, and the feelings were mutual. Needless to say, after the loss of my mother and Ruth, we remain very close to my remaining sister, Judy, and her husband, Steve Golubic.

Judy and Steve's wedding day

Judy gave up her job as legal secretary to a Wisconsin Supreme Court justice when Steve took a job in Emergency Management for Shawano County, and they moved up near Green Bay. Ruth's children moved out of Benton to the Monroe and Madison areas in Wisconsin, so the number of Perkinses in Benton diminished from years past.

The bad luck continued in 1993 when I was diagnosed with a cancerous tumor in my left tonsil. The doctors removed the tumor and part of my soft palate, opened up my neck and removed the lymph nodes, and then followed up with fifty-six radiation treatments at the Gundersen Clinic in LaCrosse. The cause of the cancer, as in most cases, wasn't clear, but research years later by Johns Hopkins supported the cause of tonsillar cancer in men to be a virus. The surgery and radiation treatments left me with a number of side effects, but I have remained cancer-free since then.

In February 2001, my uncle Bill (Glenn) Perkins died at age eighty. He was the last of my father's generation. Following the funeral service, Rose and I, along with Judy and Steve, spent three weekends cleaning up Bill's house, garage, and farm sheds in preparation for an auction. He was buried in Blue River, Wisconsin, with full military honors as a veteran of WWII.

I stayed with Beaver Builders' Supply for almost eight years and then spent about three years in the hardwood components industry, selling premade hardwood parts in truckload lots to the kitchen cabinet industry. I represented sawmill/manufacturing plants in Wisconsin and Minnesota, and traveled throughout a five-state area in the Upper Midwest. It was frustrating for me at times, working for small business owners, because they generally lacked sound management practices and often forged ahead without a business plan. Without a plan, the mills would become overbooked, the orders would miss their target dates, and I would have to replace lost customer accounts due to poor service.

As one example, I had been working on a big prospect, Triangle Pacific of Nebraska, for several months. They had four plants and built five thousand kitchen cabinets per day. I wasn't confident that the mills could handle that much volume, so before I closed the deal, I took our company president down to Lincoln, Nebraska, so he could meet the people and see firsthand what it would take for us to supply an operation of that magnitude. "No problem," he said.

In less than six months, we ran their production lines completely out of parts several times. We were running behind on future deliveries by about four days, and it was getting worse day by day. Needless to say, I lost all of that business, and of course the sales rep, being the point man, took the heat from the customer for misrepresenting the capabilities of my employer. There were other cases like that on a much smaller scale due to their "blind luck" planning, and as I approached the age of sixty-two, retirement for me was looking better and better.

CHAPTER 20

# THE OZARKS OF MISSOURI

My work took me through some southern states in the wintertime, and I would routinely phone home and talk to Rose between sales calls. She would at times tell me of a cold morning in Wisconsin, maybe ten degrees, and ask me what the temperature was in southern Missouri. When I told her it was about forty, a full thirty degrees warmer than Wisconsin, with no forecast of snow, she would respond, "Look for land!"

One of the drawbacks of living up north was the long winter, which often ran from the middle of November to April. During the winter of 2000, we had forty-seven days in a row where the temperature didn't reach ten degrees. Rose had spent most of her adult life in California and Washington State where the climate was moderate, and she didn't like those long Wisconsin winters. She did like the fresh snow, however, and insisted on running the snow blower, but as the winter went on and on, the pretty white snow turned to gray ice and left a salty slush on the highway that seemed to remain forever. As I got older, the winters were becoming more and more depressing for me as well, and I was always eager for spring to finally arrive.

Rose was also suffering from osteoarthritis in her knees and back. Our two-story home with the laundry room in the basement required her to constantly climb the steep stairways: basement to the kitchen, kitchen to the upstairs bedrooms. Perhaps it was time to look for a one-story home, and maybe in the southern part of the country with a more temperate climate.

The high taxes in Wisconsin (third highest in the nation) and the loss of personal freedom brought on by a restrictive state government in Madison also weighed in on our decision to relocate. After my mother and sister Ruth passed in 1993 and my sister Judy left the area, my Perkins family of southwestern Wisconsin had diminished in number, so we decided to sell the home in Galesville and move south.

We didn't want to move to the Deep South. Neither the tropical climate of Florida nor the Southwest desert appealed to us. We wanted to have woods nearby, and the four seasons were preferable as long as the winter was shorter. In my travels, I described the Louisville, Kentucky, area and the Ozarks of southern Missouri.

Rose found some leads on the Internet in southern Missouri, so I investigated those properties whenever I passed near the area on business trips. She accompanied me down to the Salem, Missouri, area where we decided on a nine-acre piece of property north of Salem and next to the Mark Twain National Forest. It had a separate shop, a rustic barn, and a large pond stocked with fish. The property was completely fenced and cross-fenced for livestock. The two-bedroom house was on one level with an open floor plan in the kitchen that would suit Rose much better. Property was much less expensive than in Wisconsin, and the taxes were very low, but the little house would require a lot of work to bring it up to date. Everything else about the place seemed to be a perfect fit for us, so we made an offer on the property. We closed the deal in June 2001 and put our Galesville home up for sale. I bought a cargo trailer and in late summer hauled the first of three loads of household belongings to our new location in Salem, Missouri, advertised as the "Gateway to the Ozark Riverways," a vacation destination for float trips, horseback riding, cave exploration, camping, and fishing. On the first of October, we became permanent residents of the Show-Me State. We sold the Galesville home the following April.

We put two small additions onto the house, updated the kitchen, and made improvements throughout, with Rose and I doing most of the work together. She even mixed the concrete and mortar when I laid the block foundations, helped me hoist up the rafters for the roof, and pitched in with the tricky task of hanging and taping the drywall. Rose was raised on a Vermont farm, and she isn't afraid of hard work. She likes to tell friends and neighbors that she is my cheap Mexican labor now and has taken the name, "Manuel Labor." We have three to four acres of grass to mow on our "mini-ranch," and she does most of it on the new forty-two-inch mower. I get to mow the rough areas with an old MTD. We also have a diesel tractor with several implements that we bought at various farm auctions. Whenever we are in need of a break, we simply grab the fishing poles, walk down to the pond, and catch some catfish, bass, or bluegills.

I always wanted a place like this when the kids were young but was always talked out of it because the family wanted to be in town near the schools, ball parks, and shopping. Now I spend my retirement puttering around the "Back Acres Ranch," fixing fences, trimming trees and brush, doing carpentry and my first love, woodworking. I also have to keep the old tractor in repair, rake and burn leaves dropped from our twenty-two oak trees, bush-hog the pasture and woods, feed the catfish, the deer, and a pair of wild geese that nest on our pond. They arrive in mid-February without fail. It's all a labor of love!

Quality of living became more and more important as I grew older. It had deteriorated in Seattle since the 1970s. We found adventure in our ten years in Wisconsin because Rose and I were starting over late in life. In spite of the severe winter weather, it was a rewarding time for us, and, for the most part, the quality of life there was much better than in Seattle. We found Missouri, however, to be an even better choice. We noticed that we had less government interference in our life, for example, and Missouri had managed to retain a higher degree of state's rights than in other parts of the country. A property owner's rights are paramount in the Show-Me State, and taxes are much lower than in Wisconsin. We found life to be simpler and much slower paced. And, as a bonus, the winter season was much shorter. Our Missouri home was within forty miles of the exact demographic center of the country, and we felt that by being in this central location, it would be convenient for family members and friends to visit. We were able to offer overnight accommodation for folks up north to stop by on their way to the family attractions in Branson, Missouri. They could spend some time visiting with us, enjoy a hearty breakfast of biscuits and gravy, spend additional time fishing at our pond, and perhaps glimpse some wildlife passing through our property before continuing on their trip. One of Rose's cousins from Canada, after spending a couple of days with us, said our property, with the large manicured lawn and some twenty-two oak shade trees in a pond setting, compared to a state park in appearance. We had a mixture of open pasture to the east and stands of timber north and south of the nine-acre property. Whitetail deer, Canada geese, red foxes, coyotes, and a wild turkey made regular visits to our mini-ranch. We also had some permanent residents like turtles, frogs, and bobwhite quail. A groundhog set up housekeeping in our old barn. We named him Phil despite the fact that he "slept in" every spring until the middle of March.

Since my alcohol treatment in 1984–85, and my unbroken period of sobriety, I have found an inner peace, and life has been highly rewarding. Rose and I are happy together, and although we have some occasional differences in wants and needs, we are always willing to compromise because most of the issues that crop up are never as important as our mutual happiness. My favorite saying: "In the bigger picture of life, this particular issue isn't very important." I often carry a wooden coin in my pocket upon which is engraved the Serenity Prayer: "God grant me the serenity to accept the things I cannot change, the courage to change the things I can, and the wisdom to know the difference."

Rose has supported me during my years of sobriety and was there for me during my brief bout with cancer in 1993. In some ways, she grew overly protective of me since my cancer recovery, and she knows that I, in turn, will do just about anything for her. She has frequently said, "Gary, you spoil me so." We are truly blessed with a happy life in the country and good friends and neighbors. Our adult kids are doing just great, and our grandchildren are healthy and hearty. In our twenty-plus years together, we have truly been blessed.

CHAPTER 21

# A VISIT TO THE HOMELAND

I have many fond memories of the past. I have been truly blessed. I've climbed some mountains in my life and have overcome some serious obstacles to achieve success. I take pride in my accomplishments. I have sincere regrets about some other events in my life, and I attempted to make amends. In these later years, the so-called "autumn of my life," I have focused on an earlier period of my family's history: the nineteenth century. Rose and I spend time researching family records, and these days the World Wide Web provides a better opportunity to find that long-lost ancestor from the past.

We began our research on the Perkins family by studying my uncle Willie's notes and biographical sketches that he laboriously recorded over the years. His history of the Perkins, Robbins, Hocking, and Redfern families dated back to the early 1800s. His mother, my grandmother Lilla Perkins, had provided Willie with a good deal of oral history. He queried other members of the family to obtain additional records, all of which were neatly typed and compiled in a three-inch ring binder.

I had taken a class in genealogy at one of the community colleges in the Seattle area in the 1980s, and my research was somewhat productive. Collectively, the research at that time indicated that the Perkins family was Cornish, of Celtic origin, from Cornwall, England. I think it was in the midnineties when my uncle Bill told me, "You're not as Cornish as you think you are!"

He was right. Some twenty years later, as a result of our Internet research (more credit to Rose than to me), we learned that my great-great-grandmother Catherine was Irish, born in Waterford, and that three of Thomas and Catherine Perkins's children, including my great-grandfather James, were also born in Waterford. It's likely that a young Thomas Perkins found more productive mining in the Waterford lead-mining region than his home in England at that time. It was common for the miners to emigrate between Cornwall and Ireland as mining fortunes rose and fell. Young Thomas also had the good fortune to meet and marry a young Irish lass named Catherine Creed. According to the British census of 1851, their first three children, Mary Ann, Martha, and James, were born in Waterford before Thomas returned to England with his young family. They settled in Calstock, on the River Tamar, in County Cornwall for a time. A second son, George Perkins, was born in Calstock in 1846.

\* \* \* \* \* \*

Rose and I arrived in Calstock in May 2003. We had ridden the train across the River Tamar on an ancient bridge constructed some time after the Roman conquest, perhaps the same bridge that had carried my ancestor Thomas and his family across the river some 150 years earlier. The old structure with the Roman arches was picturesque in this hilly countryside. What a wonderful view from that bridge! We stepped off the train at the north edge of town and surveyed the scene. The small train stop was little more than a covered bench, constructed of wood, and it reminded me of a school bus stop in rural America.

The village of Calstock sat on a very steep hillside along the River Tamar, with switchback streets mostly paved with cobblestone. As we trod down the nearest street toward the riverfront, we wondered if we would have the energy to climb back up to the train stop.

Gary in Calstock, Cornwall, 2003

George Perkins was born here in Calstock, Cornwall, in 1846, most likely in one of the many stone cottages that were undoubtedly constructed some two hundred years ago. We had no record of George ever coming to America, so we walked through the St. Andrews cemetery looking for a Perkins headstone with the assumption that he might have lived his entire life in Calstock and had been buried there. We found no headstone nor did we locate any parish records of him at the rectory office. We did find some tasty Cornish pasty, though, at a riverfront café. The village was holding a music festival and fair at the riverside park (on the "quay"), so we sat at a patio table, enjoying the music while eating the pasty.

We slowly climbed back up the steep cobblestone street where we met an elderly lady and remarked to her that walking in this village must keep one in good physical shape. She responded with typical Cornish wit, "It keeps you fit ... fit to drop!"

Thankfully when we reached the top of the hill, we were able to rest on the bench at the train "station" for a few minutes before the train arrived.

The train took us into County Devon, across the River Tamar from Cornwall, first to the village of Bere Ferris and then on to Bere Alston, both located on the Bere Peninsula. Originally named after an early brewery operation, the peninsula had become a major mining area by the early part of the nineteenth century. It yielded a variety of minerals, including copper, tin, silver-lead, and arsenic.

We found Bere Ferris to be a very small village set down in a valley on the southeastern sector of the peninsula where the River Tavy curled around the village to the east and south. Rose and I enjoyed lunch at the only pub in town. We could tell right off that the handful of patrons that afternoon hadn't seen an American in their area for many years, maybe ever. They were friendly and helpful in our quest to find the Perkins family home of 1851. We learned that it would "more likely have been up in Bere Alston." The postman informed us that during the plague of 1846, most residents abandoned Bere Ferris along the river to get away from the disease carried by rats and relocated up on the higher ground at Bere Alston on the northern part of the peninsula.

We had a copy of the British census of 1851, wherein Catherine was listed as "head of household." We wondered whether her husband,

Thomas Perkins, had been a victim of the plague. Their address listed on the census was 55 Pepper Street, and the location on the census indicated Bere Ferris. One of the locals explained that Bere Ferris was also the name of the district, and the district seat was located in Tavistock. Hence, the name on the census report might have been that of the district as opposed to the community. The local postman was most helpful, advising us to take the train to the next stop at Bere Alston. He assured us that we would probably find our family home up there.

This day trip, on and off the narrow-gauge train, and our two nights in Plymouth, gave us an opportunity to see a good bit of Cornwall and the home of my ancestors. It's very windy atop the high hills and bluffs overlooking Plymouth as well as most highland areas in the county, but our brief train ride took us up the scenic Tamar Valley where we found calm, sunny weather. We would have enjoyed taking a river ferry as opposed to the train, but not all of our points of interest were on or near the river.

Our base of operations during the Cornwall visit was Plymouth, a favorite holiday destination for Londoners and tourists and, of course, the launch of the *Mayflower* some 360 years earlier. We stayed in one of the many two-hundred-year-old lodgings that were now operated as bed-and-breakfasts. This one was named the West Winds. The masonry walls were about two feet thick, and the plumbing in these buildings ran vertically on the outside of the building. The rooms were comfortable, the owners were friendly, and there were no conflicts over the shared use of the one bathroom on each floor. Rose was especially thankful for that. We spent some time walking the Barbican on the Quay and visited the *Mayflower* exhibit on the pier. There was a carnival going on at Hoe Park near the West Winds, so we ventured over there to look at the art and craft exhibits and to read the inscription on the statue of Sir Francis Drake.

On one of the streets that sloped steeply down to the waterfront, we stepped into a café to sample their Cornish pasty. It tasted familiar, and the waitress told us that the simple ingredients were the same as my mom used back home in Benton: beef steak, potatoes, and onions, with a crust made with lard as opposed to vegetable shortening. The lard made the crust heavier, gave it "more body," as my mother would say, "to feed the hungry miners." This Cornish shop used what she called "Swede potatoes," a yellow variety, at their shop in Plymouth. The other popular food choice while on the coast is, of course, fish and chips. We ordered those at one of the pubs along the Barbican. Patrons are seated at common tables in the English pubs, so you have the opportunity to meet a variety of people sharing a bench seat with you and to learn a little bit more about the locality with each meal. At one of the pubs on the Barbican, however, we were seated with a young couple from North Dakota. We didn't learn much from them about the locality, but we did have an interesting conversation about the sport of curling.

Now, getting back to our visit to the Bere Peninsula, we were ready to leave the little riverside village of Bere Ferris and boarded the train to go north to Bere Alston. The train ran backward from Bere Ferris to Bere Alston. The tracks apparently dead-ended, and when the train backed out and over a switch, it was routed north to the Bere Alston station. We soon found, however, that riding backward "wasn't the half of it," as Dad would say, because after disembarking from the train, we had to walk another two kilometers up a winding hill to get to the village. The narrow gravel road was lined on each side by a ten-foot-tall, dense hedge, commonly used in Britain for centuries instead of fences. As luck would have it, Rose had a full bladder and couldn't make it to town.

She tried desperately to squeeze through a hedge, but it was too tight and too stout. It wouldn't give a bit. Then we spotted a private road that ran over a small bridge and up around a knoll. She found privacy beneath the bridge, relieved herself, and we continued to trudge up the long, winding road to Bere Alston.

\* \* \* \* \* \*

Bere Alston is a village of some three thousand inhabitants set on the picturesque Bere Peninsula, which is outlined by the River Tamar to the west and the River Tavy to the east. The deep wooded valley of the meandering River Tamar separates the counties of Cornwall and Devon. It's a diverse landscape with a high granite ridge and exposed moors to the west in Cornwall. As Rose and I paused in our uphill hike to survey the scene, it was hard to imagine the noise from over a hundred mines that operated in this region at the height of the mining boom during the middle of the nineteenth century. Tin, copper, silver-lead, and arsenic were all mined here, employing a great number of workers.

This is where the Thomas Perkins family resided during that time, in 1851. Our primary mission on this trip was to locate the family residence as determined by the 1851 British Census to be at 55 Pepper Street in Bere Alston. That location turned out to be a tenement building fronting a primary village street. (The name had been changed from Pepper Street to Cornwall Street.) In 1851, there were 512 people living on this street, mostly lead miners and their young families. Hundreds of miners and laborers walked down this road to their work and trudged wearily back at the end of their shifts.

Tenement buildings provided the most common form of housing, some dating back to the reign of Elizabeth I, and many of the miners had moved up here from Cornwall. Life was pretty tough. Children as young as ten worked at the mines, near all the smoking chimneys, the backyard pig sties, and unsanitary drainage. Bere Alston may have been a bit short of "fresh country air!" The tenements were historically owned by a king or lord, and only "freehold" tenants, those entitled to practice a trade, were allowed to vote. Before the Great Reform Act of 1832, as few as thirty male residents in the entire village were allowed to vote in the borough (village) of Bere Alston. These were known as burgage boroughs, and in the eighteenth century, most of these burgage properties had been owned by the Drake and Hobart families.

We found most of the buildings in Bere Alston to be constructed of stone, which is typical of the area, and the streets to be narrow and anything but straight. As they wound around the hilly terrain, one lost a sense of direction for a time. The village now has a population of two thousand residents, but not much has changed since the nineteenth century. The streets, narrow and crooked, have retained their charm. There are plenty of scenic country walks in Bere Alston that cross train lines, woods, and fields.

Once home to numerous pubs, the village now has only one public house, the Edgcumbe Hotel, located on Fore Street. Today, there is a comfortable modern café called Hope Cottage next door to Bere Alston United Church.

We bought soft drinks and snacks at a neighborhood market a few doors down from our family's former residence at 55 Cornwall Street. As we continued up the street and past the tenement, I tried to imagine the family, right here in this neighborhood, 153 years ago. The father, Thomas Perkins, was no longer a member of the household if the 1851 British census is accurate. It's likely that he died sometime between 1846 and 1851 because the mother, Catherine, is listed on the census as "head of household." Daughter Mary Ann, at age twenty, was still living at home and worked at a mine. In 1852, she married a local miner named Samuel Manley. Daughter Martha was ten years old in 1851, and my great-grandfather James was eight. He began his career as a mineworker three years later at the young age of eleven. It was common at that time for women and children to work at the mines, but they generally worked above the grass, breaking up ore-laden rocks with a hammer. The youngest Perkins child, George, was six years old at the time of the census. He had been born in Calstock when the family lived across the river in Cornwall.

\* \* \* \* \* \*

This visit to Cornwall and Devon had been enlightening for me, and I now felt closer to my ancestors, perhaps a spiritual connection here in the Tamar Valley. Our research had left some questions unanswered: What happened to Thomas Perkins? Did a mining accident take his life? Perhaps he was a victim of the plague of 1846. He was reportedly born in England and met and married Catherine in Waterford, Ireland. Their first three children were born in Waterford, but we've not located an Irish record of the family.

We do know that the Perkinses were miners and that James, at age twenty-one, brought his mining experience to America in 1863. He later married Eliza Jane, daughter of William Hocking, a member of another Cornish mining family. The Hockings had emigrated from Illogan, Cornwall, in 1849. It was natural, then, that many sons and grandsons of James and Eliza also took up mining here in Wisconsin. Few, if any, went below ground to toil in the shafts and drifts of the mine. They worked "up on top" in the derrick and the mill, performing work on the surface.

They worked above the grass.

# BIBLIOGRAPHY

Cambria County (Pennsylvania) Historical Society Records.

Du Maurier, Daphne. *Vanishing Cornwall*. Middlesex, England: Penguin Books, 1972.

Farrey, Loren. *A Tour Guide to the Mines*. Farrey Enterprises, 2001, Benton Mining Museum.

Hatcher, Harlan Henthorne. *A Century of Iron and Men*. Bobbs-Merrill Company, 1950.

Heritage Quest Online. Website: ProQuest LLC ©1999-2014.

Leland, John. "Writings of John Leland"

Normington, James and William Bant. *A Miner's Life*. Plymouth, England: J. H. Harris & Son, 1989.

Rowse, A. L. *The Cornish in America*. Cornwall: Dyllansow Truran, June 1991.

Rowse, A. L. *The Little Land of Cornwall*. Cornwall: Dyllansow Truran (previously published by Alan Sutton Publishing, 1986).

Smith, James Francis. *The Celtic Invasion of Rome*. Bloomington, Indiana: Xlibris, 2004.

Todd, Arthur Cecil. *The Cornish Miner in America*. Spokane, Washington: The Arthur H. Clark Co., 1995.

Vivian, John. *Tales of the Cornish Miners*. Penryn, Cornwall: Tor Mark Press, 1993.

Westwood, Jennifer. *Gothick Cornwall*. Buckinghamshire, England: Shire Publications Ltd., 1992.

Wills, Garry. *Nixon Agonistes: The Crisis of the Self-Made Man*. Marietta, Georgia: Cherokee Publishing Company, 1997.

**Websites**

Hardwoods Supply Inc.                 hardwoodssupply.com

Commencement Bay Corrugated Inc.      cbcbox.com

# ACKNOWLEDGMENTS

My wife, Rose, spent countless hours in researching the genealogy of my family. I also appreciate her tolerance and cooperation when I frequently left files, binders, and books scattered about my work area.

My late uncle Willie Perkins had transcribed my grandmother Perkins's oral history into written form, thus providing me with a head start in the Perkins/Robbins/Hocking family research.

My sister Judy Golubic was extremely helpful, not only in correcting my grammatical errors but also in rewriting some of my clumsy passages.

My granddaughter Kate Elizabeth Perkins created the background artwork for the book cover.

My stepson W. David Webb offered valuable insight into the choice of title for this book.

Friends and relatives who contributed to my many childhood experiences (otherwise known as the West End Gang):

- **Calvert, George**. A classmate and the son of a farmer where my dad worked following the close of WWII. He and I learned to drive tractors and ride horses on the farm. George reminded me of Roy Rogers.

- **Cherry, Bill**. A distant relative, classmate, and early playmate who lived next door on Galena Street. He was the "chief engineer" responsible for the design modification of the "Bum Buggy" soap box car.
- **Farrey, Carl and Gordon.** First cousins (our moms were sisters) and the brothers I never had. We were big Chicago Cubs fans.
- **Farrey, Roger and Ray.** Third cousins and "maritime engineers" who launched their home-crafted boat in the Benton Creek with only limited success.
- **Fawcett, "Leaky."** His was a few years younger but hung around with hopes of learning some valuable engineering tips.
- **Mullikin, Delos and Jack.** Second cousins on my mother's side, and you could set a watch by Delos. He always arrived at school eight minutes after the first class of the day had begun.
- **Robbins, Robert ("Pots").** He didn't work with his hands much. Pots was a great musician who later on played cornet in the US Navy band.
- **Temple, Ben**. Descendent of the village founders, the Murphys, Ben lived in the oldest farmhouse in Benton. He hosted basketball games in his gravel driveway, but we were advised to dribble around the cow pies.
- **White, Pete**. A hard worker, always ready to pitch in on our many projects, including snow-fort construction, ditch digging, and serving on the pit crew come race day. Pete was the one running around with his jacket wide open in the dead of winter.